*The Moravian Community
in Colonial North Carolina*

The Moravian Community
in
Colonial North Carolina

Pluralism on the Southern Frontier

Daniel B. Thorp

The University of Tennessee Press / KNOXVILLE

Frontispiece: Detail from illustration on page 19.

Library of Congress Cataloging in Publication Data

Thorp, Daniel B.
   The Moravian community in colonial North Carolina :
pluralism on the Southern frontier / Daniel B. Thorp.—1st ed.
      p.   cm.
   Bibliography: p.
   Includes index.
   ISBN 0-87049-605-0 (cloth : alk. paper)
   1. Moravians—North Carolina—History—18th century.
2. North Carolina—History—Colonial Period. ca. 1600–1775. I. Title.
F265.M7T44   1989
975.6'0049187—dc19   88-31608   CIP

for Carla

Contents

Illustrations

TABLES

Acknowledgments

For the past ten years I have lived with four hundred dead Moravians. In my office, in the archives, and at home they have looked over my shoulders and whispered in my ears, and without them this book would never have been written. I also had more corporeal help, though, and I especially want to thank the latter.

My oldest debt is to Jack Greene, who first encouraged me to study the colonial frontier and who left me free to do it as I wanted, stepping in occasionally to offer suggestions that were invariably welcome and helpful. At the Moravian archives in Bethlehem, Vernon Nelson taught me to read the archaic script of eighteenth-century Germans and has patiently answered my questions ever since. Mary Creech, now retired from the archives in Winston-Salem, shared with me a lifetime's knowledge of that collection, even when she seemed to doubt that I knew what I was doing. Her successor, Tom Haupert, has been even more open. Bill Hinman, at Historic Bethabara, and Paula Locklair, at Old Salem, have earned my gratitude for a decade of favors; they have provided moral support since I started this book and, most recently, helped choose the illustrations for it. And the readers and editors at Tennessee did wonders for the clarity of my thinking and my prose.

Finally, I need to thank Harold Livesay and Cyndy Bouton, who as friends and colleagues were a never ending source of enjoyment and encouragement, and, above all, my wife Carla, who shared her husband with a bunch of dead Germans and made it all a lot of fun.

Introduction

Since the early 1960s, historians of British Colonial America have generally agreed that Anglo-America became increasingly heterogeneous in the decades preceding the American Revolution. Economic developments created rich and poor where there had been only middle class before; intellectual currents eroded religious establishments; and everywhere south of New England ethnic and racial minorities threatened to become the majority. As to the consequences of this growing diversity, however, historians have continually disagreed. While one school maintains that it led competing groups into increasingly bitter and sometimes violent conflict, a second argues that it led them to tolerate one another and confine themselves to peaceful forms of competition. Neither camp has yet managed to prove its case beyond a reasonable doubt. But their efforts have generated a wealth of local, provincial, and regional studies and have furthered tremendously our understanding of colonial development.

Among recent historians of the southern backcountry, however, this has not been the case. The people and institutions of that region were certainly no less diverse than those elsewhere in colonial America. Between 1720 and 1776 thousands of English, German, Scotch-Irish, Scottish, Welsh, African, and Creole migrants trickled, flowed, and then surged into the piedmont counties of Maryland, Virginia, the Carolinas, and Georgia. They brought with them a frightful array of languages, religions, values, and customs, and they created a society as multiform as any in America—a society that one contemporary described as "a mix'd Medley from all Countries and the Off Scouring of America."[1] But the historiography of this region shows little sign of the debate found elsewhere in colonial studies. The field belongs, instead, almost entirely to those convinced that conflict was endemic to the backcountry and interested chiefly in finding its causes or debating its consequences.[2] Only a handful of writers—most notably, perhaps, Richard Beeman, H. Roy Merrens, and Robert Mitchell—have taken the other view and focused their attention on the society that emerged there in spite of the conflict.[3] The result has been a number of excellent works on the Great Awakening in Virginia and on the Regulators of North and South Carolina, but a failure to tell the whole story of life in the southern backcountry.

I am certainly not suggesting that conflict was unknown, or even rare, on the southern frontier; during the middle years of the eighteenth century the southern backcountry was probably the most unstable region in Britain's American empire. Nor do I think that historians should ignore either the origins or the consequences of that unrest; indeed Roger Ekirch's office is just down the hall from my own, and I followed with great interest his debate with Marvin L. Michael Kay concerning the roots of political turmoil in North Carolina. But I do think we need a fuller picture than we have of social developments on the eighteenth-century southern frontier; we need to put flesh on the bones that Carl Bridenbaugh uncovered almost forty years ago.[4] Bridenbaugh's *Myths and Realities* offered readers a finely balanced sketch of "the Back Settlements" as a region in which occasional outbursts of violence took place against a backdrop of different ethnic and religious groups learning to live peacefully with one another. But it was just a sketch. Bridenbaugh challenged others to provide the necessary detail, both of the violent outbursts and of the more peaceful coexistence. So far only half that challenge has been properly met, but in describing the southern frontier as part of "Greater Pennsylvania" Bridenbaugh pointed the way toward answering the other half.

Historians of the middle colonies have not been quite so dazzled by the episodes of conflict that punctuated life in a heterogeneous society. They have devoted just as much of their attention, if not more, to understanding how the various groups in such a society interacted and even competed peacefully. One of the best and most recent products of this school is Michael Zuckerman's *Friends and Neighbors: Group Life in America's First Plural Society*, a collection of eight essays by younger students of the middle colonies. The chapters of *Friends and Neighbors* describe a region in which a number of different ethnic and religious communities managed to preserve their individual identities while establishing a generally peaceful society. Ironically, however, in introducing the work Zuckerman concludes that "the capacity of the Scots to sustain a separate life among the English and the ability of the Quakers to remain within their own meetings amid multiplying masses make it unclear whether middle-colonial geopolitical units can be considered communities at all."[5]

They were communities, though, communities that operated much like a model described by the Norwegian anthropologist Fredrik Barth in the introduction to his *Ethnic Groups and Boundaries*. According to Barth the survival of any particular group (for example the Scots or Quakers about whom Zuckerman wonders) in a multiethnic society (like that of the middle colonies) does not depend on the group's isolation from others or on its ability to confront others aggressively. Groups in such an environment survive by maintaining peaceful, regulated contact across clearly defined cultural boundaries. In Barth's view, the survival of distinctive groups within a heterogeneous society requires "a set of prescriptions governing situations of contact, and allowing for articulation in some sectors or domains of activity, and a set of proscriptions on social situations preventing inter-ethnic interaction in other sectors, thus insulating parts of the cultures from confrontation and modification."[6] Evidence of just such an arrangement appears in the work of historians Laura Becker, Nancy Tomes, Ned Landsman, and the other contributors to *Friends and Neighbors*, and societies like that described by Barth were not confined to Pennsylvania and New Jersey. They were present also in the southern backcountry.

The swarm of settlers reaching the Shenandoah Valley and the Carolina Piedmont during the eighteenth century created there a patchwork of egocentric communities. Each enjoyed its own sense of identity and its own economic, cultural, and religious interests, and competition among them did lead to incidents of open conflict. At the same time, though, there occurred a Barthlike process by which individual communities sought to preserve their identities and advance their interests through peaceful, controlled contact with one another. Robert Mitchell's work on the Shenandoah Valley and Richard Beeman's recent study of Lunenburg County certainly suggest this was true on Virginia's frontier.[7] An even clearer example comes from a cluster of settlements established by the Moravian Church around what is now Winston-Salem, North Carolina.

In 1753 the Moravians purchased a large tract of land they named Wachovia. During the next nineteen years they built the villages of Bethabara, Bethania, and Salem, and every step of the way they recorded what they were doing, why they were doing it, and what they planned to do next: an archival treasure unmatched in the colonial South. The Moravian records contain autobiographies of nearly every resident of Wachovia, inventories of every building, ledger sheets from every sector of the economy, minutes of the governing bodies, and hundreds of letters written by resident leaders of the community and their superiors in Pennsylvania, England, and Germany.[8] The range and depth of material in the Moravians' various archives offers historians an opportunity to see in extraordinary detail how one community in the southern backcountry interacted with its neighbors in the final decades of the colonial period and reveals a pattern of prescriptions and proscriptions very similar to those described by Fredrik Barth and by historians of the middle colonies. While Wachovia's residents did seek to protect many elements of their community from outside influences, they also made a deliberate and sustained effort to get along with their neighbors and to integrate themselves into the legal, political, and economic systems around them.

In keeping with this view of society on the colonial southern frontier as one in which different groups tried to remain elements within a pluralistic whole, I have divided this book into two parts. The first four chapters consider Wachovia's settlers as brothers and sisters in the Moravian Church. Eighteenth-century Moravians enjoyed a strong sense of corporate identity and employed a host of what Rosabeth Kanter calls commitment mechanisms to distinguish themselves from the rest of the world.[9] This first section considers some of those mechanisms: the geography of the colony, the religious and demographic characteristics of its inhabitants, the internal governance of the community, and the rituals by which it defined and maintained its boundaries. The book's second section, chapters five through seven, treats the Moravians as citizens of a parish, county, and province in the British Empire. The residents of Wachovia knew they were part of this larger non-Moravian world and chose willingly to participate in its legal, political, and economic systems, though they were determined not to endanger the distinctive culture of their community by doing so. The chapters in the second section describe the process by which the Moravians established a variety of closely supervised links between themselves and other citizens of North Carolina, links by which to conduct those sorts of relations considered essential to the survival of the Moravian community without opening it to indiscriminate contact with outsiders.

Insofar as possible, I have tried to present Wachovia's story from both an internal and an external perspective. The Moravians' own records are wonderful, but they do reflect their authors' bias. Church members always saw the world through lenses colored by their own values and interests, and on rare occasions they even rewrote history to make it conform to those interests. Unfortunately, there are few contemporary, non-Moravian sources against which to check those of the church. Because the Moravians did all they could to reduce the role of civil officials in their community, and because no arm of colonial government reached very far or very often into settlements on the southern frontier, there are relatively few references to the Brethren in either county or provincial records. There are even fewer in the papers of Wachovia's neighbors. Most of the neighbors wrote little that has survived on any subject; as Roy Merrens so nicely put it, they achieved anonymity whether they wanted it or not.[10] And the notable exceptions around Wachovia, Quaker communities, are just as frustrating. Quaker meetings in the Carolina backcountry did leave extensive records, but the purpose and nature of those records was such that they reveal relatively little about contact between Quakers and Moravians in these early years of settlement. Nor did visitors passing through Wachovia leave much for historians, just a handful of letters, diaries, or published accounts. Not even newspapers provide much information about early Wachovia. There was at least one weekly printed in North Carolina in most years after 1751, and sometimes more than one, but almost every issue of every paper from colonial North Carolina has long since disappeared.[11] The best I can do, therefore, is use the abundant Moravian records carefully and the non-Moravian ones whenever possible.

As for the temporal bounds of this book, they define the frontier era in and around Wachovia. That certainly omits a great deal, including the eventual decline of the Moravian theocracy. But what interests me is the initial settlement of the region and the formation of attitudes and institutions that would inform its development into the nineteenth century, and I leave to others the task of describing their demise.[12] The dates I have chosen do conform more closely to Moravian than to non-Moravian milestones. The book opens in 1753, when the Moravian Church sent its first settlers to North Carolina, and closes in 1772, when church leaders replaced the temporary administrative and economic institutions of Wachovia's settlement phase with what they hoped would be more permanent ones, formally designated Salem the community's *gemein Ort* (congregation town), and declared the establishment of Wachovia complete. But the bounds of Wachovia's formative years are very close to those of the Carolina backcountry itself. Between 1746 and 1750, just as the Brethren became interested in North Carolina, the colony's Lower House of Assembly signaled the backcountry's legal emergence from the formless void by passing acts to establish Granville, Johnston, and Anson counties, the first ones west of the Fall line. And in May 1771, less than a year before the Moravians declared Wachovia settled, the Battle of Alamance and the collapse of the Regulator Movement marked the former frontier's coming of age, not through any sudden tangible change in its government or society but through a change in the region's perception of itself and the culmination of economic and demographic trends that had begun years before. Thus the period between 1753 and 1772 saw the emergence of both the Moravian community in Wachovia and the larger society of which it was a part, and I hope through discussing the former to say something about the latter as well.

Wachovia's story will not and should not convince readers that the southern backcountry was a paradise of brotherly love. At best, it will help correct the notion that life there was an unbroken sequence of riots and civil disturbances. Like any new society in America, the colonial southern frontier was an unsettled and occasionally violent place. It was also, however, a place in which thousands of strangers from a variety of nations and religions began learning to live together without surrendering all of the characteristics that defined who they were before they became Americans.

PART I

Brothers and Sisters

CHAPTER 1

The Road to Carolina

On the morning of October 8, 1753, ten men left Bethlehem, Pennsylvania, to settle in the relative wilderness of central North Carolina. With them were a number of friends and relatives who planned to travel along for part or all of the journey before returning to Pennsylvania, and somewhere ahead of them was a sturdy wagon loaded with "all that is necessary for living and cultivating the land and building houses and otherwise making a beginning" on the Carolina frontier.[1]

The men were, in many ways, superbly suited for the role of pioneers. All ten were unmarried adults between the ages of twenty-eight and forty-two—old enough to have outgrown the youthful exuberance that upset so many frontier communities but still young enough to do the work necessary to establish themselves in the wilderness. Only one of the ten, Jacob Lösch, had been born in America. The rest were northern Europeans: six Germans, two Norwegians, and a Dane. All but one of the immigrants, however, had lived and worked in America for at least three years before the departure from Bethlehem; so they took with them valuable firsthand knowledge of the American environment. They also took an amazing variety of skills with which to establish and support themselves. Among them were jacks-of-all-trades such as Henrich Feldhausen, a thirty-one-year-old native of German Holstein described as "shoemaker, carpenter, mill-wright, cooper, sieve-maker, turner, and also Pennsylvania farmer," as well as specialists like Hans Martin Kalberlahn, a Norwegian-born surgeon and physician. To-

gether, the ten had talent enough to meet most of their anticipated needs by themselves.[2]

What most distinguished the men, however, was their religion; all ten belonged to the Moravian Church. The Moravians,
known officially as the Renewed Unitas Fratrum (Renewed
Unity of Brethren), were a new church with an ancient tradition, one reaching back three hundred years to the fifteenth-
century Unitas Fratrum established by followers of the Bohe-
mian reformer and martyr John Hus (1369–1415). The Ancient
Unity, as this Hussite group was dubbed by its successor, had
attempted to simplify Christianity and make it more relevant to
the daily lives of church members by asserting that Christ alone,
not the Pope, led the church and that the Bible was the only
source of religious truth. This simplicity proved quite appealing
to the people of Bohemia and to their neighbors in the Margrav-
ite of Moravia, and by the early sixteenth century the Unity had
over two hundred thousand members, some four hundred
places of worship, and three seminaries. None of this pleased
the Roman church, however, and early in the seventeenth century the Hapsburg emperor, Ferdinand III, led a Catholic resur-
gence that very nearly eliminated the Unity in central Europe.
For the next century it survived only among refugees who fled
to more tolerant parts of Europe and in small groups that worshipped in secret rather than flee the Holy Roman Empire. That
it survived at all was due largely to the work of John Amos Comenius (1592–1670), a bishop of the Unitas Fratrum from 1632 until his death in 1670. Comenius wrote a history of the church
and a catechism of the faith and urged the consecration of new
bishops in order to preserve the apostolic succession. The great
devotion and hard work of Comenius and others kept the Unity
alive through the seventeenth century and into the eighteenth, when members of the faithful remnant met Nicholaus
Ludwig, Count von Zinzendorf (1700–1760). From that meeting
came the Renewed Unitas Fratrum, the Moravian Church of
today.[3]

Zinzendorf was the scion of an aristocratic family with a long
tradition of government service in the Electorate of Saxony. As
a youth, however, Nicholaus had been influenced less by his

family's history than by the rise and teachings of German Pietism, a reform movement that developed within the Lutheran Church during the late seventeenth and early eighteenth centuries. Scholars of the movement disagree over the precise combination of motives that gave rise to Pietism, but they do seem to agree on the broad religious, social, and political factors that went into the mix: the Lutheran establishment's preoccupation with splitting theological hairs in order to define more precisely the line between itself and Calvinism; widespread apocalyptic fears in a laity caught up in the devastation of the Thirty Years War (1618–1648); and popular resentment generated by the striking contrast between the lingering postwar poverty endured by so many Germans and the emerging Baroque splendor enjoyed by a fortunate few. Some combination of these factors resulted in a vague sense of dissatisfaction among Lutherans as early as the second quarter of the seventeenth century. Not until 1675, however, did this feeling find a voice. In that year Philipp Jakob Spener (1635–1705) published his *Pia Desideria*, which became the manifesto of a reform movement labeled Pietism by its orthodox critics. In the years that followed, other writers and preachers amplified and modified Spener's ideas, but Pietism retained a recognizable core. It remained an element within the Lutheran Church that stressed the ability and duty of individual Christians to help effect the Kingdom of God on Earth by improving the spiritual state of the world around them, "[establishing] a holy community of Christian individuals leading a geuninely godly life, based on the Word of the Lord as revealed in the Bible, sustained by pure church services and an active preaching ministry, and supplemented by individual, household, and small group sessions for devotion and edification."[4]

This was the religious environment in which Zinzendorf was born and spent his early years. Spener was his godfather; the grandmother who raised Nicholaus after his father's death and his mother's remarriage was a devout Pietist; and as soon as the boy was old enough to leave home he was sent to the Paedagogium at Halle, the citadel of Pietist learning. There he remained for six years under the tutelage of August Herman Francke (1663–1727), one of Spener's greatest disciples, and by the age of sixteen Zinzendorf had decided that God was calling him to serve as a missionary. The young count's stepfather, however, had other ideas. He found such evangelical notions demeaning and considered them especially inappropriate for the son of a noble family in a Lutheran electorate; so in 1716 he withdrew Nicholaus from Halle and sent him to Wittenberg, a bastion of orthodoxy, to study law.[5]

The twig had already been bent, though, and despite several years at Wittenberg, a European tour, and an agreement to enter the service of the Elector of Saxony, Zinzendorf had not given up his hope of serving God. In 1722 he bought the estate of Bertelsdorf, in Upper Lusatia, and set out to become a patron of philanthropic causes. One of his first acts in this new career was to offer sanctuary to a group of refugees fleeing Moravia, probably in the hope of converting them to pietistic Lutheranism. These émigrés, who reached Bertelsdorf in the spring of 1722 and began at once to build the village of Herrnhut, showed no particular attachment to the Unitas Fratrum, but they were soon joined by others who did. In 1724 a small party of Unity members arrived in Herrnhut determined to restore their ancient church to its former strength. They made little progress, though, until 1727, when Zinzendorf discovered the writings of Comenius and was immediately struck by the similarities between Comenius's work and his own recently composed regulations for the governance of Herrnhut. In fact he was so taken by what he read that he too began to consider reviving the Unity, and on August 13, 1727, as the residents of Bertelsdorf gathered to celebrate Communion, they were swept by such a sense of God's presence that Zinzendorf took it as a sign that God wished him to reestablish the Unitas Fratrum.[6]

As long as Zinzendorf was alive the Renewed Unitas Fratrum bore his stamp. He was its temporal leader, known to members as *der Jünger* (the Disciple), and was so instrumental in the formulation of its doctrine that two of the Unity's most renowned historians concluded "the theology of the Moravian Church in his day was to an unusual degree identical with the theology of Zinzendorf." Theology, however, is perhaps too strong a word. It was actually an often contradictory mix of ideas drawn by

Zinzendorf from the works of Spener, Francke, and others, filtered through his own mind and heart, and rendered nearly indefinable by his hostility to systematic theology and his reluctance to consider the Moravians a separate denomination. Zinzendorf went beyond Spener's emphasis on "the inner man" and the need "[to] feel the sealing of the Spirit and the power of the Word." The *Jünger* declared religion "a matter which is able to be grasped through experience alone without any concepts" and rejected any effort to formulate a systematic theology on the grounds that to do so would constitute an impertinent attempt "to explain and express with Words, what our Thoughts should never dare venture upon." Instead, he and his followers stressed what he called "heart religion" and sought to feel God rather than understand Him.[7]

Moreover, Zinzendorf never considered the Moravians a separate church. One of the hallmarks of Spener's Pietism was the concept of *"ecclesioloe in ecclesia"* (little churches within the church). These were groups within the Lutheran Church seeking to complete the reformation begun by Luther without abandoning the church that bore his name. To Zinzendorf both Lutherans and Moravians were little churches within a single greater church that God intended to establish. Thus, in the first decade after the Unity's renewal Zinzendorf sought and obtained recognition as a Lutheran minister and successfully defended his orthodoxy before several investigatory commissions while, at the same time, helping to organize the Unity and becoming a Moravian bishop himself. With a leader who described himself as "a Lutheran bishop of the Moravian Brethren" is it any wonder that eighteenth-century Moravians were so theologically fluid that one historian maintains "neither they themselves nor those around them knew exactly who they were?"[8]

In spite of the *Jünger's* unsystematic bent, though, several basic features of the Moravians' beliefs and practices were well established by the early 1740s.[9] First, Moravian theology was Christocentric to the point of often appearing unitarian. Luther, Spener, and Francke had all emphasized Christ and His passion in their writing and preaching but never to the extent of removing God from human consideration. To Zinzendorf, however, knowledge of God was impossible except as revealed by Christ. In Moravian theology, Ernest Stoeffler has written, "Christ . . . is not merely the revelation of God; he is the known God in his totality." Therefore, Christ was the absolute focus of Moravian attention. His life on earth provided a model that every member sought to follow; His death on the cross was the ransom for which God forgave their sins; He was the recipient of their prayers and adoration; and He was the church's Chief Elder, elected in 1741 to the position of supreme leadership of the Unity.[10]

A second distinctive feature of Moravian theology during the eighteenth century was the church's inclusive and joyous view of salvation. Zinzendorf did not share the conviction of earlier Pietists that one's spiritual rebirth came after an agonizing struggle with one's sinfulness, a struggle that many people did not win. In his view it came quickly and easily when one acknowledged the sacrifice made by Christ in one's behalf. This acknowledgment and a true love of Christ guaranteed one's salvation. Thus, Moravianism was not a religion of doubt and worry about one's ultimate fate; it was one of joy and of the certainty that one was saved.

Finally, Zinzendorf's theology was marked by its extraordinary ecumenicalism. The *Jünger* refused to believe that any church, even his own, had a monopoly on truth. To him, every Christian sect was "a particular school by means of which God meant to impart saving knowledge to his people," and the Moravians' role was to unite the awakened members of different denominations into a single "Congregation of God in the Spirit"—a sort of panchristian union rather than an organized church.[11] Toward this end the Unity dispatched two kinds of missionaries into the world, but neither was expected to bring converts flocking into the church. Missionaries in the traditional sense went to non-Christian peoples—like slaves in the West Indies or Eskimos in Greenland. They had instructions to preach the Gospel to anyone who would listen, but only the very few they believed God had called could be admitted to the Unity. Meanwhile, a second group of itinerants was supposed to organize the Unity's "diaspora," what church historians describe as a means by which the Moravians could "encourage groups of earnest Christians to organize societies for fellowship and spiritual growth" without actually admitting them to the Unity.[12] Individuals in these "societies" were supposed to maintain close and friendly relations with the Moravians while remaining members of their own confessions. In this way Zinzendorf hoped to realize his Congregation of God in the Spirit without antagonizing other, more established, churches.

As for the Moravians' religious practices, these too reflected both Zinzendorf's retention of elements from Pietism and the Ancient Unity and his own splendid originality. Their most distinctive practice, for instance, the division of congregations into choirs, was the result of Zinzendorf's elaborating on Spener's notion of conventicles. Spener believed that small groups were the best vehicle through which to revive an individual's flagging spiritualism, and in his *Pia Desideria* he suggested "having several members of a congregation who have a fair knowledge of God or a desire to increase their knowledge meet under the leadership of a minister, take up the Holy Scriptures, read aloud from them, and fraternally discuss each verse in order to discover the simple meaning and whatever may be useful for the edification of all."[13] From this rather unstructured base Zinzendorf constructed a well-defined system of ten choirs organized on the basis of members' age, sex, and marital status: infants, little boys, little girls, older boys, older girls, single brothers, single sisters, married people, widowers, and widows. In some of the ten, members lived and worked together in communal quarters; in all of them, though, they met several times each week to pray, sing hymns, and help one another lead godly lives.[14]

A second distinctive feature of Moravian religious practices during the eighteenth century was the tremendous number of services held. When John Wesley visited Herrnhut in 1738 he reported that

Every morning at eight is singing and exposition of the Scripture; and commonly a prayer.

At eight in the evening, there is commonly only mental prayer, joined with singing and expounding.

The faithful afterwards spend a quarter of an hour in prayer, and conclude with the kiss of peace.

On Sunday morning the service begins at six; at nine the public service at Bertholdsdorf. At one the eldest [a Unity official] gives separate exhortations to all the members of the Church, divided into fourteen little classes for that purpose, spending about a quarter of an hour with each class. At four begins the evening service at Bertholdsdorf, closed by a conference in the Church. At eight is the usual service; after which the young men, singing praise round the town, conclude the day.

In addition to this weekly routine, Moravian congregations also took Communion every fourth Saturday (eighteenth-century Moravians considered Saturday the Sabbath); held special ceremonies on days of particular significance to the Unity (such as the August 13 celebration of its renewal) or to the church universal (such as Christmas); and organized additional services for a week at Easter. Moreover, every congregation member was also a choir member, and every choir had its own prayer meeting at least once a week and its own festival day once a year.[15]

Wesley did more in Herrnhut than count services, though; he also noted the essential role of music in Moravian ceremonies. Zinzendorf believed that music and divine worship were inseparable. "In the Bible one sees how God speaks to Men," the *Jünger* wrote, "and in the song book how Men speak to God." In furthering this dialogue with God, eighteenth-century Moravians proved to be fantastic authors, translators, and collectors of hymns. Their *Christliches Gesang-Buch*, published in 1735, contained 972 hymns, and sixteen supplements published between 1737 and 1749 brought the number to over 2,300. Selections from these figured in every Moravian ceremony, and even the night watchmen in Herrnhut sang hymns on the hour in lieu of their traditional cry. The greatest use of hymns, however, came in the Unity's most celebrated ritual, its *Singstunde* or hymn sermon. In this the minister or a lay leader chose single stanzas from a number of different hymns and organized them, with or without prayers or lessons in between, to convey a mes-

1. The spirit of community found among the Brethren shows clearly in this eighteenth-century print of Unity members taking Communion. The artist has chosen the moment at which the communicants partake in unison and has further emphasized the communal ideal by dressing all the brothers and all the sisters alike, though in fact there was no such uniformity of dress in the church. The print also shows clearly the segregation between men and women and the separation of leaders from members that were common in early Moravian congregations and communities. (Courtesy of Old Salem Inc.)

sage to the congregation in much the same way that a conventional sermon does. Then he would deliver this message by starting each stanza himself and continuing alone until the organist and congregation joined in. Eighteenth-century Moravians also used instrumental music in their rituals, most notably in the trombone announcement of a member's death, but

hymns were their glory and a hallmark of their services in Zinzendorf's day.[16]

Finally, among the distinctive practices of eighteenth-century
Moravians one must include their use of the Lot. The Lot was a
means of seeking the Lord's response to questions or proposals.
The mechanics of its use varied from time to time and place to
place, but it generally involved drawing an answer at random
from a bowl containing as few as two or as many as twelve possibilities. Sometimes those employing the Lot drew from a number of scriptural passages placed in the bowl and tried to determine the application of the chosen passage to the question at
hand. Or they might pick from just three options—yes, no, and
a blank taken to mean that the question should be resubmitted
at a later time. Members of the Unity began using the Lot to
decide questions in church councils in 1728; five years later they
also began using it to determine if, when, and to whom members should be married. They continued to employ the Lot in
decision making until the early nineteenth century, and it was
one of the most readily visible distinctions between the Moravians and their neighbors, both in Europe and America.[17]

Following the Unity's renewal in 1727 the church gained
members steadily and extended its missionary activities farther
and farther afield. Some of those who joined had belonged to
the Ancient Unity and had migrated from Bohemia or Moravia
to Saxony. Many, however, were converts from other Christian
sects who had learned of the Brethren through diaspora ministers and had gained admission to the Unity in spite of Zinzendorf's opposition to such conversions. Preaching to a London
audience in 1746, the *Jünger* had exclaimed "I despise anyone,
who without the deepest and most thoroughly examined reason, changes over from one denomination to another." But
through that loophole of thorough examination a steady stream
of men and women entered Zinzendorf's church. During the
1730s and 1740s the Moravians established several new congregations in Germany, a handful in England, one in Holland, and
one at Bethlehem, Pennsylvania. Furthermore, Moravian itinerants were busy in Ireland, Sweden, Denmark, and the Baltic
states setting up societies that later became congregations,

while other missionaries traveled regularly among slaves in the Danish West Indies and to the natives of Greenland, Surinam, Ceylon, Pennsylvania, and various parts of Africa.[18]

Not surprisingly, all this activity upset some of Christendom's more established churches, who worried that the Unity might grow at their expense. Unity growth and activity also made better known to the world a number of Moravian beliefs and practices that made them easy targets of criticism. Their intense focus on Christ, for example, convinced many observers that they were antitrinitarians; their emphasis on the Lord's role in directing Unity actions led to charges of antinomianism; Zinzendorf's contact with Catholics in the interest of interdenominational cooperation was interpreted by many Protestants as the action of a covert papist; and the subordination of individual will to the needs of God and church resulted in accusations that the *Jünger* was a tyrant exploiting his followers for his own benefit.[19]

Ammunition for such attacks was especially plentiful during the years 1743–1750, known to the Moravians as "the period of sifting." During those years the Unity was swept by a wave of emotionalism, and its normally strong emphasis on Christ's sacrifice grew into an obsession known as "Blood Theology." Hymns, prayers, liturgies, and catechisms began to include startling references to the blood and wounds of Jesus, like these from a hymn of the period describing members' adoration of the wound in Christ's side:

Our husband's Side-wound is indeed
The queen of all his wounds;
On this the little pidgeons feed,
Whom cross' air surrounds.
There they fly in and out and sing,
Side's blood is seen on every wing.
The bill that picks the Side-hole's floor,
Is red of blood all o'er.

The Unity's emotionalism had worried some people ever since 1727, but hymns like that went beyond what most Christians were willing to accept. Even former friends of the Brethren began to abandon them.[20]

Together, the Unity's increasingly active diaspora and the excesses of "the period of sifting" led to a dramatic increase in the level of verbal, legal, and physical opposition directed at the Moravians throughout Europe and its colonies during the 1740s. In Britain and its empire the situation was further complicated by the abortive Stuart uprising of 1745, in the aftermath of which England was particularly suspicious of any group that was not fervently anti-Catholic. In the wake of "the '45," Zinzendorf's continuing effort to include Catholics in his Congregation of God in the Spirit struck many in England as Jacobism, and the Brethren found themselves under attack from all quarters. Now Methodist leader John Wesley, who had admired and very nearly joined the Unity a few years earlier, wrote his brother that "there is guile in almost all their words"; the Anglican Bishop of Exeter described them as "filthy dreamers"; and in British America both Old and New Lights blasted the Unity during the 1740s. Not all the attacks were verbal though. John Cennick, a Moravian missionary active in the British Isles, was horsewhipped in Dublin, drenched with blood in Swindon, and saved from a number of other attacks only by flight. Another itinerant, John Ockershausen, was arrested and imprisoned in York, while the colony of New York barred Moravian missionaries in 1744 and arrested two in the following year.[21]

It was this rising tide of resentment toward Moravians in the British world that first brought them into contact with John Carteret, Earl of Granville, and led to their settling in North Carolina. By the close of the 1740s the situation in Britain had become particularly worrisome to Unity leaders, and Zinzendorf had come to feel that the most effective solution to the church's problems there would be a parliamentary act recognizing the Renewed Unitas Fratrum as an ancient Protestant Episcopal church. Thus in January 1749 the *Jünger* arrived in London to direct personally the campaign to secure such an act. During the next six months he worked with several members of the House of Lords to draft an appropriate bill and to insure its passage, and one of his allies in this work was Earl Granville, who through his efforts on their behalf became in Moravian eyes "a friend of our people." Granville, however, was probably not act-

ing out of pure selflessness. His great-grandfather, Sir George
Carteret, had been one of the original Lords Proprietors of Carolina, and in 1749 Granville himself owned more than 15 million
acres of North Carolina—the entire northern half of the colony.
Most of this land was still devoid of Euro-American, quitrent-
paying inhabitants, which may explain Granville's eagerness to
serve the Brethren in Parliament. It certainly explains why he
was one of several proprietors lined up to offer them land in
various corners of the empire as soon as the Unity gained parliamentary recognition in June of 1749.[22]

Initially, church leaders had little interest in any of these offers. What changed their minds were developments later that
year in the German principality of Wetteravia. The Moravians
had leased several estates in Wetteravia since 1736 and had built
on them the communities of Herrnhag and Marienborn. Both
were thriving in 1749, and Marienborn was especially important
to the Unity as it was the center from which the diaspora was
directed and frequently the site of Unity synods. But that October the Count of Büdingen, from whom the church rented its
Wetteravian estates, died, and his successor demanded that tenants swear allegiance to his government and his faith rather
than those of Zinzendorf. This the Brethren would not do,
choosing instead to abandon Wetteravia and presenting the
church with two pressing problems. Obviously, it had to find
new homes for the three thousand or so members expected to
leave over the next three years. More important, it had to avoid
bankruptcy. Even before the Wetteravian crisis the Unity had
been in financial trouble; it had borrowed recklessly during "the
period of sifting," and merely servicing that debt was a heavy
burden. Added to that, the loss of capital invested in Herrnhag
and Marienborn made a bad situation almost fatal. Zinzendorf,
in fact, faced the very real prospect of debtors' prison. The
church, therefore, had to find some way of raising money. It was
this combination of the sudden need to relocate thousands of
refugees and the increased demand for revenues that prompted
Unity officials to consider the offers of land they had recently
received.[23]

In weighing those offers, the Moravians looked for two

things. First, they wanted a location that would permit the brothers and sisters who settled on it to practice their religion and raise their families in relative security. As one bishop put it in 1754: "We dont want extraordinary Priviledges, if only we can live together as Brethren, without interfering with others & without being disturbed by them; and if only we can keep our Children from being hurt by wicked Examples, and our young people from following the foolish and sinfull ways of the World." Second, they needed a location with good economic prospects. They did not, wrote one bishop, anticipate instant riches from some new East India Company, but they did expect the Unity's investment to produce a reliable and substantial income. "It is more often like mining works," continued the bishop; "one must invest for a long time, then one can begin to extract something. But the difference is that in a mine the yield is uncertain, and in a human colony, so to speak, it is quite certain."[24]

Conspicuously absent from these considerations was the strong missionary spirit that had marked many of the Moravians' earlier colonizing ventures and that historians have often claimed was a major factor in their decision to settle in North Carolina.[25] Certainly some members of the Unity showed an interest in bringing the Gospel to red, white, and black Carolinians during the 1750s; within the closed circle of Unity elders there was support for such missionary activity. There was none, however, in the formal pronouncements of church policy because the definitive voice there was that of Zinzendorf, and he opposed the idea.[26] Before the Unity's fiscal and legal troubles had mounted during the 1740s, the *Jünger* too had been an aggressive proselytizer, but by the 1750s his chief concerns were the spiritual, physical, and financial security of his church and its members. As a result, the 1750s saw not only talk of scaling back Bethlehem's already extensive missionary work,[27] but an apparent ban on such work in any new American settlement. Thus, in discussing the attraction of Lord Granville's property in North Carolina, Zinzendorf pointed with approval at the distance his people could put between themselves and Carolina's Indian population. Moreover, in his plans for developing a colony on the Granville land, the *Jünger* made no reference to

either missions or missionaries, and when a 1755 church conference raised the possibility of Moravian colonists in North Carolina preaching to their neighbors it was rejected at once because
"that is not the *Jünger's* inclination." [28]
Zinzendorf's inclination was toward privacy and profits, instead, and to get those he had to find a piece of land that was
neither too big nor too small and was neither too far from nor
too close to existing settlements. It had to be large enough to
include a buffer of land between a Moravian city at its center
and non-Moravian settlers around it. This would enable church
officials to decide unilaterally who could come into their community and how long they could stay, thus eliminating much of
the uncontrolled contact that is inevitable between close neighbors and was often a source of the "wicked Examples" decried
by Moravian elders. It could not be too large, though, because
if non-Moravian customers had to travel too far to reach Moravian shops they would simply go elsewhere. By the same token,
it had to be close enough to existing settlements and trade
routes for its Moravian population to import goods cheaply and
export them profitably, but not close enough to make the land
so expensive that the church could only afford a tract too small
to permit the buffer it wanted. Against these criteria Moravian
officials weighed the offers of land they had received. Some they
rejected because they promised too little room between the
Brethren and their neighbors. Others because they threatened
too much; Labrador, for instance, failed because Zinzendorf
thought "it is good for colonizing; but not for trade." Lord Granville's North Carolina holdings, however, offered exactly what
the *Jünger* wanted. [29]

Midway through the eighteenth century North Carolina was
just emerging from a century of stunted growth. Its development had long been retarded by an Atlantic coastline that consisted of low sandy islands known as the Outer Banks. Between
these islands there were few inlets large enough to admit a sea-
going vessel, and the openings there were kept changing location and appearance, making passage through the Outer Banks
a perilous undertaking that most mariners chose to avoid. Without ready access to the sea, settlers in North Carolina could

never establish the sort of export-oriented, staple agriculture that drew so many immigrants to Virginia during the seventeenth and early eighteenth centuries. Only the success of colonies farther north finally made North Carolina seem more attractive. During the second quarter of the eighteenth century thousands of Germans and Scotch-Irish came to America in search of better lives. Most entered through the port of Philadelphia and then went west to look for land. As the influx continued, though, successive waves had to go farther and farther west to find the right combination of good soil and low prices, and by the early 1730s the vanguard of this immigrant army had crossed South Mountain, some two hundred miles inland from Philadelphia, and entered the Cumberland Valley. From there, continuing west meant climbing into the heart of the Allegheny Mountains, while the route south lay along the floor of a wide, fertile valley. Migrants, therefore, tended to head south. During the next two decades thousands of recently arrived immigrants streamed out of Pennsylvania, across western Maryland, up Virginia's Shenandoah Valley, and into the northern piedmont of North Carolina.[30]

After almost a century of slow growth, North Carolina's white population suddenly jumped 140 percent between 1730 and 1750 as the German and Scotch-Irish tide reached its borders. Moreover, those who came first sent back glowing reports of what they found; so most observers expected even greater numbers to follow. Granville's land, therefore, was one of the few regions in British America that offered the Brethren exactly what they wanted: a current population and demand for land low enough to permit their purchase of a large, unbroken tract on which to separate church members from outsiders and the promise of a future population large enough to provide a market for Moravian products, services, and land sales.[31]

Serious discussions between Granville and Zinzendorf began sometime in 1750, and the two men reached rapid agreement on the broad outlines of a sale. The Unity committed itself to buying one hundred thousand acres of Granville's land and to paying a quitrent of three shillings per hundred acres in addition to the purchase price. For his part, Granville agreed to sell

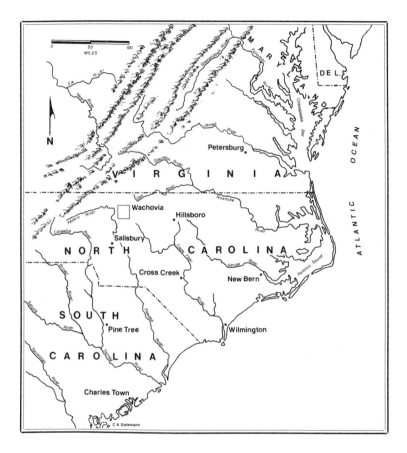

Map 1. The Southern Colonies, c. 1760

the land in a single block slightly more than twelve miles square, which would allow the Brethren to settle near its center and leave several miles between themselves and their closest neighbors. He also enhanced the colony's economic potential by giving the Brethren permission to locate their land astride a navigable river, by promising them "free Egress & Regress to all path[s] & Highways" in the area, and by permitting them to draw the bounds of their land in any way they wanted, which freed them to "cut out the barren Land" if they so desired. The only points over which there was any disagreement were the rate at which the colonists would be required to clear their land and the lengths to which the Proprietor would go to protect them from North Carolina's non-Moravian population. These too were settled, however, without too much difficulty. In the case of the former, Granville gave the Moravians six years instead of the usual three in which to clear three percent of their holdings or forfeit the grant, and concerning the latter he agreed "[to] engage to use his interest" with the general assembly to protect his Moravian tenants from persecution. With those concessions a Unity conference formally accepted the offer of land on November 29, 1751.[32]

All that remained now was for someone to go to North Carolina and find a tract that met the church's needs. For that Zinzendorf turned to Bishop August Gottlieb Spangenberg (1704–1792). There was probably no one better qualified for this assignment. Though born and educated in Germany, Spangenberg had spent much of his adult life in America and knew as well as anyone what it would take to establish a colony in North Carolina. In 1735 he had led the first party of Brethren to arrive on the American mainland, ten men sent to settle in Georgia. He remained with them just a year, though, before moving on. He first went north to investigate briefly the possibility of establishing a Moravian presence in Pennsylvania and then spent three years visiting missionaries on St. Thomas and settlers in Georgia before returning to Europe in 1739. The following year, while Spangenberg was still in Europe, the handful of Moravians left in Georgia gave in to the climate and to the threat of war and moved north to Pennsylvania, settling at what was later named Bethlehem. Thus when Spangenberg returned to America, in 1744, he went to Bethlehem. He also went as a bishop in the Moravian Church and as its leader in America, and for the next five years he directed the development of Bethlehem and the Unity's other Pennsylvania settlements. During those years Spangenberg demonstrated exactly the sort of pragmatism and common sense it took to get a colony on its feet in the New World. Unfortunately, pragmatism and common sense fell out of favor in the Unity during "the period of sifting," and Spangenberg was relieved of his duties and recalled to Europe in 1749. His fall was brief, however. The emotionalism of the 1740s was already waning, and in 1751, shortly before Zinzendorf and Granville concluded their negotiations, Spangenberg was sent back to Bethlehem. There, in 1752, he received instructions to go to North Carolina and select the land for yet another Moravian colony.[33]

Spangenberg and four others left Bethlehem in August of 1752. A sixth member caught up with them later, and the whole party made its way down Maryland's eastern shore, through Virginia, to Edenton, North Carolina. There they met Francis Corbin, Granville's agent in the colony, who was under instructions to help them in any way he could. There was, however, little Corbin could do. Pioneers arriving on the Granville Tract knew that if they registered a claim with the Proprietor he would expect regular quitrent payments, and this gave them a strong incentive not to file. Moreover, Corbin's office was more than one hundred miles east of the frontier, which made it difficult for settlers to enter their claims and practically impossible for Corbin to detect squatters. In this chaotic situation Granville's agent had no idea how much of the Proprietor's land was still vacant or where the vacant land was. The best he could do was point the Brethren west and tell them to head for the backcountry, where they might be able to find one hundred thousand unclaimed acres. For the next four months Spangenberg, his companions, and a collection of guides, surveyors, and hunters crisscrossed North Carolina in search of land. They stopped occasionally to survey promising bits, but none even approached the size Zinzendorf had in mind. Finally, in January 1753, the expedition stumbled across nearly seventy-five thousand unclaimed acres at the forks of Muddy Creek, in central North Carolina. They immediately surveyed the tract plus two others lying next to it and containing another twenty-five thousand acres between them. With these three plats and those of another ten pieces they had laid out earlier the explorers returned to Bethlehem in February 1753.[34]

By May, Spangenberg was in London, and on the basis of his

report the Unity decided to buy the Muddy Creek land and the
two smaller tracts adjoining it. Together, the three made up a
single block containing 98,895 acres. Zinzendorf asked Granville
to convey the land in nineteen separate parcels, despite the ex-
tra expense of nineteen deeds; that way if the church fell behind
in its payments it could give up a portion of the land rather than
all of it. In August the two parties finally signed the deeds, and
for £500, sterling, plus an annual quitrent of just over £148 the
Moravians acquired a new American plantation. They named it
after an Austrian estate that belonged to Zinzendorf's family; in
German it was *der Wachau* and in English, Wachovia.[35]

Wachovia lay in the southeastern corner of what had just become Rowan County, North Carolina's newest and largest
county. In 1753 Rowan included the entire northwest quarter of
the colony and stood at the edge of European settlement. This
gave Wachovia just the sort of untapped potential that Zinzendorf wanted. Its natural resources were tremendous. The soil
was a light grey loam that, though largely covered by forests in
1753, the Moravians' surveyor/cartographer later claimed would
grow anything. The region's temperature and rainfall seemed to
the Moravians ideal for the production of necessary food crops,
like wheat, and more exotic commodities, like wine and silk,
that they planned to raise for export. Its forests contained dozens of varieties of useful trees and shrubs and were extensive
enough to meet the needs of settlers for years to come. And its
streams, though too shallow or swift to be navigable, promised
abundant water throughout the year for consumption and
power.[36]

As rich as Wachovia's natural resources were, however, its
human resources were practically nil in 1753. The native Saponi
and Tutelo Indians, with whom John Lawson had stayed early
in the eighteenth century, had finally given in to European
germs and pressure and retreated toward the mountains. Few
whites had yet moved in to replace them, though. Rowan
County had approximately thirty-six hundred residents by
1753, but the majority of them seem to have lived southwest of
Wachovia, where the Great Trading Path crossed the Yadkin
River. In the northern part of the county, where Wachovia lay,

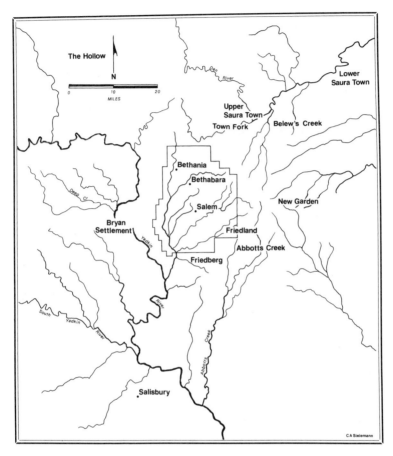

Map 2. Wachovia and Its Environs, 1753–1772

settlers were quite literally few and far between. Two men had claimed land on Belew's Creek, ten miles northwest. North toward Town Fork Creek, a half-dozen farms were strung out along the road to Virginia at intervals of a mile or more. West and southwest of the Moravians' land, near and beside the Yadkin River, was a cluster of homesteads known as the Bryan Settlement. Near Wachovia's southeast corner an unknown number of people were living along Abbotts Creek. And in Wachovia itself three families had been living when the Brethren bought the land, but two had moved on before the first Moravian settlers arrived.[37]

Over the years both mythology and history have often described early Carolinians, including those in Rowan County, as criminals, debtors, runaway servants, and other human debris from the colonies farther north. Moravian officials, too, sometimes tarred their neighbors with this brush, and a Quaker visitor who passed east of Wachovia on her way to and from the New Garden settlement during 1753–54 considered sleeping among the wild animals of the forest because they seemed less threatening to her than the "depraved" creatures she met at an inn. Such claims, however, were usually the exaggerated first impressions of newcomers. In the Moravians' case, for example, once the Brethren settled in Wachovia their almost daily references to the neighbors described them as unschooled, unchurched, and often poor, but generally as friendly, helpful, and law-abiding. There were undoubtedly those among them who were despicable, but most were probably no worse than other poor or middling Americans and Europeans of the day.[38]

Because Rowan County had such a small and scattered population it is hardly surprising that there were few signs of organized society there when the Brethren arrived. There was a county government—court, clerk, sheriff, and constables, but its powers were limited. Spangenberg commented in 1752 that throughout North Carolina "fist law" was often the only law, and modern scholars have agreed almost unanimously that on the southern colonial frontier county governments were generally weak or corrupt or both. Rowan had settlements and neighborhoods in 1753 but neither towns nor villages, and although the county court had authorized construction of a jail and courthouse, it had not yet chosen a site on which to build them. Nor did the county have many religious institutions. Presbyterians had established at least two congregations; Quakers were organizing a meeting just across the border in adjacent Orange County; and Rowan's boundaries were coextensive with those of St. Luke's Anglican parish, though there were few if any Anglicans living there and neither a vestry nor a minister to care for those who did.[39] Economically, the region around Wachovia was equally undeveloped in 1753. Most of the area's inhabitants practiced subsistence agriculture at a very low level. The average land grant in Rowan contained about five hundred acres, but only a fraction of that was cleared, and a Moravian visitor reported in 1754 that the residents "make little on their farms. . . and live from their hunting." As for economic activities other than farming and hunting, there were almost none. When Spangenberg crossed North Carolina in 1752 he commented on the scarcity of "handicrafts" between Edenton and Granville County. West of Granville, though, he said nothing, which suggests that artisans were even scarcer in that region than they were in the east. Two years later Wachovia's first Moravian residents detailed just how scarce. In letters to their superiors the colonists reported that the closest grist mill was nineteen miles away, that it was sixty miles to a store or blacksmith, and that the nearest landing for the receipt or dispatch of goods by water was 150 miles distant with no road linking it to the church's land.[40]

Into this wilderness the Unity sent its first ten settlers in the fall of 1753. Their immediate job was simply to clear a way for others to follow; they were "[to] build a house (simply out of necessity for passing through), clear some land, plant some Indian corn and purchase some cattle." Once these harbingers had prepared a base, others would follow "and with their combined strength continue the work that they began." Ultimately, these and subsequent arrivals were to build the Moravians' city upon a hill. At its center would stand the *gemein Ort* with its population of Moravian craftsmen, merchants, and administrators and their wives and children. Around that, plans called for thirty thousand acres of family farms occupied by Moravian families and around that seventy thousand acres sold to investors in the church-sponsored Nord Carolina Land und Colonie Etablissement and occupied by them and their tenants, servants, and slaves. Moravian magistrates would govern the community;

Moravian legislators would represent it in the general assembly; and the profits it drew from local and international markets would flow into Moravian coffers.[41]

By the church's reckoning it took nineteen years to complete the work those pioneers began. But finally, in the spring of 1772, Wachovia's first historian was able to declare that "on this site, after the passage of nearly 19 years, was finally attained what had been the goal at the beginning of Wachovia, to establish a *gemein Ort* in the center and on the rest to propose small villages and a patriarchal, rural life."[42] During those same years the larger community of which Wachovia was a part also grew. The sparsely inhabited, scarcely developed region that had been Rowan County in 1753 was by 1772 Rowan, Surry, and part of Guilford counties. Its population was approaching twenty thousand and included a wide range of ethnic, religious, social, and economic groups. Its economy had grown to include a mix of small farms and large plantations producing wheat for export and a variety of goods for local consumption, while the size and diversity of its nonfarm sector had also grown. Even its government had recently shown that with the help of provincial authorities it could govern effectively. And as these two communities grew, so did the links between Moravians and non-Moravians in them, not enough to eclipse the former's distinctiveness but enough to make them an integral part of North Carolina's increasingly heterogeneous society.[43]

All of that, however, lay in the future on that cold afternoon in November when Wachovia's founders reached their new home. The next day being a Sunday, they rested out of respect for the neighbors' Sabbath, but on Monday, November 19, 1753, they unpacked their tools and went to work.[44]

CHAPTER 2

The Chosen People

First came the people. Between 1753 and 1772 Wachovia's Moravian community included a total of some three hundred fifty men, women, and children who lived at different times in the villages of Bethabara, Bethania, and Salem. This was never the entire population of Wachovia, nor even all the Moravians living there. Almost from the beginning there had been residents of Wachovia who did not belong to its Moravian community. First, there were the refugees. During the French and Indian War hundreds of non-Moravians came in search of protection behind the log walls that surrounded Bethabara and its mill complex. Many of them spent months at a time with the Brethren over the course of six years until peace returned to the frontier. Then there were the dozens of families, both Moravian and non-Moravian, that bought land inside the bounds of Wachovia without becoming members of the Moravian community. The Unity had always planned for investors to settle outsiders on their land, but during the 1760s it was also forced to permit them on its own land, which it had not intended, as it discovered how terribly expensive colonization could be and how unreliable the promises were of some of those who had pledged to support the Land und Colonie Etablissement.[1]

Thus, throughout its first two decades Wachovia often had as many residents who did not belong to the Moravian community as did. But the nonmembers were always excluded both physically and emotionally from the church community. Most of the refugees were housed in a separate enclave near Bethabara's mill, about a mile from the village itself, and when the Unity began leasing and selling land to outsiders it first drew lines around Bethabara, Bethania, and Salem—lines inside of which outsiders were forbidden to settle "so that nothing becomes mixed."[2] Nor did church officials attempt to govern the lives of those who lived outside the church community, even though they lived inside Wachovia. The elders could and did regulate such people's public behavior through church ownership of their land or through the authority of civil officials who were also Moravians, but they did not try to control their private lives. Wachovia's Moravian community, then, was a discrete entity within visible and invisible boundaries. Its members included those individuals who lived under the direct and total supervision of Moravian officials, and they are the focus of this chapter.

The Moravian community was, in many ways, as diverse a group as one could find in colonial British America. They ranged in age from newborns to sexagenarians, came from a dozen different nations, earned their livings in a dozen different ways, and included born Moravians, converts to the faith, and even a few non-Moravians. But with the exception of children born in Wachovia they all shared one important characteristic; each was chosen by the Moravian Church for admission to the colony. Some had proposed themselves for service in Wachovia. Peter Stotz, for example, was a young potter living in Bethlehem when he developed "a longing toward North Carolina" in the fall of 1762. Others were proposed by various church officials in accordance with the Unity's attitude that members "[should] always keep the pilgrim spirit and whenever they could be used at any place to be ready and prepared immediately." Thus, in 1765, Susanna Maria Krause, then a forty-six-year-old widow in Herrnhut, was suddenly nominated to marry Daniel Schnepf, a forty-seven-year-old single brother who had volunteered to go to Wachovia, and was sent with her new husband to settle in North Carolina. By whatever means an individual's name came up, though, it had to be approved twice before he or she was admitted to Wachovia's Moravian community. On a few rare occasions the selection process took place in North Carolina, but most often it was in Bethlehem or in one of the Unity's European centers. In either case a board of church elders had to consider the person's qualifications first, and if the elders were satisfied they consulted the Lot to determine the Lord's will. Only those whom both God and the elders accepted were permitted to settle in or near Bethabara, Bethania, or Salem.[3]

The Lord, of course, could work in mysterious ways. The elders, however, based their decisions on a combination of spiritual and practical concerns. First, though not always foremost, were the spiritual. With very few exceptions, about which I will say more later in this chapter, one had to be a member in good standing of the Moravian Church to become part of Wachovia's Moravian community. In Moravian eyes nothing divided the world more sharply than religion. Even the language they used emphasized that division; people were either brothers and sisters or "*Fremden*," strangers. The latter were generally people who lived according to "the will of the flesh" and showed no desire to change. The Brethren, on the other hand, had shown themselves to be such ancient and active supporters of the Lord that they considered their church the "Standard Bearer of Christianity."And because their effort to settle Wachovia was an important part of their service to the Lord, it would not do to open that colony to unbelievers whose immoral behavior might taint the godly environment that Unity planners hoped to maintain there. Moreover, both the Ancient and Renewed Unitys had suffered persecution at the hands of outsiders, and one of the motives that led Zinzendorf to establish a Moravian community on the Carolina frontier was his desire to distance its members from potential enemies. Under the circumstances, he could hardly be expected to welcome non-Moravians into it.[4]

It was not enough to be just a Moravian, though. One had to be a good Moravian. The eighteenth-century Moravian Church made extraordinary demands upon its members. Its leaders routinely asked individual brothers and sisters to grant church officials the authority to determine where they would live, who they would marry, what jobs they would hold, and how they would raise their children. That sort of central direction was especially important in the establishment of new communities, though, because resources of every kind were too precious

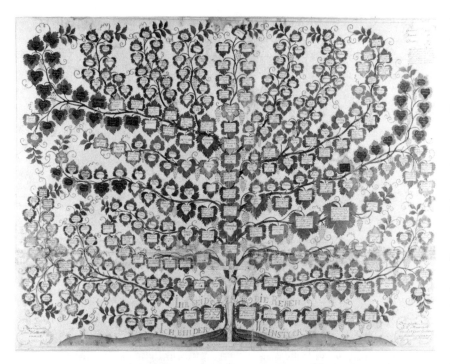

2. This Fractur Tree of the Unity, executed in 1775 by P. J. Ferber, captures beautifully the Moravians' sense of their church's history and international scope. Different shaped medallions on the leaves of the tree designate congregations, major events in church history, and societies affiliated with the Unity. Black medallions represent black congregations, events, and societies in the West Indies and Georgia. (Courtesy of Old Salem Inc.)

there to be utilized in any but the most efficient way. In choosing settlers for Wachovia, therefore, it was essential to select men and women who would accept readily the decisions of their elders and, if necessary, put the church's welfare ahead of their own. In their effort to identify such individuals the leaders of any congregation could supplement their own knowledge of church members with that of their peers in other congregations. In the eighteenth century every member of the Unity was under the close supervision of at least one official whose duty it was

3. Detail of the Fractur Tree showing the congregations and societies in North Carolina in 1775. (Courtesy of Old Salem Inc.)

to watch that individual's spiritual condition for any sign of deviance. These shepherds were required to file periodic reports on the members of their flocks so Unity and congregation elders "might never lack . . . the necessary, thorough, and reliable knowledge of our brothers and sisters." Moreover, whenever a church member moved from one congregation to another he or she was supposed to carry "a testimony from the worker [spiritual advisor] of the former place to the future one." Armed with these reports and with any other information they could gather, Moravian elders sought to identify the most spiritually fit brothers and sisters for admission to Wachovia's Moravian community and rejected those who did not measure up.[5]

Religion, however, was not the only standard by which Unity leaders judged potential residents of Wachovia. Permission to settle in the church community there also depended on one's ability to make a practical demographic or economic contribution. Serving the church demographically simply meant being of the right age, sex, or marital status to help effect whatever balance or imbalance Wachovia's planners wanted at a particular time. They might want mature, single men to perform strenuous or dangerous work one year and the next want equal numbers of adolescent males and females in order to enlarge the pool of eligible marriage partners. Whatever the church wanted, though, individuals were accepted or rejected, in part, on the basis of such demographic demands.

Economic service involved providing whatever job skills the church considered necessary or desirable at a particular stage in Wachovia's development. In North Carolina, as in Pennsylvania, Moravian leaders felt that the success of their community depended in part on church control of its economy. That control took the form of a semi-communal institution known as the *Oeconomy,* which August Spangenberg praised in 1759 as "an incomparable institution for American divinely invented for the success of His people, for the promotion of His affairs, for the confusion of His enemies, for the support of the blessed children's institutions, for the care of those who have served, for the relief of weary pilgrims, etc. and wisely maintained against all machinations of evil-minded men, where not [against] the

Devil himself." Between 1753 and 1772 most of Wachovia's Moravian residents belonged to the colony's *Oeconomy;* only those living in Bethania and a few in Bethabara were outside the system. The *Oeconomy* did not abolish private property. Members were allowed to retain whatever resources they brought with them when they entered, though there were restrictions on the ownership of land or cattle in Wachovia, and members were supposed to deposit their cash with the *Oeconomy's* directors. More than anything else, the *Oeconomy* resembled life in a company town. The church owned all the factors of production except labor, which individual brothers and sisters provided in return for food, housing, clothing, medical care, and education for themselves and their families, and directors of the *Oeconomy* decided how best to utilize all of those resources, including labor. Thus, if the directors felt that Bethabara needed a cooper they relayed their request to Bethlehem and/or Europe, and that became one of the criteria by which officials there selected a colonist.[6]

During the years of settlement the precise blend of spiritual and practical qualifications sought for Wachovia changed a number of times. In general, however, there seem to have been three periods of colonization: breaking the ice, 1753–55; broadening the base for further growth, 1755–65; and building the *gemein Ort,* 1765–72. Each of these involved the selection and dispatch of a different sort of settler, though always one chosen by Moravian officials.

During the first period, from the fall of 1753 to the fall of 1755, the principal concern of church leaders was for the basic survival of the Brethren sent to Wachovia. As August Spangenberg warned in 1753, the colony's first settlers would have to cross five hundred miles of forest inhabited by "bears and wolves, panthers and other beasts" just to reach Carolina. Then the real work would begin—"to cut down the trees among which one slept the night before, to proceed in the work until one has a house, tills a field, clears a road, encloses a garden, etc.," and all of it in the relative isolation of frontier Rowan County.[7]

In spite of the obvious incentive to choose settlers with practical skills, and in spite of Zinzendorf's directive that those selecting colonists should "pay more attention at the beginning to usefulness than to interior," there is no evidence that the elders in Bethlehem slighted religion in their choices. One year after settlement began in Wachovia nine of the nineteen men then living in Bethabara sent greetings to Spangenberg on the colony's first anniversary. Those of George Holder are typical of the rest and demonstrate clearly the strength of his religious devotion. "I am happy in the Wounds of the Lamb as a poor Sinner, that has no Right but out of Mercy, thro' the Blood of the Lamb," wrote Brother Holder. "I will let Him be my Master, and will let Him do with me, what He pleases. I cannot express myself as I would. I am poor and miserable, when I think on myself, so I am ashamed to show my Face to my Brethren. But I thank my dear Savior for what he has done on me."[8]

Moravian officials did, however, make two concessions to the environment in their selection of Wachovia's first settlers. Women were out of the question. Church leaders expected life to be rough on the North Carolina frontier, and they shared the universal assumption of their time and culture that women were too fragile to survive in such a place. Writing in 1755, Spangenberg reminded the men living in Bethabara that "the Holy Scriptures speak of it, that they [women] are weaker than we men and therefore it is important that they be more cared for." Once the wilderness was tamed somewhat women would go, but not during these first two years. For much the same reason, the elders also showed a preference for men who had been in America for several years, at least, before their departure for Carolina. They wanted men who were already "accustomed to the land, air, and work" of the New World, men like Erich Ingebretsen. Ingebretsen was a Norwegian, born at Roras in December 1721, who joined the Unity as a young man. By the late 1740s he was living in Herrnhag, and when the church decided to abandon its settlement there he was one of many Brethren sent to Pennsylvania. Arriving there in the summer of 1750, Brother Ingebretsen was assigned to the Unity's farm at Christiansbrunn, several miles north of Bethlehem, probably as a carpenter. By the summer of 1753 he had been in America for three years and with his training as a carpenter and millwright was

an ideal choice for Wachovia. Thus, 31-year-old Erich Ingebretsen became one of Bethabara's founders.[9]

The selection of men like Ingebretsen during Wachovia's first
two years gave the colony a demographic profile quite familiar
to students of the colonial southern frontier. At the close of this
first period of colonization its population was entirely male, unmarried, and largely adult. In the fall of 1755 thirty-three men
lived in the village of Bethabara. None of them were married,
and although Johan Joseph Muller and John Ranke were just
fourteen and eighteen, respectively, all of the others were at
least twenty-one. In fact, the group's median age was a mature
32.5 This was noticeably higher than the average ages found on
other southern frontiers so early in their histories and was undoubtedly a result of the elders' decision to employ men of
proven talents in Wachovia's initial stage.[10]

The Moravian community entered its second demographic
phase in the fall of 1755, when its directors shifted their emphasis from insuring the colony's basic survival to effecting the
growth and maturation of its society and economy. A year earlier, in May 1754, Spangenberg had written his colleagues in
Europe that "now the hardest nut is cracked and the ice is broken [in Wachovia]. Brethren who come there now will find
Brethren already." In Spangenberg's view Moravian pioneers
had established a firm foundation at Bethabara and it was time
to build on that foundation and to turn Bethabara into a proper
Moravian community capable of supporting the construction of
Wachovia's *gemein Ort*. This change in goals would require a
change in personnel.[11]

The elder's new emphasis on enlarging and stabilizing the
community first became evident with the expedition to Bethabara of "the Little Pilgrim Congregation," which left Bethlehem
in October of 1755. From then until the middle of 1765 the officials responsible for peopling Wachovia chose settlers who
could help realize the Unity's goal of a wealthier, more stable
colony, settlers like Gottfried and Maria Grabbs. Both Grabbs
had been born in Germany in 1716—he in Silesia and she in
Saxony. They came to the church independently and by different routes, but by 1743 both were living in Marienborn. They

were married that summer in one of the Unity's periodic "Great Weddings"—mass ceremonies uniting dozens of couples at once—and almost immediately afterward were sent to America, arriving in Bethlehem late in 1743. There they remained for thirteen years, until the summer of 1756 and the elders' decision that God needed them in Wachovia. Then, at the age of forty, Gottfried and Maria Grabbs took their nine-month-old son, William, and joined five single Brethren on the long journey to Bethabara.

In a number of important ways the Grabbs and other settlers in this second cohort were different from those who had come before them. In the first place, the men were different. To strengthen Wachovia economically required more master craftsmen; Gottfried Grabbs, for instance, was Bethlehem's miller and was sent to Bethabara because August Spangenberg wanted the mill there to generate more income.[12] Similarly, giving Wachovia's residents the ability to decide more matters on their own, instead of forcing them to wait for instructions about everything from Pennsylvania, meant sending the colony men with administrative experience.[13] Both of these qualities, artisanal skill and governmental experience, tended to increase with age; so the sixty-six brothers sent to Wachovia between 1755 and 1765 tended to be even older when they arrived than their predecessors had been. The median age of this group was thirty-five—more than two years older than that of the group that came before them. Older Brethren were also more likely to be married, and the rising age of Wachovia's immigrants was matched by a rise in the number who were married from none to 30 percent.

Second, the wave of immigrants that began arriving in 1755 included the first women sent to the colony; thirty-five of the one hundred one adults sent between 1755 and 1765 were women. For practical reasons, sisters were desirable in a Moravian community. There were certain jobs, chiefly "laundry, mending, sewing and the like," that in the view of Moravian leaders were done best by women. Men had done them during the colony's first two years, but now they "could be attended to properly." For theological reasons, moreover, women were essential to a proper Moravian congregation. The Brethren considered marriage more than just "a holy ordinance of God"; it was the means "whereby out of a creature that was but a walking sink or sewer, there is formed a temple of the Holy Ghost." Because this important step in one's spiritual progress was impossible without equal numbers of men and women, the Unity was especially interested in sending single women to Wachovia so the single men there would not become, in Zinzendorf's words, "an eternal race." Unfortunately, at the middle of the eighteenth century there were very few unmarried women in the Unity's American settlements. In Bethlehem, for instance, single brethren outnumbered single sisters by seven to one in 1753. There were plenty of unmarried women in the European congregations, but from 1756 until 1763 the Seven Years War made it too dangerous for them to cross the Atlantic. As a result, only six unmarried sisters reached Wachovia between 1755 and 1765, though in nine other cases single men from Bethabara were sent back to Bethlehem to marry and brought their brides south with them when they returned. Most of the women who arrived from Bethlehem during this period, however, were married sisters like Maria Grabbs, whose husbands too were new to Carolina.[14]

Finally, Wachovia's second group of immigrants included the colony's first children. This was actually contrary to the wishes of church leaders. Children were consumers rather than producers, and their presence in Wachovia undermined the Unity's effort to strengthen that settlement's economy. Moreover, frontier North Carolina was a dangerous place for Moravian children in the late 1750s. Cherokee warparties threatened their lives, and the absence of institutions usually found in Moravian congregations for protecting and nurturing children threatened their souls as well. Church leaders, therefore, discouraged parents from taking their children to Carolina, and most of the married couples with children, who migrated from Bethlehem to Wachovia between 1755 and 1765, did leave their offspring in Pennsylvania. In this, Gottfried and Maria Grabbs were unusual. They were one of just three couples who brought their children, and young William was one of only five who made the trip.

The second phase of Wachovia's demographic development also saw a change in Moravian policy toward the admission of outsiders to their community. Wachovia's planners had always expected non-Moravians to settle on Etablissement land, but they had not intended for Brethren and *Fremden* to inhabit the same villages. Conditions on the Carolina frontier, however, forced them to modify that stand in 1759. By the late 1750s Bethabara, which was supposed to be merely a temporary settlement from which Salem was built, had grown so large that Unity leaders were afraid it would become a permanent rival to the still-unstarted *gemein Ort*. To remedy this problem officials in Bethlehem sent Spangenberg to Bethabara in the spring of 1759 with instructions to establish a second Moravian village, Bethania, and to people it with Bethabara's surplus. On arriving in Wachovia, however, Spangenberg found himself in the middle of an Indian war and soon concluded that if Bethania consisted only of Bethabara's overflow it would be too small to defend itself. Fortunately, the same Indians who threatened Wachovia also provided a solution to Spangenberg's dilemma. The threat of Cherokee attacks had frequently driven many of Rowan County's non-Moravian settlers to seek refuge inside the log stockades that surrounded Bethabara and its grist mill. By 1759 some of these refugees had already spent three summers with the Brethren, and Spangenberg considered their presence an opportunity to serve the Lord in two ways at once. Allowing a select group of refugee families to form a society and to settle with the Brethren in Bethania would bring new souls to the Lord while providing additional bodies to help protect those that were already His.[15]

With this in mind, Spangenberg and Wachovia's resident elders used the Lot to select seven Moravian couples for transfer from Bethabara to Bethania (an eighth was chosen later). Then they decided that "regardless of all objections, we can establish several of the refugees in the new village." Ten days later, and no doubt well aware of the elders' decision, eight refugee families living at Bethabara's mill wrote the Brethren that they "perceived the truth of the Brothers' teaching" and wished to join them. The next day a meeting of Bethabara's congregation decided it was God's will to settle these non-Moravians in Bethania, and before the summer was out God's will was done.[16]

Zinzendorf objected to this innovation as soon as he learned of it, but he died soon thereafter, and the leadership that succeeded him accepted the carefully controlled admission of a few non-Moravians to Bethania and the formation of a society there. And admission to Bethania was carefully controlled. A conference of ministers described the process in 1760: "When anyone wants to move to Bethania, one examines the reason why they want that. And if no one in the conference has anything against, and if necessary, other brothers and sisters made their opinion heard and everyone else is in favor, then the Savior should be asked about it [through the Lot] in the conference." Only then were individuals granted trials in Bethania, and if their conduct endangered the souls of their neighbors or showed the Unity in a bad light they could be expelled. Non-Moravians admitted in this way were not required to join the Unity, though; they could remain mere society members. Most, however, wanted to join the church, and most became members within a few years of settling in Bethania.[17]

The changing nature of migration to Wachovia and the admission of outsiders to its Moravian community led to a number of corresponding changes in that community's demographic profile between 1755 and 1765 (Table 1). It ceased to be all male and adults only, as it had been for the first two years, and moved rapidly toward the early modern norm of a society in which males and females were present in roughly equal numbers and in which children represented about one-third the total population.[18] The most striking and important change came in the colony's adult sex ratio (the number of adult men per 100 adult women). The transition from a largely or entirely male population to one in which the sexes approached numerical equality was common in communities on the southern colonial frontier, but in Wachovia it occurred with unusual speed. Studies of other frontiers in the colonial South have shown that it

Table 1. Free Population of Bethabara, Bethania, and Salem

Year	Total	Adult Sex Ratio	Unmarried Adult Sex Ratio	Children as Percentage of Total	Dependency Ratio
1754	19	all male	all male	0%	NA
1757	72	171 : 100	all male	3.1%	.23 : 1
1759	103	146 : 100	1950 : 100	21.3%	1 : 1
1762	147	167 : 100	550 : 100	34.7%	1.27 : 1
1766	217	128 : 100	316 : 100	30.4%	.83 : 1
1771	261	114 : 100	152 : 100	21.8%	.78 : 1

often took twenty-five to fifty years for these sex ratios to reach the degree of balance found in Wachovia after just one decade. Darrett and Anita Rutman concluded from their painstaking reconstruction of Middlesex County, Virginia's population that the adult sex ratio there was 175 : 100 some fifty years after settlement began. Further west, the process seems to have moved slightly faster, but according to Robert Mitchell the ratio in Virginia's Upper Shenandoah Valley was still in excess of 150 : 100 forty years after the start of settlement there. In the Moravian community, though, it had fallen to 167 : 100 by late 1762, just nine years after the first settlers arrived.[19]

As for the proportion of children in Wachovia's Moravian population, this too rose between 1755 and 1765, though not as far as one would expect. Typically, the southern colonial frontier had very few settlers over the age of forty. As a result, once a community's sex ratio had reached the level Wachovia's had by 1762 the percentage of children in its population was usually 40 percent or more, and its dependency ratio (the ratio of children to adult women) was above 1.5 : 1. In both Middlesex County and the Shenandoah Valley, for example, by the time women made up approximately 40 percent of the adult population, as they did in Wachovia at the end of 1762, children made up nearly 40 percent of the total population and the dependency ratios were 1.55 : 1 in Middlesex and over 2 : 1 in the Valley. In the Moravian community, by contrast, there was no shortage of individuals over forty, and most of the married couples who migrated to Carolina from Bethlehem during the decade 1755–65 left their children under church care in Pennsylvania. Children in Wachovia's Moravian community, therefore, made up only 35 percent of the total population in 1762, and the dependency ratio was a mere 1.27 : 1—both figures low by frontier standards.[20]

The evolution of Wachovia's Moravian population continued after the colony entered its third demographic phase in 1765. Entry into this phase (1765–1772), like that into the second a decade earlier, was initiated by a change in the Unity's short-term priorities for Wachovia's development. On February 14, 1765 elders in Bethabara finally picked a site on which to build Salem, the colony's long-awaited *gemein Ort*, and for the next

seven years the construction of Salem dominated Wachovia's affairs, including the selection of new settlers.[21] With the *gemein
Ort* finally under way, the church no longer concentrated on
sending Wachovia the older, more experienced, married couples
it had sent during the preceding decade. They had been necessary then in order to give the young community greater stability
and earning potential. Now, however, what it needed again
were strong, young men and women to build and occupy a new
town, and this time experience was not essential because the
area around Wachovia was no longer the wilderness it had been
in 1753. Fortunately, by 1765 it had become much easier for the
Unity to provide such people. Peace had finally returned to the
North Atlantic; so it was easier to transport European Moravians to America, including single women. Moreover, an important new source of personnel had emerged as the population of
Bethlehem aged. The Pennsylvania settlement had turned
twenty in 1762, and every year more of its children reached an
age at which Unity leaders felt they could send them to North
Carolina without their parents—at least 12, though usually
fourteen, for boys and sixteen for girls. Thus, between the
middle of 1765 and the close of the *Oeconomy* the Unity sent to
Wachovia the young, unmarried men and women it would take
to build and occupy Salem.

As individuals, the brothers and sisters who made up this
third wave of immigrants were people like Gottfried Praezel and
his future wife, Maria Elisabeth Engel. Praezel was a weaver by
trade and a native of Upper Lusatia, where he was born in 1739.
In the fall of 1765 church elders in Herrnhut tapped him for
inclusion in the first party of Brethren to go from Europe directly to Carolina. After assembling in Zeist, Holland, Praezel,
seven other single brothers, and one married couple took ship
for London. From there they sailed on to Charles Town, and
then set out on foot for Wachovia. On the way north, they met
a wagon sent from Bethabara to fetch them and finished their
journey of four months aboard it. Nine months later Praezel and
his traveling companions were part of the crowd that welcomed
Maria Engel and fifteen other older girls and single sisters (sent
by the elders to establish a choir) as they completed a four-week

hike from Pennsylvania. Once Salem became Wachovia's *gemein Ort*, in the spring of 1772, both Praezel and Engel moved there with their respective choirs; they married in 1783, and lived there until they died, he in 1788 and she in 1823.

As a group, Praezel, Engel, and the others were they youngest settlers yet sent to Wachovia. Among males the median age at arrival was 31.5, a year younger than the first cohort and nearly four years younger than the second, while the age of female migrants fell even further, from 31.5 before 1765 to just 21 afterward. This was not, however, the result of families arriving with young children; only 17 percent of the individuals in this third wave were married when they arrived, compared to 46 percent in the second, and none brought children. Rather, it was the large number of adolescents and young adults arriving between 1765 and 1772 that brought down the average age. This was also the most sexually balanced group of immigrants to arrive in the Moravian community during its early years. Between 1765 and 1772 just over 46 percent of the church members sent to Wachovia were women or girls, compared to 35 percent of those sent during the preceding decade, and the Unity was finally able to send a significant number of single women to the colony.

The arrival in Wachovia of such a relatively large number of female settlers, many of them unmarried, led to a marked and welcome change in the most stubborn component of the colony's frontier demographics, the sex ratio among unmarried adults (Table 1). Although the adult sex ratio in the Moravian community had become more balanced with the arrival of married couples during the late 1750s and early 1760s, the ratio among unmarried adults had remained distressingly imbalanced. In 1762 it was still 550 : 100, which if maintained would have condemned three-fourths of the unmarried men in Wachovia to bachelorhood for life unless they broke church rules and looked beyond the Unity for a spouse. The arrival of parties like that including Maria Engel, however, began to change this. By late 1766 the ratio among unmarried adults had improved to 316 : 100, and at the end of 1771 it was 152 : 100. The latter figure was still far from perfect—threatening to keep a third of Wachovia's unmarried men in that state forever. It was an improvement, though, and left unmarried men in Wachovia in a better situation than their counterparts on other southern colonial frontiers.[22]

By the time Salem became Wachovia's *gemein Ort,* in April of 1772, and the colony's frontier era closed, its population was far more mature demographically than one would expect in a community just nineteen years old. Its adult sex ratio stood at 114 : 100, high for a stable, early modern population but low for one on the southern colonial frontier, and children made up less than a quarter of its population, comparable to levels usually found in eighteenth-century Europe and in older communities in the American colonies and below those common on the southern colonial frontier.

One final element in Wachovia's Moravian community about which something must be said is the handful of blacks enslaved there. Eighteenth-century Moravians had no doubts about the morality of slavery. God had created the institution, and to question His handiwork would be presumptuous if not blasphemous. Like most Europeans and Euro-Americans of their day, Zinzendorf and his followers believed that God had created a rigidly structured universe in which every creature occupied a particular place in a hierarchy that rose from the lowliest worm to the men and women created in His image. The gradations on this Great Chain of Being did not stop with the distinctions between species, though. Among humans at least they were so precise that each individual had a distinct niche, and it was a terrible mistake to ignore them. "The natural caste remains as it is," claimed Zinzendorf. "If one wishes to make a gentleman out of someone who was born to be a peasant, one inflicts upon him a mask with donkey ears." And slavery was just another divinely ordained niche. As August Spangenberg explained, "it is not by chance, rather from God, that one man is a master and the other a slave."[23]

Nor did the Brethren doubt which people God had chosen to occupy humanity's lowest order. After visiting slaves on the island of St. Thomas in 1739, Zinzendorf wrote that God "Punish'd the first Negroes wth Slavery." Zinzendorf evidently accepted the then current doctrine that Noah's son Ham had been cursed for looking upon his father's nakedness. According to the story, Ham's descendants were a people whom God had both blackened and ordered to live as the servants of servants as punishment for their ancestor's transgression. In the Moravian view, therefore, black and slave were synonymous, and black slaves owed both their color and their station to God's judgment on Ham.[24]

This did not, however, place slaves beyond the pale. The Brethren considered blacks fully human and believed they were ignorant of the Lord only because they had been born in Africa, a continent His word had just begun to reach. The stereotypic evil behavior of black slaves was due not to any inherent flaw in their humanity but to the fact that they were generally born among heathens. "One of ye Heathens cannot do so much good as one who has learn'd from his Infancy to do some good & has not been suffer'd to get so many bad Customs," wrote Zinzendorf. "For a Heathen is used from his Infancy to do ye bad & has never learn'd it any better." Once they acknowledged Jesus as their Savior, though, blacks would receive the power to abandon the stubborn, lazy, and unfaithful ways of their earlier lives, and they would hate sin as much as they had loved it before.[25]

To Zinzendorf, the archetypal example of a Christian slave seems to have been Anton, a servant of Count von Danneskiold-Laurvig, director of the Danish West India–Guinea Company, and the first black Zinzendorf ever met. The *Jünger* came to know Anton in 1731, when the former came to Copenhagen to offer King Christian VI his services as "a free volunteer in the service of the Lord." Anton was hardly a typical slave; he had been born in the Danish Antilles, undoubtedly spoke Danish as his native tongue, and was already a Christian when Zinzendorf met him. Nevertheless, the count apparently took him as a model for Christianized blacks and assumed that others could become just as civilized as he. Like Anton, however, they would remain slaves in spite of either conversion or education and would have to continue serving their masters and mistresses

with "Love & Quietness." The Moravians' god might deliver his
black children from "ye Slavery of ye Devil" but not from that
of their fellow men.[26]

These Moravian attitudes toward slavery and blacks made it
easy for Wachovia's planners to imagine a peaceful, multiracial
community in the colony—one in which whites benefitted from
the labor of blacks and "heathen" from the care of Christians.[27]
Imagining this was even easier because such a community already existed in Bethlehem. In the fall of 1753, when the first
colonists left Pennsylvania for Wachovia, the congregation from
which they went owned five of its members. These communicant slaves lived on an ill-defined middle ground between freedom and slavery. Their daily lives were clearly unlike those of
most slaves in America, but they were still property with no
guarantee they would not be sold to less benevolent masters.
As Spangenberg explained in 1760: "At Bethlehem, we too have
negroes. Because of our love to them we do not free them, for
they would be in a worse condition if they got free as if we kept
them. Actually they are not slaves with us, and there is no difference between them and other brothers and sisters. They
dress as we do, they eat what we eat, they work when we work,
they rest when we rest, and they enjoy quite naturally what
other brothers and sisters enjoy."[28]

Congregational records offer little support for Spangenberg's
claim that the Brethren kept their slaves out of love, and the
bishop's letter ignores completely the mental cruelty that went
with slavery—the constant fear of sale and the indignity of losing one's name and heritage, for example. But the description
of material equality between free and enslaved church members
does seem accurate. Slaves in Bethlehem who were also members of the congregation lived in the appropriate choir houses,
occupied positions in their choirs' internal hierarchies, and even
participated in Unity synods. Except for the appellation "der
Mohr," they seldom stand out from their white coreligionists in
the mundane details of daily life.[29]

In North Carolina, though, the Moravians encountered problems they had not foreseen, and as a result blacks did not become an important element in Wachovia's population during the

period covered here. Part of the problem was financial. Slaves were expensive and Unity finances were too strapped to pay for many. But the major factor limiting the use of slaves in Wachovia was a growing concern among church leaders there that bringing such people into their community might endanger its spiritual health.[30]

Between 1758 and 1766 the Reverend John Ettwein, then Wachovia's resident executive, took several extended trips through southern North Carolina and South Carolina. There he discovered slaves who were nothing like Zinzendorf's Anton. They were neither Christianized nor Europeanized. Many spoke African languages still and preserved their traditional music and dance, which the Brethren considered "the Devil's work," and because their masters were seldom concerned about their spiritual welfare they often lived and died in total ignorance of God's word. Not surprisingly, Ettwein worried about the effect such people might have on a Moravian community. He also worried, as did others of his day, about the apparent tendency of slave owners to develop unchristian habits themselves. Speaking of South Carolina Germans he had met, Ettwein wrote in 1763: "I wish their Children may turn out a good Race but am afraid the Negroes have too much Influence upon them and I have observed that often where a Man has Slaves his Children become lazy & indolent etc. What I saw and heard of the Negroes [in South Carolina] made me very uneasy. If some care was taken of their Souls their Servitude might be a blessing unto them but I [could] hear nothing of that and even of no Prospect for such a Thing."[31]

In spite of their fears, Moravian settlers in Wachovia eventually began to employ slaves. Initially, they seem to have done so simply to cope with a persistent shortage of labor in the colony. During the 1750s and early 1760s there were seldom enough workers in Bethabara to meet the *Oeconomy's* demand, and elders there wrote frequently to their superiors asking for more. Finally, in 1763, the overseer of Wachovia's *Oeconomy*, Abraham von Gammern, hired a female slave to help in Bethabara's tavern, and while extant records say nothing about the motives behind this decision they do reveal that the hiring of a second slave in 1764 was definitely motivated by the need for more workers. Minutes of the Helpers Conference, which set economic policy in the *Oeconomy,* contain the notation that "Mr. Blackburn [James Blackburn of Town Fork] has offered to lease us his negro for the winter, we will certainly need him in the cow yard, Br. Gammern may therefore make an agreement with him." And three years later, in 1767, the necessity for someone to help Jacobus van der Merk in the mill prompted the same conference to decide it would either have to hire another slave or shift one of the brothers to the mill.[32]

Six years after they began leasing slaves, the Brethren in Wachovia decided to buy their first, and that decision involved much more than a simple search for labor. In 1769 Sam, whom the *Oeconomy* had leased since 1766, "expressed a desire to learn to know the Savior."[33] This, of course, was precisely what Zinzendorf had envisioned in the 1740s and 1750s—Moravians bringing Africans out of the darkness, and Sam appeared to be as good a candidate for salvation as they were likely to find in North Carolina. Having been in Bethabara for three years already, he had had plenty of time to learn something about the Unity, and church leaders had had ample opportunity to look for signs of heathenism in his behavior. Presumably, both he and they believed he could live according to church precepts because on August 9, 1769, the *Oeconomy* bought Sam for £120, paying £20 "in goods or dealings of any kind in the Store or elsewhere in the Town of Bethabara" and £100 in cash due one year later. At the time of the sale Johann Michael Graff wrote that the elders hoped Sam "shall also become the Savior's own," and two years later that faith began to bear fruit. Late in 1771 Sam was baptized and christened Johann Samuel, and the following April he was received into the congregation, though not until 1774 did he take communion for the first time. Sam's example may also have convinced the Brethren to take chances on four other blacks shortly before the *Oeconomy* closed. Between March and October of 1771 they bought Franc, Sambo, Sue, and Sue's daughter Sukey. In none of these instances did the elders explain their action, but they must have hoped that the four would follow Sam's example and become good, albeit enslaved, Moravians.[34]

From its founders, then, to its slaves, Wachovia's Moravian community included truly chosen people. Members were hand-picked for their devotion to the church and for their ability to serve it. And Unity officials, having taken such care to select the right men and women for admission to Wachovia, were determined to provide them with the institutions they would need to protect the community they had become.

CHAPTER 3

The Church Family

As Christians, Moravian officials knew all about temptation. They knew that simply choosing the right people to settle Wachovia would not insure that the Moravian community there retained its distinctive values and characteristics, because even the most carefully selected brothers and sisters were liable to err if left alone for too long. The church, therefore, had to make sure that every individual was part of a group and understood clearly that it was the duty of members to watch one another and assist one another in adhering to the course chosen for them by God and Count von Zinzendorf. In the eighteenth-century Moravian world, including Wachovia, the two most important groups in the provision of such supervision and assistance were the family and the choir.

Family, the older and more familiar of these institutions, served an important symbolic function in Zinzendorf's Moravian Church. In seeking to intensify the emotional link between his followers and their God, the *Jünger* often employed anthropomorphic language to make theological concepts more concrete, and family relationships were a frequent source of such allusions. The Trinity, for example, became a family—God the father, Holy Ghost the mother, and Christ the son—while both the relationship between Christ and the church and the relationship between Christ and the souls of individual Moravians were described as marriages. A Moravian family, therefore, was as living icon with multiple and overlapping meanings. As father and husband, a man represented both God and Christ and was, himself, a bride of Christ because in Zinzendorf's theology all souls were female and married to their Savior. Women were brides of Christ in their own right, but as mothers and wives they also symbolized His mother—the Holy Ghost—and the whole Moravian Church in its capacity as the Bride of Christ. The marriage itself between an earthly husband and wife not only embodied the loving relationship that existed between Christ and His church, but was also so strongly identified with the eternal union between Christ and the souls of individual believers that the temporal version was often described by Moravians as a "proxy marriage." And when children arrived, they not only represented the purity and innocence of Christ but completed a domestic version of the Trinity according to Zinzendorf.[1]

Moravian families were more than just religious symbols, though. As important as that role was, it was only one of their functions. Families in the Unity were also an essential vehicle for the socialization and supervision of individual members. This was especially true in the case of children; to Zinzendorf the family existed "for the sake of the children . . . and for the perpetuation of the fellowship of believers through them." Schools run by the Unity might provide most of a child's academic training as well as much of his or her formal theological education, but it was the parents' duty to instill in their offspring an acceptance of Moravian social ethics. Zinzendorf's Unity made tremendous demands on its members. They were expected to suppress most of their personal desires entirely and surrender to God, through His ministers, the power to decide where they would live, what trade they would practice, who they would marry, and a variety of other questions affecting their private lives. Such total reliance on God's will—the willingness to go through life "with a childlike, trusting heart and always with a clear view of the Savior"—did not come from ministers or teachers telling children what God required of them. To insure the successful transfer of a proper Moravian spirit from one generation to the next, someone had to show children on a daily basis what it meant "[to] belong to a pilgrim folk," and parents were in the best position to do so. In the close confines of a family, parental example exerted a powerful force on children, even before the latter were conscious of it. Moreover, if the twig failed to grow as it was bent, parental supervision offered the best hope of providing early detection of the deviation.[2]

Children, however, were not the only ones to benefit from the intimate supervision provided by a family. Moravian husbands and wives were expected to keep an eye on one another too. Church elders had no illusions about the ability of men and women to lead godly lives day in and day out. They were bound to slip from time to time. By marrying, individual members gained an ally in their effort to resist temptation—someone who could watch their behavior for signs of backsliding and provide loving correction when such signs appeared or, if that failed, report the problem to congregational officials. For this reason Unity leaders regarded married life as an especially effective mechanism for settling individuals whose actions endangered their souls and as a means of reinforcing the faith of church members whose duties forced them to have extended contact with outsiders.

Finally, Moravian families, or at least married couples, were essential to the smooth operation of daily life in church communities. Moravian theology required separating unmarried men and women as completely as possible. Ideally, adolescent and adult members of the two sexes were to have no contact before marriage beyond their joint presence at congregational services, where they sat on opposite sides of the aisle. Married brothers and sisters were the only adults in the congregation allowed to have contact with members of the opposite sex; so certain positions in the community could only be filled by married men and women. For example, any minister responsible for an entire congregation had to marry or be barred from meeting with half his flock. Even the brother who supervised the communal kitchen and cellar under Bethabara's *Oeconomy* had to be married "because he has to have contact with the sisters."[3]

The other group found among eighteenth-century Moravians was their choirs, subdivisions of the congregation based on age, sex, and marital status. Choirs have existed among the Brethren for more than two centuries, but historians still cannot agree on their origins. Some scholars maintain that they began as a temporary measure for housing and feeding a great many people in a hurry when refugees from Moravia and Bohemia started to arrive in Herrnhut during the 1720s and early 1730s, and that spiritual and social functions were added later.[4] Others contend, more convincingly it seems, that the system emerged from Spener's conviction that small groups were the most effective forum for encouraging spiritual growth. As a student at Halle, Zinzendorf had organized several groups for prayer and spiritual edification along lines suggested by Spener in his *Pia Desideria*. Later this preference for small groups resulted in the formation of "bands" in Herrnhut divided on the basis of age and sex to reflect different stages in the life of Jesus, and eventually some of the bands grew into communal institutions whose members lived and worked together in an effort to help one another in their spiritual progress.[5]

Whatever their origins, choirs soon became a ubiquitous and useful institution in Moravian settlements. In established congregations there were choirs for every age and sex: infants, young boys, young girls, older boys, older girls, single brothers, single sisters, married couples, widows, and widowers. From birth to death church members belonged to a choir, passing as they aged from one to another as naturally as they passed through the biological stages of their lives. And when they died, their passing was announced by an anthem peculiar to their choir, and they were buried in God's Acre, the congregational cemetery, in a section reserved for members of their choir. Functionally, Moravian choirs worked like families to divide large congregations into smaller units so their members could supervise one another more easily. But unlike families, one did not need to be born into a choir. Anyone migrating to a Moravian community would find an operating choir into which he or she fit, which made the system immensely beneficial to the church. The eighteenth-century Unity frequently transferred members from one congregation to another, and choirs insured that wherever they went these individuals would be under the sharp but compassionate eyes of church officials from the moment they arrived. Moreover, the system provided a wonderful means by which to socialize adult converts. Choirs brought these newcomers into immediate and intimate contact with the elders and all but eliminated the possibility they would slip between the cracks of a large congregation. And if any choir outgrew its ability to provide the close supervision its members required, it could be further divided into smaller groups known variously as bands, classes, or rooms, each of which was small enough to restore the necessary degree of intimacy.

In fact, choirs were such an effective means of socializing members that for a time it seemed they might replace families altogether in the Unity. The 1740s, the Moravians' "period of sifting," saw a general rise in the church's evangelical spirit, but around Zinzendorf's son, Christian Renatus, there emerged a party within the Unity that sought to intensify dramatically individual members' relationship with their Savior. Wherever these extremists gained control they transferred many of the family's social and economic functions to the choir, and in some congregations choirs and other communal institutions became virtually surrogate families, stripping real ones of all but their reproductive function.[6]

Eventually, however, the elder Zinzendorf concluded that too great a reliance on choirs threatened the Unity's long-term survival. In his opinion, children raised in the spiritual hothouse of the choir system were forgetting that a hammer or plow was as much God's tool as a Bible was. They were enamoured of the missionary ideal and seemed less willing to enter professions requiring manual labor than were youths brought up by their parents, many of whom performed such labor themselves. And though missionaries were important to Zinzendorf, the church also needed farmers, builders, and craftsmen. By the early 1750s the *Jünger* had begun restoring the family's role in raising children, hoping that this would also restore the tradition of sons following their fathers into the fields or workshops. "Otherwise," he wrote, "we get nothing but princes, priests and officers and no common soldiers."[7]

This renewed concern for the family was very evident in Zinzendorf's plans for Wachovia; there he intended to restore the proper balance between family and choir. Both he and Spangenberg considered family life the preferred state for Wachovia's residents. As Spangenberg assured one of his colleagues in 1754, "we do not intend to let the young people in Wachovia remain single till the end of the world, rather to bring them into a patriarchal family condition." Yet all the colony's planners knew there would always be individuals in Wachovia who had no family—young adults who had not yet married, widows and widowers, and the wives of men travelling on church business. To keep watch over these people the elders wanted a full complement of choirs. In Wachovia the two institutions would once again complement, rather than compete with, one another; each would work to promote Moravian values among a particular sector of the colony's population. And because church officials expected both families and choirs to serve an essential role in Wachovia's success, they intended to take an active role in the formation and operation of both.[8]

In the case of families, the elders' role began with making sure that brothers and sisters married within the church. Endogamy, marriage within a specific tribe or similar social unit, had been important to the Unity since its renewal in 1727 because of Zinzendorf's belief that one's spouse was an important ally in one's effort to lead a godly life. It became especially important, though, after the "period of sifting," as parents resumed a leading role in raising Moravian children. The congregation in Bethlehem received a sharp reminder of that fact shortly before the first of their number left for Wachovia. "In particular," wrote Zinzendorf, "I positively forbid the intermarriage of members of our Single Sisters' choir with natives of Pennsylvania," and told them that any woman who ignored this ban "must be left to her own devices."[9] There was no comparable enunciation of policy in early Wachovia, but it was clearly an unspoken rule of life there. Nothing brought disciplinary action faster than marriage outside the church. In the first nineteen years, only one member in North Carolina, a forty-year-old gunsmith named Andrew Betz, made the mistake of choosing a non-Moravian mate. When he did, his superiors decided "to act according to the commonly accepted manner and rules": within three weeks they had excommunicated Betz from the church and expelled him from the colony.[10]

Endogamy had its price, though; insisting that members marry within the church obliged Moravian leaders to establish and maintain a sexually balanced adult population in Wachovia. During the colony's planning stage it seemed that providing the right mix would be relatively easy. There were too many single men in Bethlehem and too many single women in many European congregations. If the two surpluses were simply brought together in North Carolina then everyone could be happily married. Unfortunately, just as church leaders decided it was safe to bring single sisters to the Carolina frontier, the Seven Years War broke out and convinced them that the threat of naval action made it too dangerous to risk sending women from Europe to America. Left to its American resources alone, the Unity could not provide enough brides for the men in Bethabara. Throughout the late 1750s and early 1760s the elders in North Carolina worried about this dearth of single sisters, writing their peers in Bethlehem in 1760, for example, that the marriage of several brothers "is one of our daily wishes and greatest desires." The situation finally improved after 1763. Peace returned to the North Atlantic, permitting emigrations from Germany again, and the aging of Bethlehem's children provided another source of potential brides. Large parties of single sisters and older girls, therefore, arrived in Wachovia in 1766, 1768, and 1771, and by the latter date the single brothers there had a realistic hope of marriage within the church.[11]

Moravian officials did more for marriages than manipulate the demographics of Wachovia, though. Every match in the church community required at least their consent and usually their active participation. In spite of efforts to segregate unmarried men and women in the congregation, it was possible for a couple to meet and seek to marry on their own. This seems to have happened twice among the members of Wachovia's Moravian community between 1753 and 1772. The best example is that of Hans Martin Kalberlahn and Anna Catherina Antes, who married in Bethlehem during the summer of 1758. Kalberlahn, then thirty-six years old, was visiting Bethlehem after five years as Bethabara's physician. While there he was called upon to treat Sr. Antes, thirty-one and a member of the Single Sisters Choir, when she was injured in a fall from her horse. As the sister recalled later in her memoir: "He took care of me, we liked each other very much, and as soon as I was sufficiently recovered we were married." There was, however, more to it than that. The couple had to convey their request to marry to Bethlehem's elders, who may also have sought the Lord's opinion through the Lot, and the wedding had to wait until permission was granted. Fortunately, it came soon, and the ceremony took place in July of 1758, followed nine months later by Kalberlahn's return to Bethabara with his bride.[12]

In most of Wachovia's marriages, however, the elders were far more active than they were in the Kalberlahns' case. Of the thirty-three weddings held between 1753 and the end of 1771, a total that includes nine held in Bethlehem for brethren like Kalberlahn who lived in Bethabara, at least twenty-one (64 percent) were apparently arranged by church officials. (And this does not include at least six couples who were married in Bethlehem or in Europe specifically so they could accept calls to Wachovia.) In each of these cases the elders decided that a particular brother should marry for his own or the community's good, chose a mate for him, and secured the consent of both parties.

Typical of this pattern was the union between George Baumgarten and Maria Fiscuss in 1765. The preceding summer Johannes Schaub had asked to be relieved of his duties in the tavern, and the Helpers Conference began looking for someone to replace him. Because patrons of the tavern were nearly all non-Moravians visiting in town it was essential that the tavernkeeper have a wife to help him resist their influence. The conference, therefore, had to choose either a married man or a single brother who would marry before assuming the post. When the Helpers Conference first met to consider a successor to Brother Schaub it suggested two single men, Baumgarten and Jeremias Schaff, and instructed the single brothers' pastor to speak with each of the two about this matter. Little else was done, however, until January 1765, when the conference suddenly revived the issue. This time Baumgarten's was the only name that came up for the tavern, and this time members also discussed Maria Fiscuss as a possible mate. Four days later one of the elders approached Baumgarten about taking over the tavern, and the latter agreed. He must have known that to do so would require him to marry, but he was not yet told that his superiors were considering Fiscuss for him. Sometime during the next two weeks both Baumgarten and Fiscuss learned of and agreed to the match, and on February 12 the Helpers Conference decided that the wedding would take place the following Sunday. By early March the couple was married and settled in the tavernkeeper's small house.[13]

Officials in Wachovia were not marriage-happy, though. They would not, for instance, force an unwilling individual to marry. It was, of course, extremely difficult for someone to resist the wishes or suggestions of his or her elders in a community as closely knit and supervised as Wachovia and one in which a communal economy operated. But Herman Lösch did it. In 1760 Brother Lösch was a thirty-one-year-old widower whose wife of one year had died in a typhus epidemic that swept through Bethabara the year before. The disease also left several widows in its wake, and officials of the Moravian community wanted Lösch to marry one of them. Lösch, however, preferred returning to his native Pennsylvania for a new bride, and his superiors eventually let him go.[14]

Nor would the elders sanction a marriage if conditions in the congregation were not conducive to its success. Throughout the late 1760s, for example, they sharply restricted family formation in Bethabara, in spite of the fact that single women were arriving in larger and larger numbers, and seem to have done so because of a housing shortage in town. The church's aim by then was to provide separate quarters for each couple because that accorded best with Count von Zinzendorf's theory of child-rearing. Once work began at Salem, though, all construction stopped in Bethabara except for that considered absolutely essential, a category that did not include family housing. Between the beginning of 1765 and the end of 1769 only four couples were permitted to marry in the Moravian community—the smallest number in any five-year period of Wachovia's history—despite the backlog of unmarried brothers and the arrival of single sisters in larger numbers than ever before. And none of the four exceptions required new construction in Bethabara: Christoph Kirschner was chosen to marry a widow in Bethania and move in with her; George Baumgarten married to assume his post in the tavern; Jacob Bonn was the new doctor and lived alone in the apothecary; and George Holder married after being selected to operate a Unity farm outside Salem. Officials in Bethabara had held up Peter Hauser's marriage in 1762 until they got an answer from Bethlehem as to whether or not the newlyweds could share a house with the groom's father, and in the latter half of that decade they apparently refused to create any new families before they could house them properly.[15]

Unity efforts to promote marriage in Wachovia did not, however, blind officials there to the need for mechanisms to end a relationship that threatened the souls of its partners or their children. Though Gillian Gollin's study of Bethlehem implies that divorce would have violated the sanctity of marriage, and Robert Woosley's work on ethics among the Brethren in Wachovia states categorically that "permanence" was a hallmark of Moravian unions, evidence from Wachovia suggests a more tolerant attitude toward separation and divorce. Because a family at war with itself could not be a Christian family, and therefore could not be a proper environment in which to raise Moravian children, Unity officials apparently believed that at some point it was better to end a bad marriage than to force a family to live in the disharmony it created. The most significant indication of this attitude is contained in Count von Zinzendorf's 1755 instructions for the design of Wachovia's *gemein Ort*. Among the buildings he planned for the town was an institution for children "whose parents do not get along together." Unfortunately, he did not say what to do about the couples themselves. Thomas Haupert, archivist of the church's southern province in the United States, has suggested on the basis of several couples' histories that eighteenth-century elders may have granted de facto divorces by sending the partners in an unhappy marriage to different congregations, sometimes on different continents.

Whether or not this is true cannot yet be proven, but in the case of early Wachovia it is something of a moot point, anyway, as there is no evidence that any couple there had marital problems severe enough to warrant a separation.[16]

Having done so much to create families in Wachovia, church officials had no intention of leaving them alone. Elders continued to play an active role through the creation and maintenance of an environment and institutions conducive to families' comfort and tranquility. While this continuing attention to the needs of families was due in part to concern for the well-being of adult members, the children's welfare seems to have been paramount. Children, after all, were the reason Zinzendorf gave for the existence of families, and his views on children were an important factor in determining both the quality and the form of life in Wachovia's Moravian community. As an orthodox Lutheran, which he always claimed to be, the *Jünger* believed in original sin and in the need for children to be cleansed by their Savior through baptism. But he also believed that every child was born with a perfect soul, and it was the latter belief that informed his attitude toward childrearing. As long as either Zinzendorf or his memory dominated the church its members raised their children according to his "principle of free development." Because children were inherently good, ran the theory, the secret of raising them properly was to provide appropriate examples to guide them and then stay out of their way as completely as possible. Of course parents and teachers had to protect youngsters from bad examples and from hurting themselves and had to punish "acts of willful disobedience to known requirements," but beyond that they were to grant them as much freedom as possible to develop on their own, as God intended. This would only work, however, in an environment from which both spiritual and temporal hazards had been removed.[17]

The pattern and personnel by which and by whom Wachovia was settled removed many of the spiritual dangers that might otherwise have threatened the children living there. In laying out the colony and in selling its surplus land, the church made sure that Bethabara, Bethania, and Salem each remained protected by a buffer of land around them on which none could settle without church permission. And from behind these barriers, as detailed in the preceding chapter, the elders tried to screen potential settlers and admit only good Moravians and a few trustworthy non-Moravians. This, the Unity hoped, would create a godly enclave within which it would be possible to let children develop freely without their constantly encountering what Spangenberg called "the foolish and sinfull ways of the World."[18]

The church also created an environment in which members faced fewer of the worldly problems that so often threaten families. Nearly every resident of Bethabara and Salem belonged to the *Oeconomy*, and from it they received everything they needed to live a healthy an comfortable life. Housing was not palatial, but it was dry and warm and protected against Indian attack. Clothing was not elegant, but it was sturdy and clean. Food was abundant; in 1764–65 residents of Bethabara consumed an average of 6.4 pounds of flour, 3.8 pounds of meat, .8 pounds of butter, and .5 gallons of beer per person per week plus unrecorded quantities of milk, fruit, and vegetables, and if a family had children its milk ration was doubled. The *Oeconomy* also included a doctor and a midwife in its ranks and provided medical services for its members, including long-term care for those struck by disease or accident. All in all, the system offered economic security from cradle to grave and insured that no couple would lack the material resources to care properly for themselves and their offspring. Moreover, it promoted domestic tranquility by banishing economic problems that might undermine a marriage or lead to quarrels that set a bad example for the children. Spangenberg, at least, showed a clear understanding of the *Oeconomy*'s contribution to happy families when he wrote the elders in Bethabara about Carl and Anna Maria Opitz. In 1759 the Opitzs had moved to Bethania. The economy there was under some church supervision and control but was not part of the *Oeconomy*, and by 1761 Carl and Anna Maria were having problems adjusting to it. "Opitz and his wife shall hardly survive in Bethania if they cannot be in harmony with one another," Spangenberg explained. "Therefore it occurred to me whether one should take them into Bethabara again. They could be in the *Oeconomy* again."[19]

For the sake of the children, church officials also tried to insure that each family in Wachovia had its own home and garden, or at least separate quarters in a larger building. This too was necessary if children were to enjoy the free development Zinzendorf wanted for them. The first married couples to reach Bethabara had to live together in the *gemein Haus*—one dormitory-style bedroom for the men and one for the women. With the latter were the colony's first children. Spangenberg soon ordered a change, though. "For if the children run all about in the Sisters' Choir and carry on this and that, they will be reprimanded too much," he feared. "That is not good. It is better to remove everything from their path so as not to excite their curiosity." Within a few months, therefore, mothers and children had moved to a separate room in the *gemein Haus*. That too was only temporary, however. To Spangenberg, even two families living together "[was] not good for the children"; so each was assigned its own home or apartment just as soon as they became available over the next few years. And by the close of the 1750s dormitory-style housing for married couples seems to have ended in Bethabara except as an emergency measure taken when the number of newlyweds temporarily overwhelmed the housing supply in town, as it did in 1762 after seven couples were married there in a single ceremony. In the Unity's two other Carolina settlements, Bethania and Salem, separate accommodations for each family were standard from the beginning. Not every family received its own house though. Ministers' families in particular often lived in rooms of the *gemein Hausen*. In 1766, for example, Br. and Sr. Ettwein lived with their daughter Maria in one room of Bethabara's *gemein Haus*, while the Graffs lived in another with their two children.[20]

Nor did every family have its own garden, which the church also regarded as a device to enhance the free development of children. While discussing his plans for Salem in 1765, Frederic Marschall explained that locating each house on its own lot "is not only an economical arrangement, but particularly good for the children, who can thereby have room for their recreations under oversight." That oversight could be appropriately loose, though, because children playing in their yards would be relatively safe from the dangers of shops and traffic around them.[21]

The church in Wachovia, as it did elsewhere in the Moravian world, also operated a number of institutions designed to assist parents in the task of socializing and educating their children. Moravian children normally lived with their parents until about age thirteen. During those years parents were expected, through their example and direction, to preserve the child's "original innocence and baptismal grace" while instilling in him or her "[a] personal experience of love and service for Christ." No one, however, expected either parent to raise them without substantial help from the congregation. The demands of building a frontier community, combined with long hours spent in congregational and choir services, meant that neither mothers nor fathers could always watch their children properly, and that was a source of frequent concern for Wachovia's administrators. "The children cause us great grief," wrote three of Bethabara's leaders in 1760; "it seems to be almost impossible that parents in the *Oeconomy* can raise their children usefully for the congregation, especially where their are so few as here; one weeps when one thinks about how it goes with the few children [here] and we still do not know how to help: there are just so few people." And two years later, when Philip and Magdalena Transou arrived from Bethlehem to settle in Bethabara with their three children, elders in the latter place sent them to Bethania instead because Bethabara still lacked the appropriate mechanisms to assist parents in raising their children.[22]

The most important such mechanism in Wachovia during the years of the *Oeconomy* was the day school, which children entered almost as soon as they were weaned. The Unity of Zinzendorf's time followed the pedagogical theories of John Amos Comenius, the great bishop and educator of the Ancient Unitas Fratrum. To Comenius no child was too young to learn. He certainly did not believe that a three-year-old could absorb the same information as a twelve-year-old or even that the two would respond to similar teaching styles, but through games and pictures even children too young to read could begin to learn. And when a child's soul was at stake there was no time to lose.[23]

Early in 1760 Wachovia's elders decided it was time to establish day schools for Bethabara's children, one for its three boys and another for the five girls; and two months later, as six Moravian families prepared to move to Bethania, they ordered the establishment of schools there too. Schools for younger children were also established in Salem when it became the colony's *gemein Ort*. By 1772, then, schools for the younger children were operating in all three of Wachovia's Moravian settlements. These institutions were actually a cross between a school and a modern daycare center. Classes were held at least five days a week, if not six, but only in the morning "because," as one brother explained, "at that age they cannot yet spend the whole day in school studying." In the afternoon there were supervised activities: going for a walk, working in a garden if the weather was nice, or cleaning cotton indoors if it was not. These non-classroom experiences were not only educational, but contributed to a child's physical development too, which the Moravians felt was an important part of one's total development. Unfortunately, there are few references to the academic regimen of Wachovia's schools for younger children. Students in Bethlehem learned reading, writing, and arithmetic at this age and sometimes grammar, history, geography, and nature studies as well. The only subject specifically mentioned in Wachovia's primary schools was arithmetic, which the children began in 1768. It seems safe to assume, however, that reading and writing were part of the curriculum too and that religious training was also an important part of the school day, as Zinzendorf believed that the example of the child Jesus should be "the daily food in the children's classes."[24]

At age thirteen or fourteen Moravian children entered a new stage in their lives. For many of the adolescents in Wachovia this meant separation from their parents; practically every teenager in Bethabara and Salem before 1772 had been sent there from Bethlehem without his or her parents. And for all of Wachovia's children, those with parents in the colony and those without, adolescence usually meant leaving their parent's home, though it seldom meant release from either parental or congregational supervision. For boys it was time to begin an apprenticeship or fulltime work on the farm. Girls were expected to assume a greater role in domestic chores, and some were put out as servants in other families or in congregational enterprises like the tavern.[25]

As in so many other matters, the primary responsibility for deciding when and to whom a child in Wachovia would be found lay with the church. Among the duties of the Helpers Conference, and later of its successor the *Aufseher Collequim*, was the task of determining how best to allocate the *Oeconomy*'s resources, including the labor of its children. Wachovia's craftsmen and the Brethren responsible for its agriculture and construction work regularly notified the conferences of their labor needs, and the latter tried to meet those needs from the pool of adolescents in or expected in the colony. In November of 1764, for example, a party of teenage boys arrived from Bethlehem, and within three weeks the Helpers Conference met to place them with various masters in the *Oeconomy*. Four of the eleven boys were assigned without reservation, while the other seven were put in trades "on trial." Six weeks later the conference reassigned those who were not working out in their original positions, and five weeks after that ordered the new apprentices bound to their masters.[26]

Sometimes Unity officials consulted the children involved in these arrangements or their parents, though not often. Among the eleven youths given masters in the fall and winter of 1764–65, only one was allowed a voice in his fate. John Nilson was first placed with Bethabara's tanner, but by the time the Helpers met to fine tune their allocation of apprentices young Nilson had informed them that he wanted to be in the tailor shop instead. The conference agreed to consider the request and must have consented to it because by 1766 Nilson was an apprentice tailor. Similarly, when Christian Renatus Heckewalder reached Bethabara in October 1766 he was sent to work with Melchior

Rasp, a stonemason, because he "chose to learn the trade of
Mason." In most cases, however, apprentices in Wachovia's
Oeconomy played no part in choosing their masters.[27]

As for parents, the surviving evidence presents a confused
picture. In at least one instance, that of Elisabeth Fiscuss, the
Helpers Conference refrained from making an assignment until
someone spoke to the girl's father and then accepted his opinion
that she was too young. But Elisabeth was one of the relatively
small number of teenagers in Wachovia whose parents lived in
the colony too. In most cases the parents were in Bethlehem and
did not participate in the choice of a trade for their offspring,
though at least one believed he had a right to. In 1773 Andreas
Schober, who lived in Bethlehem, learned that four years earlier
officials in Bethabara had put his son Gottlieb with a linen
weaver to learn that craft. The elder Schober was furious and
wrote Frederic Marschall:

> I cannot do otherwise than to ask you how it comes about that you
> have bound my son without asking me or informing me. I believe
> that it is well known that we are not in Germany, and thus no one
> has authority to bind my children . . . and in addition to a profes-
> sion which may possibly be against his temperament. What do you
> think? If a father is to bring up his children until they are 12 or 13
> years old and would hope that for some years they might earn well
> for him and then another comes along and engages them. It's hap-
> pened this time, but as long as I live it shall not happen again, for
> no man may contract my children against my will.

Schober notwithstanding, most adolescents in Wachovia were
assigned to artisanal or agricultural duties without their parents' participation.[28]

Separation from one's parents did not mean the end of fami-
lylike supervision, though. Children apprenticed to learn a
trade entered a master/servant relationship modeled on that existing between parents and children. "The master is like a
brother in our family, so one gives him the children *in loco par-
entis*," Bethabara's Helpers Conference explained in 1769. And
like parents, masters were expected to serve as examples to

their charges, demonstrating proper Christian life, and to provide them with adequate food, clothing, and other essentials. Children put to farm work generally labored in the *Oeconomy*'s common fields and lived in choir houses under the close and constant supervision of their brothers or sisters.[29] Nor did adolescence mean the end of classroom supervision. Congregations in Wachovia began providing classes for the older boys and girls as their numbers increased in the mid-1760s. In 1766 Bethabara opened a school for teenage boys, and the following year Bethania opened two—one for boys and one for girls. Salem lagged behind for some reason; not until 1774 or 1775 did it have a school for older boys, and it is unclear that one for girls opened at all during the colonial period. Classes for the older children were usually held in the evening, after the day's work was done. If the boys' school in Bethabara is representative, every night during the winter students met for two hours of reading, writing, and arithmetic lessons. Beginning in 1771 both sexes also began to receive instruction in "the foundation principles of salvation." That, however, seems to have been in a separate meeting held in addition to the other evening classes.[30]

For most of Wachovia's children the Unity's role in socialization went no further than educating them and maintaining the sheltered environment in which they and their parents or masters lived. The church was prepared, however, to assume full parental responsibilities if the need arose. In other Moravian communities this happened quite often because of the many missionaries sent to regions considered unfit for children (indeed many of the couples sent to Wachovia from Bethlehem left their children there when they went south). Neither Bethabara nor Salem dispatched any missionaries until after the *Oeconomy*'s close, though; so the church there took over only for children who had lost one or both of their parents. Parental death began in Wachovia as early as 1759, but not until 1761 did elders there feel the need to establish a regular means of dealing with the problem. Until the latter date church officials handled individual cases as they arose by calling on other members to help

raise these children. Thus when Polly Rogers succumbed to typhus, in 1759, and her husband returned to Bethlehem, the elders asked Sister Kalberlahn, herself recently widowed by typhus, to care for seven-month-old Johanna Rogers. When
Barbara Kraus died, though, in October 1761, leaving a widower
and two small children, John Ettwein wrote that her death
"forced us to beginn a Nursery." Ettwein did not say why the
death of Sister Kraus forced the Unity to act; Matthaeus Kraus
was not the first man left with young children, and nothing suggests that he was physically or emotionally unable to care for
them. Rather, it seems that the decision to set up a nursery in
1761 was simply a result of the growing number of orphans in
Bethabara; the young Krauses were numbers four and five.[31]

The new facility took up two rooms in the *gemein Haus* when
it opened. In one room Sisters Kalberlahn and Biefel, both widows, cared for three young girls, while in an adjoining chamber
Sister Luck, also a widow, and Sister Ettwein looked after two
orphan boys and Ettwein's own son. For girls the nursery functioned in the *gemein Haus* until the early 1770s, by which time
all of its inmates were old enough to live with a choir or to be
bound out to a family. The boys' institution, however, had a
rockier history. For unknown reasons it had closed by the fall of
1762 and remained closed until 1770. In the interim at least one
boy, Gottlob Kraus, lived in Bethania with Gottlieb Bachoff, the
congregation's lay reader, and his wife Rosina. Nothing is
known of the others, though, until Bethabara officials reported
in 1770 that emigration to Salem had freed enough space for
them to reestablish the boys' nursery. That same report also provided the only known description of the daily routine in Bethabara's orphanages:

> The institution now cares for three orphans, Gottlob Kraus and the
> two sons of the Widow Dixon. They are in the charge of the Single
> Brother, Wurtele, who also conducts the day school, and the young
> Single Brother Nilson is his assistant, going there after work hours,
> to sleep, and also alternating with Br. Wurtele in taking them to
> services. In the morning the Brn. Graff, Lorenz [Bagge], and Reuter
> have classes for them and the other boys; in the afternoon Br. Wur-
> tele takes them out to cut wood, or, for other work.

Within two years, though, the boys' nursery closed again because the children living there had outgrown it. Like the girls, they were old enough by 1772 to begin service as apprentices or servants and went to live with their masters.[32]

In Wachovia childhood ended at about age twenty-one, but it rarely ended with marriage and the formation of a new family. Between 1753 and the end of 1771 the median age at first marriage for brides in Wachovia's Moravian community was 27.5 and for grooms thirty-six. There is only one known case during this period of any individual marrying before age twenty-one; so for Wachovia's teenagers admission to the colony's adult population usually meant leaving family supervision for that of a choir.[33]

Choirs actually predated families in Wachovia by several years, having arrived in 1753 with the first party of single brothers sent to Bethabara. Gradually, as settlers of different age, sex, and marital categories arrived, other choirs did too: Married People, Little Boys, and Little Girls in 1756; Widows and Widowers in 1759; Older Boys in 1764; Single Sisters and Older Girls in 1766. With the arrival of the last two, the diarist in Bethabara was finally able to proclaim that the village had "a complete congregation." In Salem the process was repeated between 1766 and 1772 as the Unity transferred to Salem a large part of Bethabara's population, and with it a full complement of choirs. Bethania, too, had some choirs, but did not yet have a complete congregation in 1772.[34]

Like families, Wachovia's choirs were a means of bringing individuals into close and regular contact with a group small enough to see what they were up to and concerned enough to point out their mistakes. This was especially important for those groups in the adult population who had no family in the colony—widows, widowers, single brothers, and single sisters. For them choirs were the chief means by which individuals received proper supervision, and it is not coincidence that they were the groups in Wachovia whose members lived as well as prayed together. Each of the four ate at a common table, slept in a common dormitory, spent their evenings in a common parlor, worshipped in a common *Saal*, and, as the single brothers'

Principia explained in 1775, "[tried] to live as a House of God in proximity to Jesus in love and harmony with one another."[35]

Even in the nonresidential choirs, though, there were frequent opportunities for members to observe one another. During Wachovia's first decade each choir assembled at least once daily for group prayer. Sometime between 1762 and 1770 the number of meetings dropped to five per week when the elders decided to replace Saturday and Sunday choir sessions with meetings of the entire congregation. Even with the reduction, though, choir members still saw one another at least five times a week in their own, more intimate, services. Moreover, the larger choirs—the Single Brethren, Older Boys, and Married People—were further divided into bands and classes, each of which contained five to twelve members and met regularly "for religious purposes."[36]

Supervisory duties did not, however, fall entirely on the members of a choir. Choirs in Wachovia had recognized leaders who were responsible for the spiritual well-being of their charges. At the top of each was a *Pfleger* or *Pflegerin*, pastor. They were appointed by the Unity and known collectively as "the Workers" in a congregation. Each was assisted by a *Chor Diener*, choir attendant, who helped the pastor during services and assumed all of his or her duties in the event of death or sickness. If both *Pfleger* and *Diener* were indisposed the elders could appoint someone to fill in for them so "that still somebody has the supervision at home." And in the larger institutions each band or class had its own supervisor, who reported to the pastor any problems that surfaced in meetings of those smaller groups.[37]

The Workers could learn a great deal about their flocks merely by watching them on a daily basis, but their most valuable window into the souls of parishioners was probably the interviews they conducted with individual members prior to Communion. The Brethren regarded Communion as a celebration of their fellowship with one another as well as a sign of their relationship with God. They tried, therefore, to limit participation to those who were at peace with their neighbors and to exclude any who harbored unchristian grudges toward another. Between 1753 and 1772 Wachovia's brothers and sisters took Communion approximately once a month, and it was the Workers' duty each time to speak privately with every member under their care, which gave them an excellent opportunity to look for signs of any deviation from the Moravian way. There were also several occasions between 1753 and 1772 on which Unity officials in Pennsylvania or in Europe directed the pastors in Wachovia to send them special reports on the spiritual condition of every congregation member, which required another round of interviews. In 1768, for example, the Unity Directory, its collective executive at the time, sent word to the elders of every Moravian congregation that "it has been especially commended to us according to the Synodal commission to watch over the walk of faith in the Congregations and Choirs." The letter continued:

> If this purpose is to be attained according to the spirit of our Lord, then reports are of necessity required of the state and inward life of grace of the individual brothers and sisters as well as how the life of every individual choir is constituted at any time in order that we might never lack during the coming discussions the necessary, thorough, and reliable knowledge of our brothers and sisters . . . Therefore, we are asking you to send us a report as described above.[38]

Together, the families and choirs described in this chapter were essential to the Unity's ability to protect the spiritual and moral values of Wachovia's Moravian community. Surrounded as they were by non-Moravians and tied to them by social, political, and economic links, the Brethren needed some way to maintain close supervision over one another lest individuals succumb to the sinful ways of the world. More important, they had to find a way of maintaining that close supervision as their community grew larger. American history is full of groups such as the Moravians that have tried to function in the world without surrendering the characteristics that distinguish them, and one of the great problems confronting such groups has always been their own growth. As the community expands, its leaders lose the ability to maintain face-to-face contact with their followers. The Moravians, however, found a way to expand without sacrificing the close supervision of individual members. Through their families and choirs they managed to redivide their community as fast as it grew so that individual brothers and sisters remained in groups small enough to ensure intimate contact between church members and church leaders.[39]

To modern sociologists Wachovia's families and choirs provided "the capacity [for church leaders] to socialize loyalty to themselves into deeper levels of the personality." To the brothers and sisters living there they offered "assistance in consecrating the daily life." Whichever view one adopts, though, families and choirs were an important factor in the Moravian community's ability to function peacefully in a heterogeneous province without surrendering either its identity or its values. The reinforcement of community norms provided by families and choirs allowed the Moravians to open themselves to some forms of contact with their neighbors in the knowledge that they could successfully resist the unwanted change that such contact might threaten.[40]

CHAPTER 4

"Under Their Own Laws and Ordinances"

Riding herd on the families and choirs of Wachovia was a Moravian government that regulated both community and congregation in the colony. The elders who planned Wachovia knew that in order for their efforts to succeed someone would have to coordinate the activities of individual members and harness their energies for the common good. That sort of coordination is important in any common venture, but in Wachovia's case it was especially important because settlers there had to be protected from spiritual as well as temporal danger. The brothers and sisters faced not only the threat of Indian attack, disease, starvation, and other physical dangers, but also threats to their religious values both from inside and outside their community. So before a single colonist left Bethlehem, church leaders there and in Europe proposed an administrative structure that would reach from the *Jünger* himself to individual men and women living in Wachovia.[1] In the years that followed the form of that government changed frequently as officials and committees came and went and changed their names. Its basic structure, however, and the beliefs informing it remained the same. Throughout Wachovia's first two decades its government consisted of a theocratic oligarchy directing a multitude of subordinate officials under the immediate supervision of a resident executive and the ultimate direction of Unity leaders in Europe.

First and foremost Wachovia's government was a theocracy. The Brethren themselves described it as such, and the description fits both its purpose and its personnel. To the Moravian residents of Wachovia every aspect of an individual's life was an

extension of his or her religion, and the object of their community life, in the words of John Ettwein, was "to live for Him and
to serve Him according to His will." The function of its government, therefore, was to determine God's will and to carry it out.
Of course the best way to do that would have been simply to
turn government over to Him, and because Christ was the
Unity's Chief Elder He did sometimes take an active role,
through the Lot, in Wachovia's governance. On a day-to-day basis, though, the task of governing the community fell to the
Brethren themselves, and it seemed to them that the surest way
of seeing that everything went "according to the direction of the
Holy Spirit and Savior" was to draw its leaders almost exclusively from the ranks of the clergy.[2]

The identification of an individual as a leader in Wachovia's
government, as opposed to one who merely served in its ranks,
is based on whether or not that individual played a significant
role in both its spiritual and secular affairs. Moravians had a
penchant for compartmentalized authority. This meant their
communities invariably had two administrative hierarchies, one
spiritual and the other temporal. The real leaders were those
men and women holding positions near the top of both because
only they participated regularly in both secular and spiritual decision making. In Wachovia, twenty-three men and women met
that criteria between 1753 and the end of 1771, and all but one
were either ministers or the wives of ministers. The lone exception, Anna Maria Kraus, was an official of the Single Sisters
Choir and could, therefore, be neither ordained nor married.
This ministerial elite dominated Wachovia's government during
the years of the *Oeconomy*. Every incumbent of the colony's three
most important offices—*Oeconomus* (executive of the colony),
Vorsteher (overseer of its business and finances), and *Ordinarius*
(pastor of the congregation)—was a minister, and ministers or
their wives held at least half the seats on each of the colony's six
most powerful committees.[3]

It is unclear from the surviving records exactly what role the
women in this group played. In numbers alone they were a major element, even a majority at times. Moravian wives were their
husbands' "helpmeets" and not only shared any congregational

offices the men might occupy but continued to hold as widows the positions they had assumed as wives. As a result, women not only constituted one-third of the colony's total leadership pool but were frequently a majority of the leaders resident in Wachovia at any particular time. In the summer of 1767, for example, seven of the Elders Conferences' eleven members were women. There is, however, little evidence that women's authority matched their numbers. When speakers can be identified in the records they are usually men, and although Anna Maria Kraus, *Vorsteherin* (feminine of *Vorsteher*) of the Single Sisters Choir, had been in both the Helpers and Elders Conferences during the late 1760s, when the *Oeconomy* closed in 1772, Brother Jacob Meyer was named Curator of the Single Sisters with responsibility for advising the sisters on economic matters and representing them in the council that regulated Wachovia's economy. Women, it seems, were more often seen than heard among Wachovia's leaders, and real power evidently lay with their male colleagues.[4]

A man's ordination did not provide automatic entry into the colony's leadership, though; three of the ministers living in Wachovia during its first two decades held no important secular posts and, therefore, do not rank among its leaders. Nor would ordination keep an individual at the top if he did not perform effectively. The clearest example of this is the case of Jacob Lösch.

Lösch, an ordained minister, arrived with the first party of Moravian settlers and came as Wachovia's *Vorsteher*. In that capacity he was responsible for oversight of the *Oeconomy*'s trades and crafts, administration of its communal agriculture, keeping its books, and handling its money. Soon after Lösch assumed his duties, though, his superiors began to worry that he was not up to the job. His bookkeeping was especially worrisome and moved Spangenberg to write in 1755 that Lösch "[was] more fit to be the subject of a book than to keep the books." The following year, therefore, his responsibilities were reduced somewhat, when Bishop Mattheus Hehl visited Bethabara. Hehl found that the colony's increasing population and expanding *Oeconomy* had "overgrown" Br. Lösch. "It was good and necessary, therefore," wrote Hehl, "that his office was divided into departments, that qualified people were installed in each department, and that Br. Lösch retained *the Vorsteher's* office." Complaints continued, however. The last straw was a book-keeping error in 1761–62 when Lösch forgot to enter some £200 in the annual accounts, and the apparent result was Spangenberg's decision to name a new Congregation *Vorsteher* and make Lösch merely the Plantation *Vorsteher*—a subordinate responsible only for the *Oeconomy's* farm. Further evidence of Lösch's fall came three years later, in 1765, when the Unity left him off Wachovia's new Elders Conference. This was the colony's most powerful board at the time, and Lösch was the only minister present who was not included in its ranks. And the omission was deliberate. Frederic Marschall, Wachovia's *Oeconomus*, specified that Lösch "does not really belong in the Elders Conference." Clearly the Unity wanted men and women of God to govern its communities, but it also insisted that they be men and women of the world.[5]

With so much power in the hands of the ministers, Wachovia's government was also oligarchic. This tendency was temporarily suspended during the colony's first two years, when it had few ordained men, its population was small, and its goal simply to survive. During these years the Unity granted extraordinary power to Bethabara's Congregation Council—a body whose meetings were open to every member of the congregation and in which every member was to have "freedom to display his thoughts and his opinions freely and unhindered." This permitted a much greater degree of popular participation in the governing process than was normal in Moravian communities of the day. Meeting in September of 1754, for example, the congregation decided that its members should concentrate on building more housing instead of trying to establish another farm, and early the next year another session of the Congregation Council determined what kinds of help the colony should request from Bethlehem.[6]

The unusually democratic situation did not last long, though. By late 1755 officials in Bethlehem had decided that Wachovia's settlers had cleared their first hurdle. They had established themselves in the wilderness, and there seemed little doubt that the colony would at least survive. It was time, therefore, to move beyond mere survival and to bring Wachovia into line with Moravian norms; so Bethlehem ordered a range of demographic, economic, and political changes in the colony beginning that fall. In demographics this meant dispatching married couples to Wachovia. In economics it meant establishing operations that would turn a profit rather than just those needed to live. And in politics it meant removing the Congregation Council from decision making and replacing it with a smaller conference over which the ministers could keep a tighter rein. "In congregation councils," explained Bethlehem, "the danger is that when what comes there goes against the generally held view of things that they are not willing to support the Savior's vote." The Carolina Brethren, therefore, were instructed to establish a smaller, more select conference and to place Wachovia's government in its more reliable hands.[7]

It took almost a year to get this new board off the ground, but in late 1756, after a false start and at least one name change, the Helpers Conference finally emerged. This was the first in a series of small conferences established to direct the colony's affairs. Over the next fifteen years it was joined by the Select Conference, the Weekly Conference, the Elders Conference, the Personal and Choir Conference, and the Diacony Conference. Some of these were simply new names for old boards, and the six merged and split in such a way that different numbers existed in different years. In some combination, though, they ran Wachovia after 1756, and their assumption of power meant that control of the colony passed into the hands of a very small group. Lacunae in the records, absenteeism, and the presence at some meetings of individuals summoned for their expertise on a particular matter make it impossible to state precisely how large a group made the decisions in Wachovia after 1756. Nevertheless, it was clearly a small one. At its center were the twenty-three men and women identified above as leaders, those who held positions at the top of both spiritual and temporal hierarchies. All were never present at once, though. There were never more than eleven in Wachovia at the same time, and between

1756 and 1772 the median number present each year was 8.5. These individuals sat on whatever select conferences were in existence. With them were a smaller number who belonged to conferences governing one side of the community but not the other, supervising economic but not religious affairs or vice-versa. Thus, the regular membership of Wachovia's decision making bodies was usually from nine to eleven men and women, though individual absences often kept the number down to five to seven in any particular meeting.[8]

And the Congregation Council? With the establishment of the Helpers Conference the Congregation Council became largely a forum in which decisions were announced rather than made. For example, minutes of a meeting held in late 1756 open with a statement that "the following were made known" and a recitation of actions taken recently by the Helpers Conference. The same council meeting closed with a promise from Wachovia's acting executive, Christian Seidel, that the Congregation Council would remain a means by which the brothers and sisters could make their opinions known to the leaders. But Seidel mentioned no larger role for it, and after 1756 it was no longer a major component in Wachovia's government.[9]

The same Bethlehem conference that gave Wachovia's elite the authority to govern also gave it an essential component of the power to do so—the Lot. The Lot's great power in governing a Moravian community lay in its ability to give human decisions the sanction of divine backing. There were so few rules regarding its use that the elders in a Moravian congregation could exert tremendous influence on the process. They decided when to use the Lot; they decided the number and wording of the potential answers from which they drew; they interpreted the single response they did draw; and they decided whether and when to resubmit questions answered with a blank. Yet the final decision was taken as the will of God, and anyone who dissented faced possible charges of apostasy as a result. This not only assured community leaders of divine support for virtually any decision they made, but also reduced substantially the likelihood of a potentially divisive issue factionalizing the community. Once a decision was made good Moravians were expected to say *"thus* has the Savior disclosed His sense to His people" and to accept it.[10] During Bethabara's first two years any matter sufficiently important to warrant use of the Lot had been decided in Bethlehem or Europe. In 1755, however, officials in Bethlehem decided that "things can occur [in Wachovia] that one cannot foresee now" and empowered the colony's executive, Christian Henrich Rauch, to use the Lot "in extraordinary cases where there is no clear certainty in his heart or the matter cannot be decided through discussion with the Brethren." When Rauch left Bethabara, in 1756, authority to use the Lot went with him, but elders in Bethlehem soon restored it for good. In 1758 John Ettwein received instructions to establish a small body, the Select Conference, that was authorized to use the Lot when "there occur peculiar circumstances, e.g. with the refugees, Indians, etc. about which the brothers and sisters cannot communicate with us first and about which the have, heretofore, still no plan."[11]

Between 1758 and the close of the *Oeconomy,* Wachovia's leaders employed the Lot fairly often but in reference to a limited range of issues. They used it most frequently to decide on the admission of new members to the church or the readmission to Communion of those members who had been disciplined by exclusion from the Lord's Supper. Use of the Lot was also common, almost universal in fact, when the question of marriage arose; only twice during this period did the elders approve matches without asking the Lord's opinion.[12] Concerning more worldly affairs, only questions about how to start Bethania or where to build Salem regularly merited consulting the Lot. In other matters, officials in Wachovia preferred to follow the instructions given to Brother Rauch. First they tried to decide the issue through discussion and the emergence of a consensus; only if that failed did they turn to the Lot.

In spite of its preference for rule by ministerial elite, the Unity did not oppose all forms of popular participation in Wachovia's government. Church leaders saw the advantage of granting residents a voice, though not a vote. By establishing small, subordinate boards whose members came from the congregation at large, ministers serving on major administrative bodies could tap the special talents of any brother or sister without giving him or her license to effect change without the elders' consent. As August Spangenberg explained in 1756, "in regard to certain matters . . . a committee of the Congregation Council [should] be appointed made up of individuals who must either compete in carrying out the project or at least have some comprehension of it. Then each one of them should express his opinions and the best possible use should be made of their views. We have often taken similar action in Bethlehem with profit." In Wachovia, ad hoc committees like this helped the colony's ministerial clique decide, among other things, where to locate a new barn and what sort of "night lamps" were needed in Bethabara.[13]

Unity officials also believed that using popular fora to ratify the decisions of select conferences made it easier to implement those decisions. In the elders' eyes, the Congregation Council, for instance, contributed to the governance of Wachovia long after smaller bodies had taken over its role in decision making. It helped to insure, as Mattheus Hehl explained, that "one has the heart of the brothers and sisters in a matter that one undertakes." Wachovia's elders were prepared to go against community opinion if their Lord demanded it, but they preferred to govern with the support of their constituents because it made the job easier and increased the likelihood they would accomplish their goals.[14]

Government in early Wachovia was also distinguished by a marked tendency toward fragmentation of authority. As Wachovia grew the Unity created new offices and conferences to administer particular sectors of the colony, most of them quite narrow. The result was an array of subordinate officials exercising limited authority under the oversight of a few more powerful ones, which is exactly what the Unity wanted. Its leaders had already established such governments in Herrnhut and Bethlehem, and from the beginning they sought one for Wachovia too.[15] This was certainly not the result of any desire on their part to encourage popular participation in directing the colony. Nor is there any indication that Moravians used the many branches of Wachovia's government as a testing ground for potential leaders. Rather, they used this arrangement to make it easier for the colony's ministers to govern the community effectively. Lower ranking officials and committees were usually responsible for small and specific areas of business and were expected to confine their attention to their particular jurisdictions. They did not, however, enjoy any significant authority to act within their spheres. They were expected to gather information, pass reports and requests on to higher authorities, and leave major decisions to men and women at the top. Thus the cadre of ministers that governed Wachovia gained detailed information on which to base its decisions without surrendering any of its authority and maintained a monopoly on knowledge of the entire colony. Once decisions were made they went down along the same hierarchy for execution, and any problems that arose could be isolated and corrected. The result was an almost military chain of command and accountability that was crucial to the colony's smooth operation.

Moreover, this penchant for compartmentalizing responsibility provided multiple checks on the behavior of congregation members. Because government in a Moravian settlement usually consisted of two parallel hierarchies, one for spiritual affairs and the other for temporal, any individual occupied positions on both and was under the close scrutiny of at least two officials or committees. Jacobus van der Mek, for example, was under the eyes of three. Van der Merk, a millwright, lived in Bethabara from 1754 until his death in 1772 and for most of that time was married. At any given time, therefore, he was in close and regular contact with the congregation's *Vorsteher*, who met regularly with all the community's master craftsmen, the *Pfleger* (pastor) of the married brothers, and Bethabara's House Conference, which was responsible for its domestic economy. Each of the three was a separate entity reporting through its own channels to the ministers who governed Wachovia. This sort of redundancy greatly reduced the chances that any problem would go unnoticed and increased those of maintaining the community's Moravian values.

There were, however, limits to the fragmentation of authority that marked Wachovia's government. The Unity also wanted its

colony to have an *Oeconomus*, a single executive with the ability
to coordinate all the various committees and conferences. Without such an official, worried the elders, settlers in Wachovia
might never accomplish the goals set for them. There had to be
someone, in the words of J. P. Weiss, "who should have the
whole plan in view so that he can follow Heaven's sense in the
future."[16] What Weiss and others thought Wachovia needed was
a little Zinzendorf—an *Oeconomus* with unrestricted authority
and extensive powers—but it took time to get one.

For some unknown reason the first party of settlers sent to
Wachovia contained no such figure. In spite of the planners'
express wish for unified authority in Wachovia, the colony operated under a dual executive for its first two years. Jacob Lösch
managed its temporal affairs, while Adam Grube and his successor, Jacob Friis, handled the spiritual, and none of the three
had the final word. This awkward arrangement lasted until
1755, when Bethlehem decided it was time Wachovia conformed to Moravian norms and sent it its first single executive.
But they did not send an *Oeconomus*. Only Zinzendorf could
choose such an important official, and in 1755 the *Jünger* had
still not made up his mind whom to send. Instead, Bethlehem
appointed a "Helper in everything" to serve as an interim executive. The Helper's jurisdiction was just as broad as that of an
Oeconomus; there was "nothing too large, nothing too small,
nothing too external, nothing too internal, nothing too apostolic, [and] nothing too servile" for his attention, according to
the conference that chose him. But the Helper did not enjoy the
autonomy of an *Oeconomus*. Unlike the latter, the former remained subordinate to officials in Bethlehem; so without an
Oeconomus Wachovia would never be a fully mature Moravian
community.[17]

Throughout the late 1750s it seemed Zinzendorf was always
about to name an *Oeconomus* for the colony. He never did
though. When the *Jünger* died, in 1760, the post was still vacant,
and it remained vacant for three more years, until a Unity conference selected Frederic Marschall for the job in 1763. For another five years, though, the job was effectively empty because
Marschall's duties in Bethlehem prevented his leaving. Until

Marschall could be spared Wachovia continued under a *Vice-Oeconomus*, first John Ettwein and then Mattheus Schropp, who was really just the Helper in everything under a different name. Finally, in 1768, Marschall arrived in Wachovia to take up his duties.[18]

As *Oeconomus*, Marschall was the highest ranking Moravian official in Wachovia and was responsible for the entire colony. But in the church hierarchy he was a *Senior-Civilis*, an ordained position equal to a bishop, but expected to concentrate on the material welfare of his flock. Marschall, therefore, wrote his deputy before leaving Bethlehem that on reaching Bethabara he had no intention of playing a significant role in the daily rituals of the congregation there. "I would not employ my time with preaching or conducting meetings," he told John Ettwein, "just as that is not my practice here [in Bethlehem]; for it is not fitting for a *Senior-Civilis* to be occupied in the same manner that a spiritual leader or church executive is." Marschall spent little time on daily business affairs either, though. Instead, he met with members of the select conferences to formulate long-range plans for the colony, both temporal and spiritual plans, and left their execution to more specialized conferences and officials below him. The *Oeconomus*, then, seldom employed the full powers given him, but after 1768 he was there if needed.[19]

One thing that did not change when Frederic Marschall arrived was Wachovia's subordination to Unity officials in Europe. Eighteenth-century Moravians considered themselves a far-flung empire in the service of God; one diarist even wrote in 1761 "the sun never sets upon His people." And wherever the Lord sent them, brothers and sisters remained under the direction of His spokesmen—Count von Zinzendorf until his death and then a succession of committees and synods. Once Marschall arrived, though, the process did get easier.[20]

Until then European officials often administered Wachovia through Bethlehem, sending word of their general expectations to the latter where specific steps were formulated and sent south for implementation. And in the beginning Bethlehem made an amazing number of Bethabara's decisions. In September of 1756, for example, a meeting of the Congregation Council in Bethabara decided that settlers needed a distillery, a spring house, a buttery, and a barn, and it ordered construction of the first three. The barn, however, was a different matter. "Because this must be done permanently and be planned with a view to the entire plan," the council decided, "we can and will resolve nothing concerning it here, rather we will send plans and proposals to Br. Joseph [a name given to Spangenberg] in Bethlehem and await a decision on them." Three months later their answer arrived. On the last day of the year Martin Mack and Nicholaus Garrison arrived from Pennsylvania with a letter from Spangenberg containing forty-one instructions for specific courses of action, including the bishop's ideas on barn construction. "You should not build the barn too close to the living quarters," wrote Spangenberg, "otherwise it will be inside the stockade. But above all you should not build it of log in the Pennsylvania style, rather make a frame and nail boards to it."[21]

During the next decade Bethlehem's instructions grew steadily less detailed as leaders there gave Bethabara a freer hand in deciding how to accomplish Unity goals. And things became considerably less complicated in 1768, when Frederic Marschall arrived to serve as the colony's *Oeconomus*. This finally removed Bethlehem from its intermediary position. Marschall and the various conferences in Bethabara began making decisions that had previously been made in Pennsylvania. But there remained three areas of business over which Unity leaders in Europe exercised close control: distribution of the church's land, construction of the colony's *gemein Ort*, and the selection of Wachovia's higher officials. In each of these, decisions were made in Europe until long after the close of the *Oeconomy* and relayed to Wachovia to be carried out. Furthermore, from time to time Unity synods issued directions affecting all of the church's congregations. In 1769, for example, a synod meeting in Herrnhut ordered a variety of changes in Moravian liturgy and governance in order to reverse an apparent decline in the members' spiritual commitment, and early the next year, when word of this reached Bethabara, the changes were made.[22]

The preceding discussion has identified some of the ideals that informed Wachovia's government but has said relatively little about how that government actually operated. The most effective way to address that issue is to outline the administrative apparatus at a particular time and consider how its parts worked together to direct the colony's affairs.

Table 2 represents the government of Wachovia in 1764 and the lines along which information and instructions passed between leaders and members. At the top was John Ettwein, the colony's *Vice-Oeconomus*. Frederic Marschall *Oeconomus-designate* did visit Wachovia late in 1764, but for most of the year Ettwein was its resident executive. He was the Unity's spokesman in Carolina, and he was responsible for orchestrating efforts to carry out the church's grand design for its colony.

In theory at least, the Congregation Councils of Bethabara and Bethania also had general supervisory duties in 1764. Since losing the authority to make decisions, though, Bethabara's had lapsed into almost complete inactivity. It was supposed to be a forum in which members of the congregation could ask questions, air grievances, and make suggestions about a wide range of topics. But since 1756, residents of the village had been losing interest in their emasculated Congregation Council. As early as October 1756, a month after the Helpers Conference took over decision making for good, Mattheus Hehl reported, "it seems the Brethren almost had not the least desire anymore concerning it [the Congregation Council], because it is no longer what it was in the beginning." In 1764 Bethabara's Congregation Council never met; its most recent meeting had been in July 1763 and the next was not held until October 1765. In Bethania there was a little more activity; its Congregation Council met once in 1764 to discuss the village's debt to Bethabara.[23]

Neither the *Vice-Oeconomus* nor the Congregation Councils were the real power in Wachovia in 1764. That role belonged to the seven ministers, wives of ministers, and widows of ministers who made up the colony's ruling elite that year. Joining Brother Ettwein at the top were his wife Johannetta; Johan Michael Graff, *Ordinarius* and *Pfleger* of the married people; Gertraud Graff, wife of Johan Michael and *Pflegerin* (the feminine of *Pfleger*) of the married people; Anna Bischoff, widow of David Bischoff, who had been Bethania's pastor from 1760 until his

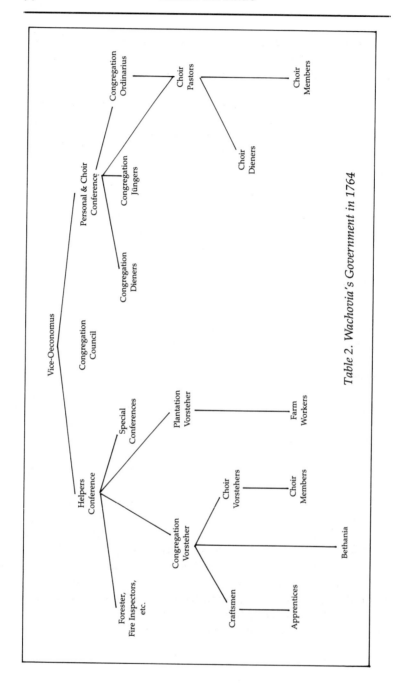

Table 2. Wachovia's Government in 1764

death in 1763; Gottlieb Hoffman, single brothers' *Pfleger* until his recall to Bethlehem in November; and Lorenz Bagge, who replaced Hoffman. Like Ettwein, each of these men and women was a member of both the colony's chief conference on temporal affairs and the major board handling spiritual matters; and as one or the other they met on seventy-three different days during the year.[24] The median interval between such meetings was four days, and only eleven times during the year did it exceed seven. In addition to those formal occasions, members of this elite must have spoken informally to one another on a daily basis. Bethabara was, after all, a small village, and the Graffs and Ettweins lived in the *gemein Haus,* while Hoffman and Bagge were across the square in the single brothers' house. It is unclear where Sister Bischoff lived that year, but it cannot have been very far from the others.

Directing Wachovia's secular business in 1764 was the Helpers Conference. During the year ten individuals served on this conference. They were the seven first-rankers named above plus Abraham von Gammern, *Vorsteher* of the *Oeconomy;* his wife Julianna; and Jacob Lösch, former *Vorsteher* of the *Oeconomy* and now that of its farming operations. The last three had all been or would be members of the first rank in other years, though in 1764 they operated in the material world only. In addition to these regular members, Frederic Marschall sat with the Helpers when he was in town as did Johannes Fromelt, *Oeconomus* of the Single Brothers Choir in America, who came with Marschall to inspect the colony.

The Helpers Conference met fifty-two times in 1764. It did not, however, meet weekly. Sometimes it met two or three times in a single week; about 20 percent of the time more than a week passed between sessions; and on one occasion thirty-seven days did. The agendas included a variety of matters affecting the physical welfare of Wachovia and its residents. Principal topics of discussion that year were long-range economic development, room and job assignments, construction of new buildings and the repair of existing ones, maintenance of economic and other relations with non-Moravians, and defense of the community against Indian attack. The Helpers did handle spiritual issues from time to time. It was they, for example, who decided to admit George Hartman, one of Wachovia's neighbors, to the Unity. Most religious matters, however, fell to other bodies. Decision making in the Helpers Conference that year usually involved discussing a question until some consensus emerged. There is no record of the members voting on anything in 1764, and they used the Lot in just five of their fifty-two meetings that year.[25]

Once the Helpers Conference had made a decision it was passed to the proper subordinate for implementation. Chief among these subordinates was the Congregation *Vorsteher,* Abraham von Gammern, who was himself a member of the Helpers Conference. As *Vorsteher,* von Gammern was responsible for the daily operation of crafts and trade in the colony and for bookkeeping in that sector of the *Oeconomy.* In carrying out these duties he met regularly with Bethabara's master craftsmen and storekeeper to set prices, check their books, and listen to their needs, opinions, and suggestions. *Vorsteher* von Gammern was also responsible for monitoring the material needs of individual *Oeconomy* members. With the help of his wife, who watched the communal stores; the keeper of Bethabara's public store; and a handful of Choir *Vorsteher* and *Vorsteherin,* he administered the distribution of clothing, household supplies, and artisanal materials. This was no doubt very similar to the process described by Frederic Marschall in 1769, by which time von Gammern had died and been replaced by a committee. "In each choir," wrote Marschall

> a Brother or Sister is appointed, who ascertains what clothing is needed, and to whom requests for other necessaries are made. These appointed Brethren and Sisters meet at stated times for conference. When all needs have been considered . . . a list is given to the merchant [in the Bethabara store] of all the various things which he shall bring from Charlestown for the Congregation Store. From these the tailor and seamstress receive what they require for their work; and the requests include pins, shoe-buckles, combs, buttons, tea, coffee, sugar, indeed all kinds of necessaries.[26]

Finally, von Gammern also chaired the Bethania Committee in 1764 and thus was the key liaison between Bethabara's Helpers Conference and the residents of Bethania. The latter were not members of the *Oeconomy,* but they were still under the jurisdiction of officials in Bethabara, including that of the Helpers Conference. In 1762, after governing Bethania directly for three years, Bethabara had established the Bethania Committee "for the promotion of external [i.e. nonreligious] order" in the new village. The committee consisted of four men—two chosen by Bethania and two chosen by Bethabara—under a chairman sent from Bethabara, and until his death in 1765 von Gammern was that chairman. This committee handled secular matters concerning Bethania that the Helpers Conference felt could be safely decided there. These were largely internal economic issues, such as the distribution of land and the adjustment of boundaries, or questions concerning the maintenance of civil order in the village. More important issues were still decided in Bethabara by the Helpers Conference, and von Gammern was the intermediary through whom its decisions or requests made their way to the people living in Bethania.[27]

The Helpers Conference also directed a number of lesser officials with specialized and restricted responsibilities. Among these were the Plantation *Vorsteher,* Jacob Lösch, who was responsible for daily operation of the *Oeconomy's* farm; an Inspector of the Forests, charged with watching for trespassers trying to exploit the hunting and grazing potential of church land; and Fire Inspectors to insure that buckets and ladders were available and in good repair. The Helpers could also appoint ad hoc committees to investigate particular problems. In 1764 it did this just once; in December it named five brothers, two of whom were members of the Helpers Conference, to recommend ways of replenishing the *Oeconomy's* grain supply.[28]

On its spiritual side Wachovia's government contained a similar though smaller network of officials. At the top in 1764 was the Personal and Choir Conference. This board consisted of the seven brothers and sisters identified above as the colony's first-rank leaders plus Brothers Marschall and Fromelt when they were in town. All of these people also sat on the Helpers Conference, but as the Personal and Choir Conference they considered different matters in a different way. In 1764 this conference met once every fifteen days or so, though it exceeded that average one third of the time. Its agenda was strictly limited to religious topics, and its members spent most of their time on just three issues: setting the congregation's liturgical calendar, ruling on the admission of new members, and considering requests or suggestions for marriage among members of the Moravian community. This was also the forum in which Wachovia's ministers consulted the Lot. Most questions concerning marriage or admission involved the Lot, and it was used at fifteen of the twenty-four meetings in 1764.[29]

The most important subordinates on Wachovia's spiritual side that year were the *Ordinarius* and the Choir *Pfleger* and *Pflegerin*. The former was pastor of the congregation, and the latter were pastors in the various choirs. All of them were members of the Personal and Choir Conference, and in their individual capacities it was their duty to effect the decisions they made collectively. Each held services for his or her choir with the assistance of a Choir *Jünger* and perhaps a Choir *Diener*. The *Pfleger* and *Pflegerin* were also the administrators most responsible for watching individual brothers and sisters for signs of backsliding. This, of course, was a perpetual responsibility, but it was most visible when the congregation prepared for Communion. In February 1764, for example, Brother and Sister Ettwein spoke to each member of the married peoples' choirs in Bethania, while in Bethabara the Graffs spoke with every married member, Gottlieb Hoffman with every single brother, and Anna Bischoff with the other widows. Choir *Pfleger* and *Pflegerin* were also crucial to the flow of information and instructions between Wachovia's leaders and individual members of the congregation. If one member of the congregation had a complaint against another, the approved means of dealing with the trouble was for the aggrieved party to speak to his *Pfleger* or her *Pflegerin*, who would take the matter to the Personal and Choir Conference for resolution. And working in the other direction, *Pfleger* and *Pflegerin* were often the instrument through which the Personal and Choir Conference contacted individual brothers and sisters about matters concerning them, such as marriage or violations of Unity ordinances.[30]

Ultimately, of course, one of the chief functions of Wachovia's government was to insure that colonists there obeyed Unity tenets and directives; so if any of its branches discovered a deviant individual it had to have the authority to discipline him or her. That authority lay exclusively with the colony's ministerial elite, though it does not seem to have mattered which hat they wore when they exercised it. In 1764, for example, both the Helpers Conference and the Personal and Choir Conference corrected wayward members. Yet the Moravians' determination to maintain community standards did not result in an Orwellian campaign to discover and punish transgressors. If anything officials erred on the side of moderation, believing as they did that the Lord's "chief command is to *love* and [chief] prohibition is against *judging.*" Their first concern was always the errant brother or sister, and only when a member had proven intractable or a genuine threat to the whole Moravian community would elders take any action to protect a congregation at the expense of an individual. And even then, they were urged to use restraint. As Bishop Spangenberg wrote John Ettwein in 1762: "whatever you do, dear Brother, do not let it come to an entire break with any Brother or Sister; do not throw down the bridge, but leave a way by which they can return when they come to themselves."[31]

In keeping with Spangenberg's admonition, the elders in Wachovia used a variety of responses against backsliders in the congregation. The simplest option seems to have been talking to an offender. When, for example, the Helpers Conference learned that John Richter had his own cattle, contrary to the rules of the *Oeconomy,* the conference directed one of its members to speak to Brother Richter and secure his promise to get rid of the animals. Richter apparently did so, and nothing else was said about the matter.[32]

If discussion failed the most common sanction was to bar an individual from Communion and other church rituals. Writing to the Charles Town merchant, Henry Laurens, John Ettwein explained, "if anyone does not walk worthily, the Gospel, he is not to be admitted to the Lord Supper till he repents and mends tho' he is a Communion Brother or Sister. If he is not admitted

to the Holy Communion, he has till he is admitted again also
no Admittance to the Private Meetings of the Communicants
viz. our daily Liturgy . . . And thus ev'ry Meeting is an admonition to such who have not Admittance." Minutes of Wachovia's various conferences contain frequent references to brothers
or sisters who have been excluded from the Lord's table, but
they rarely indicate the nature of the offense for which this punishment was levied. During the years of the *Oeconomy,* the only
instance in which exclusion from Communion can be linked to
a particular offense was in 1763, when August Schubert was excluded because he beat an apprentice he suspected of theft
rather than turn the case over to the proper officials.[33]

The next step available to the elders seems to have been the
registration of a formal reprimand against an individual. Unfortunately, it is unclear how or where this was filed, and there was
only one recorded instance of a reprimand before 1772. Of that
incident, extant sources report only that it was for "very unbrotherly" conduct, "especially in consideration of the actions
with the sisters."[34]

When all else failed, Wachovia's leaders had both the authority and the power to expel any member whose actions threatened the general welfare of the congregation. As long as members remained in the *Oeconomy,* and it owned the land on which
they lived and worked, any offender could easily be removed if
necessary. The church had to find a new way to exercise control
once individuals began leaving the *Oeconomy* and leasing land
in Bethania or Bethabara. Starting with Bethania's establishment
in 1759, therefore, rental agreements in Wachovia contained
clauses such as that found in a Bethabara lease signed by Jacobus van der Merk in 1763. "[The lessee] binds himself and en-
gages to observe strictly the Law of God & Country," it declared,
"as also in a Special Manner the particular Rules of the Society
as statutes of the Place. Upon which the Duration of this Agreement chiefly shall depend for in Default or willful & obstinate
Transgression all Grants, Promises, & Articles on the Part of
Abraham v. Gammern [for the Unity] shall be declared void."
And because it proved impossible to include such restrictive
covenants in deeds of sale, the Unity refused to sell any land in

Bethabara or Salem and sold that in Bethania only to individuals approved by officials in Salem.[35]

Expulsion from Wachovia could take several forms. An individual might be permitted to leave without being formally expelled, ordered back to Pennsylvania while remaining a member of the Unity with the possibility of readmission to Wachovia, or dismissed from both the colony and the church. During the years 1753–1772, at least ten men were expelled or encouraged to leave Wachovia because of their behavior. The first example came in 1758 or 1759; during the next decade six more had to leave—one each in 1760, 1762, 1765, 1767, 1768, and 1769; and in 1771 three more were dismissed. In about half these cases a reason for the action was recorded. It seems that those returned to Pennsylvania were guilty of a degree of self-interest that made it impossible for them to live in Bethabara's communal economy. George Lösch was sent back to Pennsylvania until he promised to be "obedient and orderly," while John Lanius was returned to his parents after he ran away from his master and was disobedient. Those expelled from both Wachovia and the Unity, on the other hand, were guilty of more serious breaches. Andrew Betz was cast out for marrying a non-Moravian, for example, and Henrich Feldhausen for giving in to "carnal desires" and falling into "all kinds of sin and shame."[36]

The clearest example of how Moravian officials used these escalating powers in an effort to reform individuals without having to expel them from the church community is the story of August Schubert, who was finally permitted to leave in 1765. The elders in Bethabara tried repeatedly to effect a change in his behavior and gave up only when he became a threat to the congregation.

Schubert came to Bethabara in 1760 to replace the recently deceased Hans Martin Kalberlahn as the colony's physician. It certainly did not help Schubert that his predecessor had lived a life of exemplary virtue, had died caring for victims of a typhus epidemic, and was remembered with affection bordering on adoration. Schubert, by contrast, was a man whose own *Pfleger* called him "very arrogant" and complained that he "does not go well with the brothers and sisters." Within two years of his arrival in Bethabara, Schubert had used his medical position to extort from the elders "a better house and comforts," and earned a reprimand for behaving in a "very unbrotherly" manner. Early the next year, 1763, things got worse when Schubert suspected his thirteen-year-old apprentice had stolen some money from him. Rather than bring his suspicions to the elders, Schubert beat the boy and threatened to rub salt and pepper in his wounds if he did not reveal where he had hidden the money. When the elders learned of Schubert's action they had a long talk with him and barred him from Communion in the hope that would bring a change.[37]

Neither Schubert's attitude nor his behavior got any better, though, and by 1764 officials in both Bethlehem and Bethabara had decided that Brother Schubert needed a wife. In May a choir conference in Bethlehem reached that conclusion. By the time its directive reached Bethabara, however, the Personal and Choir Conference there had already decided the same thing and had begun talking to the doctor about potential mates. The elders eventually chose Anna Elizabeth Kraus, a widow living in Bethabara, and the two were married the day after Christmas.[38]

Marriage only made Schubert worse. Five months after his wedding things finally came to a head. On the evening of May 16, 1765, Johannetta Ettwein asked Sister Schubert if she planned to help weed the flax the next day. The latter replied that she had too much other work to do and snapped at Sister Ettwein: "It is easy for you, you don't have anything else to do; the work is about to kill me." She then broke off the conversation, went home and, in the words of John Ettwein, "told her husband goodness only knows what." Whatever Anna Elizabeth said it got the doctor "all stirred up," and he went in search of *Vice-Oeconomus* Ettwein, whom he quickly found at Michael Sauter's house. Schubert demanded to speak with Ettwein; so the two went out in the garden, where the doctor "talked of nothing but how tired God knew he was of the *Oeconomy*" and how determined he was to be free of it. Schubert also complained that his wife was "very harassed" by the other women, including Sister Ettwein, and that she "had enough work in their garden and that she could do absolutely nothing else" except perhaps help with the milking during the summer. Ettwein assured Schubert that no one would ask more of her than that, and when the two men parted that evening Ettwein believed the matter was resolved.[39]

But the following Monday Schubert wrote the Helpers Conference demanding that he and his wife be released from the *Oeconomy*. The conference replied that they had no authority to permit that until after the move to Salem. Schubert wrote again, however, pressing two demands: "1. That I may regard myself as a practitioner and servant of medicine among you; 2nd. that I be permitted to acquire the clothing necessary for my wife and myself." The first inclination of the Helpers Conference was to ignore the letter, but as the members discussed it further they concluded that the doctor had become "a dangerous individual." In a letter written later that year, John Ettwein explained that Schubert and a few others had "tried to cast insinuations on the ministers and did all they could to stir up a faction against us." If that is what the Helpers Conference thought Schubert was up to, then it is hardly surprising that its members came to regard him as "a dangerous individual." He was no longer just a threat to himself; he had dragged several others into his sinful ways and threatened to undermine the theocratic base of Wachovia's government. The conference, therefore, asked the Lot "Should we open the door to him?" The response was yes, and two members informed the doctor that he was free to leave Wachovia whenever he wanted.[40]

Schubert chose to leave almost immediately, but before going he sought to have the Helpers Conference declare that it was expelling him. This it refused to do, replying only "we do not wish to do or say anything with regard to his intentions of leaving." Thus if Schubert had a change of heart the way would be open for his return. The prodigal never asked forgiveness, though. Husband and wife returned to Pennsylvania, settled between Bethlehem and Philadelphia, and cut themselves off from the Brethren. As for those in Bethabara who had supported Schubert, two couples at least stayed away from Communion one Sunday "because of the affair," and according to Adelaide Fries they and another sister were "under discipline until the end of the year."[41]

Cases like that of August Schubert were rare in early Wachovia. Of course there were problems; records of the Moravian community include frequent references to individuals or groups who violated church standards or regulations. But officials in the colony seldom needed heavy pressure to bring errant brothers and sisters back to the church's way. Settlers were, after all, chosen for the strength of their commitment to the Unity, and once they got to Wachovia the overlapping supervision and support of family, choir, and church and the economic power of the *Oeconomy* provided constant refreshment for anyone's lagging spirits. As a result, the normal function of Wachovia's government was to direct highly motivated individuals rather than to coerce reluctant ones. And despite occasional problems with weak or frustrated members the Moravian community there remained strong and loyal until well into the nineteenth century.

The preceding chapters have concentrated on Wachovia's Moravian community as a separate enclave within North Carolina's frontier population and on the tools and techniques its leaders employed to promote and protect that separateness. This was certainly part of Wachovia's early history, but only part. Moravian leaders had always intended to establish links between church members in North Carolina and outsiders. They sought only to control those links, not to abolish them, to routinize contact rather than stop it. The next three chapters explore that side of Wachovia's history—how the Brethren participated in the economic, political, and social systems of Rowan County and North Carolina without destroying the distinctly Moravian community they were building at the same time.

PART II

Citizens and Subjects

CHAPTER 5

Moravians in the Marketplace

Trade is one of the oldest and most common forms of contact across cultural boundaries. Since before recorded history, societies that disliked one another, distrusted one another, and often tried to destroy one another have also done business with one another. It comes as no surprise, then, to find that economic relations were the oldest, the most visible, and probably the most important source of regular contact between members of Wachovia's Moravian community and the world around them. Just two days after the Brethren reached what later became Bethabara they bought meat and corn from a Mr. Haltem who lived north of them on or near Town Fork Creek. From that small beginning, trade between Moravian and non-Moravian residents of North Carolina rapidly grew to involve hundreds of people and brought the Brethren and their neighbors into daily contact. And trade was only one of the economic ties between these two communities. They also established relationships as debtors and creditors, employers and employees, and landlords and tenants, relationships that were always important and sometimes crucial to the well-being of Moravians and non-Moravians alike. Long before 1772 Wachovia's Moravian community was fully integrated into the regional economy of western North Carolina.[1]

The brothers' and sisters' entry into North Carolina's economy neither surprised nor upset church leaders. Moravian communities in Herrnhut and Bethlehem had done business with their neighbors since the 1720s and 1740s, respectively, and Wachovia's planners expected its residents to do likewise. It

would, in fact, be essential that they do so. If Wachovia was ever
to be both autonomous and profitable, as Zinzendorf wanted it
to be, then the Brethren would have to strike a balance between
isolation and participation. It was certainly important to achieve
a level of economic self-sufficiency. As Gillian Gollin explained
in her study of Bethlehem, "the Zinzendorfian model of an exclusive community . . . [involved] a determination to establish
a degree of independence from the outside which would permit
the Moravians to pursue their religious goals unhampered by
the limitations imposed by a dependence upon non-Moravian
resources." If carried too far, however, the search for autonomy
might interfere with the equally important search for profits.
Absolute self-sufficiency would require the Brethren to dupli-
cate services that were already available from non-Moravians in
the area. It might also force some of the Brethren, most of whom
were artisans, out of their shops and into unskilled positions
that earned the church less than it could get by leaving them in
their lucrative crafts and hiring non-Moravians for the unskilled
jobs. For Wachovia to develop as Zinzendorf intended, it had to
be part of the economy around it.[2]

This is not to say, however, that individual brothers and sisters had to be part of it. It is essential to distinguish here between the Moravian community and individual members of that
community. In the case of the former, church officials expected
and encouraged contact with the outside world; in the case of
the latter they did all they could to prevent it. The elders were
afraid that few brothers or sisters could resist what one Moravian writer called "the American spirit of unlimited freedom."
They tried, therefore, to routinize economic relations in order
to eliminate contact between individual Brethren and their
neighbors without interrupting the communal contact they considered essential to Wachovia's success.[3]

First, Unity leaders tried to channel contact through Wachovia's *gemein Orten,* initially Bethabara and then Salem. Because the residents of those villages were brothers and sisters
considered to have the strongest faith, it stood to reason that
they also had the best chance of resisting the bad habits of visiting strangers. Furthermore, as the seat of Wachovia's govern-

ment and home to most of its ministers, the *gemein Ort* contained an impressive array of institutions designed to help individual members resist temptation. Residents lived under family, choir, congregation, and community supervision, and if anyone showed signs of weakening, those sentinels were close enough to detect the problem and to take action before major spiritual damage was done. Finally, the Unity planned to seek corporate status for its *gemein Ort*. A charter would give Moravian officials the authority to make ordinances for the town that were also binding on non-Moravians within its bounds, and as Frederic Marschall explained in 1767, "[if] people know we can as a corporation make external [i.e., temporal] ordinances in the town that also bind strangers as long as they are there . . . then they have more respect."[4]

Channeling outsiders into this designated forum involved both a carrot and a stick. The carrot was for nonmembers and involved locating in a single place everything that might attract them to the colony. Zinzendorf intended from the start to concentrate Wachovia's craftsmen, stores, and business leaders in its central city. Beyond the *gemein Ort* he wanted farms and small villages only—nothing that would attract outsiders. The stick was a number of policies adopted by the Unity to insure that none of its other settlements in Wachovia rose to rival its *gemein Ort*. When Bethania was established, in 1759, Spangenberg made sure the new village would offer little in the way of competition. It was forbidden a tavern, store, mill, apothecary, or anything else that might divert visitors from Bethabara; even its own residents had to go to Bethabara to exchange their farm products for finished goods. And as Salem became the colony's *gemein Ort*, church elders in Europe explained that "Bethabara remains the farm where agriculture, farming, and brewing can be carried on." In the end Bethabara was allowed to retain its mill and tavern and a branch of the store (the body of which went to Salem), but the rest of Wachovia's nonfarm economy and all of its business leaders moved to Salem. Bethabara continued to receive visitors after its demotion, though their number declined rapidly, and the village soon slipped into an insignificance that barely competed with Salem for the attention of outsiders. Thus when J. F. D. Smyth passed through the older community, in 1772, he wrote, "being informed that Salem was the principal [town], I immediately proceeded on."[5]

This effort to confine visitors to particular locations continued inside the *gemein Ort*, too. By the 1790s officials in Salem had gone so far as to define precisely which parts of town were open to outsiders and which were not. There is no evidence of such an explicit demarcation during the years of the *Oeconomy*, but there was an unmistakable desire to restrict cross-boundary contact in the *gemein Ort* to a few specific locations, especially the store and tavern. This was most clear, perhaps, in the pass system announced in 1768 to deal with beggars arriving in Bethabara. Indigents admitted to the village received "tickets" permitting them to enter but only to go to the store "lest they come to the houses to beg." A much larger problem, however, involved outsiders who stayed the night. The longer one stayed among the Brethren the more time one had to cause mischief; so overnight guests were allowed only in special quarters separated from the brothers and sisters. Those quarters were one of the first things the Moravians built in Carolina. Just three months after arriving, the colonists in Bethabara started a "strangers' house" (*fremden Logis*) so they would no longer have to share their cabin with visitors, and they located it on the opposite side of the clearing in which they lived—at a slight remove, anyway, from their own cabin. Three years later, when the Brethren erected Wachovia's first tavern, it was even more important that they keep some distance between it and themselves because the tavern would not only house outsiders but also serve them beer and liquor. Bethabara's inn, therefore, went up two hundred yards from the center of town, not far enough to put its patrons beyond the ken of their hosts but far enough to insulate most residents from drunken visitors. And when the Brethren built a tavern for Salem, it too went up on the edge of town.[6]

It was not enough, however, to keep outsiders in certain parts of the colony; Moravian officials also wanted to control who they saw when they got there. The first step toward that end was to bar most residents of Bethabara and Salem from the likeliest points of contact. Instructions given to Bethabara's storekeeper show clearly that his operation was intended to serve outsiders and to discourage its use by church members. There was also a clear understanding that the tavern was off limits to the brothers and sisters, though not until 1775 is there evidence of a formal regulation to that effect. The idea was to conduct as much business as possible through a few designated contact specialists. Nearly all business dealings between outsiders and the Moravian community were handled by the *Vorsteher* or by the storekeepers and shopkeepers of Bethabara or Salem. These specialists were chosen, in part, for their ability to resist the sinful ways of non-Moravians. Unfortunately, it is impossible to say exactly what the elders thought made an individual more resistant. The only demonstrable criterion to emerge from the Moravians' records was marriage. Because the church regarded one's spouse as an important ally in the struggle against Satan, it was especially desirable for members who came into frequent contact with outsiders to have a wife or husband who could provide them spiritual reinforcement. Not all of Wachovia's contact specialists were married, but most were, and several wed specifically as a prerequisite for assuming positions that exposed them to non-Moravians. In 1762, for example, Spangenberg wrote from Bethlehem to inform Bethabara's Weekly Conference, "we have decided on Br. Angel for the tavern, but he should marry toward that end."[7]

It is impossible to say whether or not this effort to restrict economic relations between Moravians and non-Moravians had any effect on the extent of those relations. It almost certainly reduced the frequency with which they occurred between some Brethren and strangers visiting their community; that was what it was supposed to do. There is no evidence, however, that it affected the extent of contact between the Moravian community, as a community, and outsiders seeking to do business with it. Between 1753 and 1772 cross-boundary contact was an integral and essential feature of Wachovia's economy, despite significant changes both in that economy and in that of the region around Wachovia. During that period Wachovia's economy went through three distinct stages of development. First, came two years during which the colonists tried simply to survive; then came a three-year period marked by efforts to broaden the colony's local economic base; and finally, a third period arrived during which it entered the Atlantic economy. And in each of the three there were extensive economic links between Wachovia's Moravian community and the world around it.

During its first phase Wachovia economy was relatively simple. This was due to the relatively simple state of the economy around Wachovia and to the Unity's long-range plan for its colony. Bethabara's founders reported that most of their neighbors were "poor," raised little on their farms but corn, depended on hunting to survive, and had little to spare for trading with craftsmen such as the Brethren hoped to be. Church leaders, therefore, considered it essential that Bethabara quickly become as self-sufficient as possible in meeting its basic needs. "When we have everything that serves for the body's nourishment and needs," wrote Spangenberg, "then we will think about commodities and commerce." That self-sufficiency was not to extend beyond basics, though. Unity plans for Wachovia's eventual development called for its merchants and craftsmen to live in its permanent *gemein Ort*, not in Bethabara. Thus, any crafts established in the latter place would eventually have to be dismantled and reestablished someplace else once a site was chosen for the *gemein Ort*. For that reason, Spangenberg directed that only what he called "necessary crafts" were to go up in Bethabara. Everything else could wait. As he explained to Bethabara's residents in 1755:

> It is good, of course, that you have a mill and smithy, and perhaps make-shift means to furnish the articles which you cannot obtain there yet must have. But whenever you can manage and adapt yourselves to the circumstances, by all means do so. For example, if you can make do with iron kettles, with some copper vessels, and such milk containers as you can fashion of wood until such time as the pottery can be built at the right place where it belongs, this will save you a lot of time in the first place and then lead to better results.[8]

As a result, the Moravians' chief economic activity during their first two years in North Carolina was farming. In small fields around Bethabara they raised corn, wheat, rye, barley, oats, buckwheat, millet, flax, hemp, tobacco, and cotton. Corn was by far the most important of these early crops because of the relative ease with which it could be prepared for human consumption. Most of the Brethren, however, preferred the taste of wheat to that of corn, describing the former as "the proper grain for bread." Moreover wheat was the first crop they planted when they got to Wachovia. But until they built a grist mill, the only place they could turn wheat into flour was at a neighbor's mill on the Yadkin or on Town Fork Creek, which was expensive and inconvenient. Corn, on the other hand, they could grind in their own "Indian mill." So until they finished their own grist mill, in November of 1755, the Moravians relied on mush and bread made from corn, and corn made up two-thirds of their grain harvests.[9]

In addition to their field crops the Brethren planted hundreds of fruit trees, a medical garden, and a vegetable garden that produced beans, potatoes, peas, cucumbers, melons, salad greens, pumpkins, and cabbage. And in the woods around their settlement they kept cattle, horses, pigs, and sheep.[10]

Wachovia's first economy was not entirely agrarian, though; it did contain Spangenberg's "necessary crafts." Most of the men in the first party sent to Wachovia possessed both farm and non-farm skills, and among them were a doctor, two shoemakers, two millwrights, two carpenters, a cooper, a sievemaker, a turner, a tailor, at least one tanner, and a baker.[11] Spangenberg hoped that the combined talents of these men would be enough to meet most of Bethabara's immediate needs. It soon became clear, however, that the colony also needed a blacksmith and that the millwrights needed help; so in 1754 two of each were sent from Bethlehem. The smiths were busy in makeshift quarters within a few weeks. The millwrights also went to work at once, but it took them longer to finish their job. Not until November 1755 did Bethabara's grist mill run for the first time, and another eighteen months passed before the rest of the complex—saw mill, bark mill (for grinding oak bark from which to extract tannin for tanning leather), oil mill, and flax breaker—was finished. For the first several years, all of these nonfarm activities were subordinate to agriculture; "the crafts are good," wrote Spangenberg, "but the farm always goes first." And the highest priority was to ready Bethabara for larger parties of brothers and sisters.[12]

This emphasis on laying the groundwork for a larger colony did not preclude the rapid establishment of economic relations between the Moravians and their neighbors. In fact, it practically guaranteed them. In enlarging their operations in Bethabara the Brethren had to buy a variety of materials from their neighbors: cattle, horses, and pigs for breeding stock; tobacco plants; and a variety of seeds and trees. Moreover, because they spent so much of their time and energy clearing additional land, putting up more buildings, and otherwise preparing for additional settlers, the men in Bethabara did not raise enough food to meet even their own needs, much less enough to feed future arrivals. Corn, for example, was their chief crop and dietary staple until 1756; yet in 1754 they grew just three-quarters of the corn they needed, and in 1755 less than half. Month after month they bought barrels of corn from their neighbors to cover the shortfall. They also bought hundreds of pounds of beef, pork, and bear meat plus smaller quantities of flour, cornmeal, rum, butter, and seeds.[13]

Cross-boundary trade went both ways, though, even in Wachovia's earliest days. Bethabara's founders brought with them a range of manufactured goods and artisanal talents in short supply on the frontier. Furthermore, as they added to their resources in anticipation of future colonists they made themselves that much more attractive to potential customers. The result was a steady stream of outsiders, three hundred to four hundred people a year, arriving to trade with the Brethren. Some came to buy manufactured goods from the *Oeconomy*'s storehouse: blankets, axes, hoes, tinware, and other items brought or shipped from Pennsylvania for the Moravians' own use. Others made the journey to visit Bethabara's growing community of craftsmen. By the fall of 1755 the tailor, blacksmith, cooper, tanner, and shoemaker were all accepting non-Moravian customers when their schedules permitted it, and according to August Spangenberg people for twenty miles around were waiting to use the brothers' grist mill when it opened that November. But the greatest draw during these early years was Hans Martin Kalberlahn, Bethabara's Norwegian-born surgeon. Kalberlahn had been sent to Wachovia to care for its Moravian settlers. From the moment he arrived, however, he was besieged by outsiders, some of whom had reportedly travelled over one hundred miles to see him. Others who needed his services were too ill to travel; so Kalberlahn made housecalls, sometimes riding twenty miles or more to see a patient. He made these calls over the objections of his superiors in Pennsylvania, who believed "there occur that way too many things that cut across our congregation plan and are involved with at least danger, where not damage, to the soul." Whether in or around Bethabara, Brother Kalberlahn diagnosed people's ills, dispensed medication, pulled teeth, set broken bones, and performed a variety of surgical operations regardless of a patient's religion.[14]

It is difficult to measure precisely the volume of all this trade because of questions about the Moravians' bookkeeping. It is unclear, for example, just how they treated exchanges in kind. They definitely calculated barter like cash in 1754; after that it is impossible to say for sure. The records are good enough, though, to show that in 1754–55 the volume of trade between Bethabara and its neighbors was growing and that the balance of this trade clearly favored the neighbors. In 1754 the total value of goods and services exchanged between Moravians and non-Moravians around Wachovia came to approximately £185, Virginia. In 1755 the figure was about £315, an increase of 70 percent. Most of the increase came in sales to the Brethren, though. In 1754 Bethabara's *Oeconomy* paid outsiders almost £130, Virginia, and earned from them just £55. The next year earnings rose 54 percent to approximately £85, Virginia, but expenditures went up 77 percent to £230. In both years the only reason Bethabara could balance its books was that Bethlehem sent it large sums of cash—nearly twice as much, in fact, as it earned from its neighbors.[15]

Moravian business records are also good enough to show the geographic extent of early trade between Wachovia and the

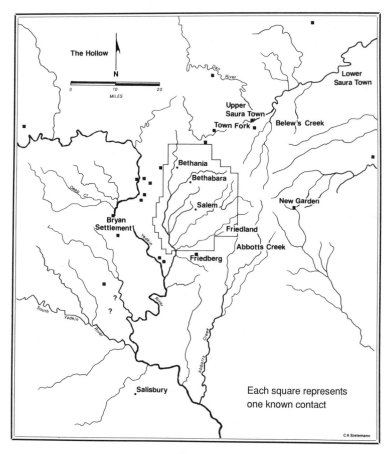

The Hollow

N

0   10   20
MILES

Lower
Saura Town

Upper
Saura Town
Town Fork

Belew's Creek

Bethania

Bethabara

Salem

New Garden

Bryan
Settlement

Friedland

Abbotts Creek

Friedberg

?

?

Salisbury

Each square represents
one known contact

C A Sielemann

Map 3. Wachovia's Non-Moravian Business Contacts, 1753–1755

world around it (Map 3). In 1754–55 the Brethren identified by
name fifty-three of the people with whom they did business in
Bethabara's hinterland. The homes of twenty-one of these can
be located from other references to them in the Moravians' records and maps, while two more of the names match or resemble
those of known landowners in Rowan County at the time and
may or may not be the same individuals. Most of these people

lived within twenty miles of Bethabara—along Town Fork Creek, to the north and northeast, and near the Yadkin River, to the west. A significant number lived beyond that twenty-mile radius, though. There were fairly regular dealings between Wachovia and the Quaker settlement at New Garden, twenty-five miles east of Bethabara. A Mr. Wallik, perhaps the Martin Wallock who lived thirty-five miles away in the Forks of the Yadkin, sold corn to the *Oeconomy.* Somebody crossed the fifty-odd miles between Bethabara and the home of a Mr. Drollinger, who lived near the Haw River east of New Garden, for him to sell brandy to the Brethren. And William Owens came from the Mulberry Fields, almost sixty miles west of Wachovia, to sell deerskin and buy linen in 1755. Beyond this immediate hinterland the Moravians' only business contact with outsiders during the *Oeconomy's* first stage was their importing iron from Pennsylvania via Wilmington in 1755.[16]

Trade was not the only economic bond between the Brethren and their neighbors, though. As customers, patients, and sightseers flocked to Bethabara, the Brethren found themselves playing innkeeper to them. They certainly had not intended to do this, but within a month of their arrival, the Moravian colonists began complaining about the inconvenience of housing visitors in their one small cabin and the expense of feeding them from *Oeconomy* stores. To separate themselves from the aliens in their midst; the Brethren built a "strangers' house" in February of 1754, and to reduce the financial burden of their hospitality they decided in September of that year to begin charging a small fee for lodging. Thus, by late 1754 the Moravians were operating a de facto tavern, though they had no license to do so until 1756, and providing food and lodging to scores of non-Moravian guests.[17]

The rapid growth of trade between Brethren and strangers also led to the rapid formation of credit relations between them. This came in spite of strong objections from Unity officials in Pennsylvania and Europe. Loans to outsiders were especially worrisome to the church because so many people refused to honor their obligations and left the Brethren either to absorb the loss or initiate legal proceedings. "We either become cheated or entangled with people," concluded a 1755 conference in Beth-lehem. Taking loans from outsiders was just as dangerous be-cause they gave potentially hostile creditors leverage over the Brethren and threatened the latter's autonomy. Unity elders, therefore, urged Wachovia's settlers to use only cash or com-modities in their dealings with strangers, but that proved im-possible from the start.[18]

Most of the non-Moravians who patronized Bethabara's shops, doctor, and tavern were small farmers. They often needed credit to carry them from one harvest to another, and even in flush times might have nothing the Brethren needed or wanted. In such an economy, insistence on immediate payment would often make it impossible for people to buy, and such a policy was neither good business nor good religion. If the Breth-ren refused to do business with a man when he needed credit, how could they expect him to come back when he did not? And how could a good Christian deny his neighbor the supplies or care he and his family needed simply because they were tem-porarily unable to pay? Without extending credit to their neigh-bors, the Brethren could help neither them nor themselves; so they regularly came through with the necessary loans. In fact, the first money they earned in Wachovia, ten days after their arrival, was two bushels of corn that a patient of Brother Kal-berlahn's promised to pay later, and during the next two years their records frequently mentioned Jacob Lösch or another member riding out to collect money due the *Oeconomy* or debt-ors arriving to work off what they owed.[19]

The Brethren, too, often ran short of cash. During Wachovia's first two years, the *Oeconomy* borrowed from outsiders at least as much as it lent. The first party of colonists took with it £300, Pennsylvania. The money did not last long, however, and the inability of customers to pay immediately for what they bought in Bethabara meant that very little flowed in to replace it. As a result, the Brethren, too, were forced to buy on time. "As soon as we had no more money," wrote Jacob Lösch, "I went to three men [and] said to them that because we now had no cash we would honestly pay them as soon as we can; to which they were agreeable." By January 1754 the Brethren were already in debt to a Mr. Guest, one of their neighbors, and by the summer of 1756 their indebtedness to outsiders had reached £45.11.10, Virginia, which they owed to eight creditors for purchases of butter, salt, corn, cattle, and hemp.[20]

Finally, these first two years also saw the start in a long line of non-Moravians hired to work for the Brethren in Wachovia. In October of 1755 the congregational diarist reported that three men had agreed to work felling trees and splitting shingles for three weeks in return for a pair of shoes each from the *Oeconomy's* cobbler. Others were paid in cash for their labor. Matthias Eders and Valentine Zinn, for example, each received £1.2.6, Virginia, for shingle making later in 1755. While employed in Bethabara, all these men stayed in the strangers' house and, presumably, ate meals there that they picked up in the community kitchen. In spite of one recent writer's assertion that the use of outside labor in Wachovia "represented a continental drift in Moravian aspirations," there is no evidence that either the colonists or their superiors considered it anything out of the ordinary. According to Gillian Gollin, Herrnhut employed dozens of non-Moravian construction workers during the 1740s and 1750s, and when Spangenberg came to North Carolina in search of land, in 1752, he hired locals as hunters and chaincarriers. As long as the two groups did not live together in Bethabara, and as long as the outsiders remained day laborers who could be expelled quickly if necessary, Moravian leaders did not object to the presence of non-Moravian workers and often hired as many as they could afford.[21]

The economic links that developed between Moravians and non-Moravians during Wachovia's first two years grew even more extensive after 1755 as the colony's *Oeconomy* entered its second phase, one that lasted until the end of 1758. During the first phase, Wachovia's residents had been free to ignore immediate profits and concentrate, instead, on the long term through tasks like clearing land and breeding cattle. They owed this luxury to their superiors' belief that money invested in the Nord Carolina Land und Colony Etablissement would support the colonists for five years, by which time their capital improvements would be generating an income large enough to sustain them. This confidence soon proved ill-placed, however, as the colony's childhood was cut short by the Etablissement's failure to attract as many investors as it was supposed to and by the failure of those who did join to pay promptly for their shares. Letters written by Cornelius van Laer, the company's codirector based in Europe, to Spangenberg, his counterpart in America, are a fund-raiser's nightmare. They detail van Laer's unending search for loans and contributions to fill the gap between anticipated and actual revenues—including one campaign among the sisters in Zeist that netted three gold rings, two gold snuff boxes, one snuff box trimmed with gold, and "many things made of silver." Further delays arising from the need to convert currencies and transfer them from Europe to America so slowed the process that no Etablissement funds reached this side of the Atlantic before the spring of 1755.[22]

In the meantime, Unity officials expected Bethlehem's *Oeconomy* to pay Bethabara's bills. This the Pennsylvanians managed but only at considerable expense to their own community, and throughout 1754 and 1755 Spangenberg complained to his colleagues in London and Zeist. He did more than grumble, though; late in 1754, after Bethlehem had supported Wachovia for a year without receiving a penny from the Etablissement, he declared "[we] can move no further in the Carolina affair until we receive remittances and loans [from Europe]." Six months later, when the long-awaited torrent of European capital finally began and turned out to be a trickle, he concluded that Wachovia would simply have to begin supporting itself much sooner than expected.[23]

Thus Wachovia's *Oeconomy* entered its second phase. Between early 1756 and late 1758 church leaders in Bethlehem and Bethabara took steps to increase the latter's ability to attract earnings from the local economy. The most important part of this process was the enlargement of Wachovia's nonfarm activities. For example, Spangenberg suddenly decided it was time to send a potter to Bethabara. The Brethren there had been asking for one since early 1754 both to provide earthenware for their own housekeeping and as a source of income for their community. Officials in Pennsylvania had repeatedly denied their request on the grounds that pottery was not a "necessary craft" and that if they built a pottery in Bethabara they would just have to move it again a few years later. As recently as June of 1755 Spangenberg had refused again to send a potter to Carolina, but by September he had a change of heart. He decided the settlers in Bethabara would have to bear more of their colony's cost; so he sent Gottfried Aust to open Wachovia's first pottery. Another indication of the new desire to increase Wachovia's earnings came a year later when residents began advertising the prices they would pay for local products, in an apparent bid to attract more trade, and to require that items they took be at least "marchantable," suggesting that they planned to resell at least part of what they bought.[24]

The search for additional revenue also affected the *Oeconomy*'s agriculture, most notably in the almost total elimination of corn cultivation in Wachovia between 1755 and 1758. Corn constituted 68 percent of the Moravians' grain harvest in 1754, while wheat accounted for only 9 percent. By 1758 the roles were reversed; corn had fallen to 9 percent and wheat had risen to 60. Certainly, part of this decline was a result of the brothers' stated preference for bread made from wheat, but that cannot be the whole story because the Brethren continued to use large quantities of corn even after they stopped eating it themselves. Their livestock consumed hundreds of bushels each year; their distillery turned an unknown quantity into liquor; and they probably used cornmeal in the tavern. In spite of their continued use of corn, however, the Brethren grew almost none, and this was more a matter of economics than taste. Given the average yields and prices of the two grains in Wachovia, an acre of wheat was worth 45–50 shillings compared to thirty-six for an acre of corn. In that situation it made better economic sense for the brothers to devote their resources of labor and land to the production of wheat and to buy the corn they needed. And that is exactly what they did.[25]

With the arrival of more artisans and the increased production of wheat in its fields, Wachovia's economy was ready to stand on its own. By the latter half of 1757 it had a mix of farmers and craftsmen who were earning more than they spent, and in May of that year Spangenberg told the colonists that they should expect no more help from either Bethlehem or the Nord Carolina Land und Colonie Etablissement. "From now on I consider your economy to be like a young, very well equipped married couple," wrote Spangenberg. "So be industrious and take pains faithfully to assist the Saviour's cause in your turn."[26]

Coming of age certainly did not diminish Wachovia's economic ties to the world around it. Those ties grew even stronger during the *Oeconomy's* second phase, as Bethabara grew and consolidated its position as an economic center of the Carolina backcountry. Trade, the most visible economic link between Moravians and non-Moravians, increased significantly in both volume and extent. Most of the trade into Bethabara was still food from the surrounding region. Late in 1757 Spangenberg noted with approval that "the neighborhood is accustomed to bringing its grain, cattle, butter, and the like to Bethabara," and during the first half of 1758, 65 percent of *Oeconomy* expenditures in North Carolina were for food products like meat, grain, butter, eggs, and sugar. Some of this still went to feed the brothers and sisters themselves because until the 1758 harvest they did not produce enough food to meet their own needs. In 1757, for example, they raised 345 bushels of wheat, by then the principal grain in their diet, but on the basis of their known consumption patterns probably needed twice that just to feed themselves. The *Oeconomy* made up part of the shortfall, 174 bushels, from the toll collected at its grist mill, and may have had some wheat on hand from previous harvests, but that still left it short and helps explain why Bethabara bought 237 bushels of wheat from outsiders during the first five months of 1758. The Brethren also bought from their neighbors grain to be processed and resold in Bethabara's tavern. Throughout the period 1756–58 the Moravians sold food and drink to their guests, and if they had to buy wheat and rye for their own use, then they must also have bought what the tavern required. Not all the *Oeconomy's* purchases were food, though. It also continued to hire non-Moravian workers and to buy hemp, hides, linen, and "store things" from their neighbors and from peddlers passing through.[27]

In exchange, the Brethren offered a growing variety of goods and services. During this second phase of the *Oeconomy,* Bethabara opened both a grist and a saw mill, a pottery, and a legitimate tavern while continuing to operate its tannery, blacksmith, cobbler's shop, tailor's, and apothecary, and to sell small quantities of imported goods from its storehouse. In terms of income derived from outsiders, the tavern quickly became the most important of these operations. It was a plain log structure built to replace the "strangers' house" and was located some two-hundred yards northwest of the village proper in an apparent effort to isolate its unchurched patrons from the brothers and sisters living nearby. It opened in the spring of 1757. By the end of that year its average monthly income of just over £9, Virginia, represented about half the *Oeconomy's* earnings from non-Moravian trade. The following year the tavern's share of *Oeconomy* earnings dipped slightly to 42 percent, but it was still the most reliable moneymaker in Bethabara, bringing in £12–13 every month through sales of liquor by the drink and in bulk and from feeding and housing visitors. A fading second behind the tavern was Bethabara's blacksmith, who made and repaired a variety of metal implements, shod horses, and may have repaired guns. Just behind the smith was the pottery, which sold plates, bowls, pitchers, and other earthenware to the neighbors. Last among the *Oeconomy's* major economic attractions during this second phase was its grist mill, which like the pottery and blacksmith had been built with one eye on the Moravians' own need for its services and one on its potential earnings from outsiders.[28]

Given the growth of population both in and around Wachovia and the diversification of Bethabara's *Oeconomy,* it is hardly surprising that the volume of trade between Moravians and non-Moravians rose significantly during the *Oeconomy's* second phase. The estimated total in 1758, based on figures for the first six months of the year, was £1150, Virginia—three times what the trade had been worth in 1755. A more important change, however, came in the balance of that trade; between 1755 and 1758 it shifted in the *Oeconomy's* favor. In 1755 the Brethren had spent about £230 while earning just £85 in trade with their

A View of Bethabara.

4. This view of Bethabara, probably done in 1757 by Nicholas Garrison, shows the relationship between Brethren and strangers in early Wachovia. On the right is the heart of the Moravian community: the Single Brothers' House, the *Gemein Haus*, and some, though not all, of the other congregational structures. On the left, outside the stockade and 200 yards from the Brethren, is the tavern complex, built to serve outsiders visiting Bethabara without admitting them to the village proper. (Used with permission of the Archives of the Moravian Church in America—Northern Province)

neighbors. By 1758, based again on reports for the first six months, the *Oeconomy*'s estimated income from outsiders was £600, and its expenditure to them was £550.[29]

There were also important changes in the territorial extent of Wachovia's trade with non-Moravians. During the second phase of the *Oeconomy*'s development, trade between Brethren and strangers became both more concentrated and more widespread. The concentration came in Bethabara's immediate hinterland (Map 4). Here there was a marked increase in the density of business contacts within twenty miles of town, and especially in the strip of land between Wachovia's western edge and the Yadkin River. There was growth farther out in Bethabara's hinterland. Trade increased, for instance, between the Moravian town and Quakers around New Garden; wagons from the latter community began bringing wheat to be ground in Bethabara's mill, and individual Friends, like Hannibal Edwards, purchased and sometimes ordered goods through the *Oeconomy*. But the trend was clearly toward greater geographic concentration close to Wachovia's borders. At the same time long-distance trade between Moravians and non-Moravians increased between 1755 and 1758. The Brethren stepped up their dealings with Wilmington, two-hundred miles southeast of them, and the Bethabara diarist reported that people were coming from as far away as South Carolina's Broad River, over one hundred miles southwest of Wachovia, to buy pottery.[30]

This is precisely the pattern one would expect to find as the population grew and the economy developed in western Carolina. Both Hillsboro, seventy miles east of Bethabara, and Salisbury, forty miles southwest of the Moravian community, were growing just as rapidly as it was. Shops, stores, and taverns opened in both during the second half of the 1750s. Moreover, individual mills, taverns, and stores began to dot the countryside between these larger villages. John and Alexander Lowrance, for example, opened a tavern/store just south of the Forks of the Yadkin in 1757. As these new operations appeared they must have attracted some of the Moravians' more distant customers; people who had previously gone to Bethabara's store or mill probably began visiting closer ones as they opened, which

5. The mill, not quite a mile outside Bethabara, was another place at which Brethren and outsiders met. The mill not only ground corn and wheat for both groups but served an important role disseminating information between them: announcements were often posted here, and during the French and Indian War dozens of refugee families lived here for months at a time under Moravian care. (Used with permission of the Archives of the Moravian Church in America—Northern Province)

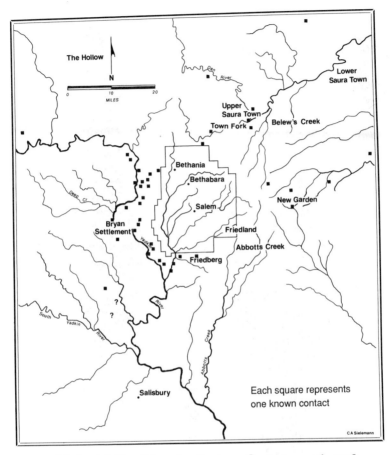

Map 4. Wachovia's Non-Moravian Business Contacts, 1756–1758

led to a contraction in some aspects of Bethabara's hinterland. This process did not, however, affect all the craftsmen in Bethabara. Those like the potter, who had no competition among newcomers, continued to draw customers from afar. In fact the improving roads and communication that came with rising population meant that people at even greater distances than before might hear of them and visit them. Furthermore, improvements in transportation made it easier for backcountry settlements like Bethabara to trade with coastal communities like Wilmington. The effect of all this was just the sort of trading pattern found around Bethabara during the Oeconomy's second phase.[31]

As trade between the Moravians and their neighbors continued to grow during these years, so did credit relations between them. Brethren and strangers alike were still short of cash at times, and although Unity officials disliked either borrowing from or lending to outsiders they still had no choice but to do both. Thus, by the end of 1758, the Brethren owed £45, North Carolina,* to a total of eighteen non-Moravians and were owed in turn just over £90, North Carolina, from fifty-five individual non-Moravians, a trading company in Wilmington, and the government of North Carolina.[32]

Although some of the dealings described above did take place in coastal towns like Wilmington, at the end of the *Oeconomy*'s second phase Bethabara had still not entered the Atlantic economy. The Brethren had known all along, however, that it would have to eventually. "If a province does not have what it needs and does not produce decent and profitable things for export," wrote August Spangenberg in 1758, "then nothing can arise [there], and up until now that has been the case with North Carolina." And soon after he wrote that, early in 1759, Unity officials decided it was time Wachovia's *Oeconomy* entered its third phase and began participating fully in world trade.[33]

In making this transition the settlers in Wachovia had to do three things at once: find something they could export profitably, improve their ability to collect the products of Bethabara's hinterland, and establish better links with coastal markets by which to move goods in and out of their colony. "If this proposal can be accomplished," Spangenberg told Cornelius van Laer "then the Brethren can send objects of the province in return [for manufactured goods] to Pensilvania, New York, etc. or a sloop might bring goods to Carolina and take flour, beef, pork,

---

*Sometime in late 1758 the Brethren began keeping their records in North Carolina currency rather than Virginia. By Moravian accounts, Virginia money was worth slightly more than North Carolina, and the latter converted at a rate of 93 percent: i.e., £1, North Carolina, became 18 ½ shillings, Virginia.

tar, etc. to the West Indies, there it could discharge the goods and would bring rum, sugar, molasses, salt, cocoa, and the like back to New York, Pensilvania, etc."[34] And all three steps bound them ever more securely to the non-Moravian economy around them. The first problem was to find an export, or exports, on which to base this trade. The Brethren had been thinking about this since before they came to Bethabara, and like many of those who preceded them to Carolina had thought first about a trio of semitropical products: wine, silk, and olives. Wine production came first because the Brethren found grapes growing wild in Wachovia when they arrived. During the summer and fall of 1756 Bethabara's residents gathered wild grapes, and by Christmas they had made and sent to Bethlehem a bottle of wine that Spangenberg declared "had a good color, good bouquet, good taste, and pronounced essence." Serious viniculture did not begin, however, until mid-1757. At that time the Brethren chose a spot on the southern face of a hill overlooking Bethabara, cleared land for a vineyard, and began to plant. Spangenberg had suggested they stick with indigenous varieties rather than "Br. Cossart's French vines" because the former were already accustomed to the climate. Instead they planted "200 domestic and 200 wild vines," but nothing came of them. In the years that followed, Bethabara's vineyard disappeared from the colony's records. The colonists did report making wine from currants and wild grapes for their own use, but they said nothing about their vineyard, and wine never became "the great commodity for export" that church officials had hoped it would be.[35]

Silk and olives proved equally grand failures. Unity elders were especially anxious to produce "the silk about which the English nation is so concerned" and through Henry Cossart acquired both white mulberry seeds and "silkworm seeds" from southern France. From Nimes, via Paris and Westminster, the seeds travelled to Bethlehem, where those for the trees at least were planted sometime between 1754 and 1756. In 1757 a dozen saplings made the final journey to Bethabara, and the following spring Jacob Lösch reported they were "breaking into leaf nicely." Lösch also wrote that "Br. Bachoff already has about 200 young silk worms," but that is far as silkmaking went. Records after 1758 report no further progress and offer no explanation for their silence. Olives never even made it that far. Henry Cossart apparently provided these seeds too, and in the fall of 1759 Bethabara's gardener, Jacob Lung, planted them. According to one report, the seeds failed to germinate because Lung ignored Cossart's instructions concerning when to plant and planted them in the wrong location. Whatever the reasons, though, the attempt failed, and efforts to raise olives in Wachovia came to nothing.[36]

The Brethren could not trust entirely in experiments that might or might not yield practical exports. Their superiors wanted results and wanted them soon; so while waiting on the outcome of their trials with wine, silk, and olives, residents of Bethabara had also been looking for sources of less exotic but more immediate returns. Initially, the greatest promise seemed to lie with flour and breadstuffs. The Brethren had already shipped flour to the lower Cape Fear valley at least twice in 1757, taking it to pay storage and handling fees on a load of iron sent from Bethlehem through Wilmington. That had been an ad hoc arrangement, though. Now they meant to make a real go of it. The *Oeconomy*'s mill was fully operational, its farmers were producing larger and larger crops of wheat, and grain growers in the neighborhood were beating a path to its door with their wagons. All that remained was to install a more efficient bolter at the mill so it could produce what the Brethren described as "merchantable flour." Such a bolter, described as an "English bolter," had arrived in Bethabara in 1757 and gone into storage, evidently because it was unnecessary in the local trade. In August of 1759, though, the Helpers Conference decided to begin sending a wagon to the coast approximately once a month for trade and correspondence, and six weeks later it ordered the English bolter installed. By October the job was finished, and in November the inaugural shipment of zweiback and ship's bread left for the Cape Fear.[37]

Over the next fifteen months the Brethren sent three more loads of wheat, flour, and flour products to the coast, but the trade east never amounted to much. There were very few shipments, just six from 1761 to the close of the *Oeconomy*. Further-more, they represented only a fraction of the Moravians' trade with strangers. During the twelve months beginning June 1, 1762, for example, the *Oeconomy* shipped just twenty-one bush-els of wheat to the Cape Fear while grinding and selling four hundred fifty bushels to outsiders in Bethabara. Wachovia was just too far west to compete profitably with wheat and flour producers closer to the coast, and the fact that this trade contin-ued at all after 1760 was due to special circumstances described below.[38]

Perhaps the most conspicuous failure as an export commod-ity, however, was cattle. Historians have long maintained that America's first cattle barons and cowboys lived on the Carolina frontier, but neither title fits the Brethren. They did raise cattle in Wachovia, buying their first animals just a month after arriv-ing and building a herd that eventually topped two hundred head. Given the size of the community, however, this was not an especially large herd. It was fewer than three head per per-son—about twice the number found on farms in southeastern Pennsylvania at the time but only half that found in Texas a century later. More to the point, the Moravians never organized any of the overland drives by which cattle reportedly made their way from the southern backcountry to markets as far north as Philadelphia. They did consider sending animals to Pennsylva-nia, and under pressure to find an export the Helpers Confer-ence did decide in 1759 to send thirty head to Bethlehem. The danger of Indian attack led them to cancel the drive, however, and they tried again, apparently because of uncertainty about the prices they could expect in northern markets. It was prob-ably just as well because the Brethren had never shown any particular aptitude as drovers. In 1754 Jacob Friis described for Gottlob Königsdorfer his experience as "your first Cowherd in Carolina." "I had two Brr. to help me," wrote Friis; "it went badly, first one Cow ran away, and when we would bring her back 3 or 4 ran away, at last they all became rebellious and ran home to their calves, at last I stood alone and was obliged to go home after them."[39]

After these numerous failures, the Brethren finally did discover a profitable export. It was the deerskin that neighbors brought to pay for goods purchased in Bethabara. The Moravians had known since their arrival that deerskin was one of the few products of the backcountry for which there was a demand in Europe. As one wrote later, "Merchants love skins better than gold." They also learned, however, that few of the Brethren had the skill necessary to hunt deer profitably. Elders in Bethlehem, therefore, directed the colonists not to waste their time trying. They did encourage Bethabara to accept skins in trade, though, and before 1759 this policy brought a modest flow of hides into town. The Brethren took pelts when they were offered and sent them north to Bethlehem, but they seldom went out of their way to look for them.[40]

Sometime between 1759 and 1761, however, all that changed. It was becoming clear by then that Moravian efforts to raise an export were not going to meet Unity expectations, and this may have prompted church leaders to put more emphasis on collecting skins from Wachovia's neighbors. When residents of Wachovia first made contact with the upcountry agents of Charles Town merchants in 1759, information provided by the agents about trade with that city, the premier American market for deerskin, may have inspired the Brethren to deepen their involvement. Whatever the reason, though, by 1761 Bethabara's *Oeconomy* was aggressively pursuing skins for export, and during the next decade the Brethren collected thousands of hides from outsiders trading in their village. They accepted quantities as small as a single skin or as large as a thousand, took them dressed or in the hair, and twice a year, usually, loaded the skins into wagons and took them to market.[41]

Lacunae in the colony's records make it impossible to calculate either the exact volume or value of the traffic, but one can establish its lower limits. During the decade 1761–71 the Moravians reported exporting 45,600 pounds of deerskin. They also sent to market three shipments of unknown size, which if they equalled the median of recorded loads brought Bethabara's total to 54,600 pounds. Based on the latter figure, the *Oeconomy*'s mean annual export of deerskin during the years 1761–71 was 4,964 pounds. That represents just over 6 percent of the annual mean total of skins shipped from Charles Town, the Moravians' chief market, during the period 1765–69 and over 9 percent of the mean between 1770 and 1775. Wachovia might not have cornered the market in deerskin, but it did control a significant portion of the trade. As for the monetary value of the trade, based on the median prices paid for dressed and undressed skins the estimated total of 54,600 pounds was worth between £6,370 and £9,555, North Carolina, and the mean annual total of 4,964 pounds was worth between £579 and £869. This is, admittedly, a wide range of possibilities, but even the lower figures make deerskin the colony's most valuable export by a wide margin. After several years of looking and several failed experiments, Wachovia's Moravian settlers had finally found something to sell the world.[42]

Closely linked to Bethabara's search for a profitable export was its campaign to improve the collection and distribution of goods in its hinterland, especially through the establishment of a public store. Of course the Brethren had taken local products in trade almost since the day they arrived in North Carolina. In the beginning, however, the process had been relatively disorganized. Outsiders brought what they had to offer to the particular craftsman whose services they needed. If they wanted store goods they went to the *Oeconomy's Vorsteher*, who provided what he could either from "a large chest" built in 1755 to hold "things we have to sell" or directly from *Oeconomy* reserves stored in a loft above the bakery. These arrangements worked well enough, but when Spangenberg directed the colonists to enter international trade he wanted them to do so according to "good principles of commerce." And to him that meant centralizing the process. Thus, when he visited Bethabara in 1759–60, he effected several changes in the *Oeconomy* designed to improve its performance as an entrepot, and chief among them was the decision to establish a public store and to charge its keeper with "[all] matters of purchase and sale" from outsiders.[43]

Located near the single brothers' house, Bethabara's store was never much to look at. It began as "a poorly built, one story log-house . . . [with] no regular ceiling, but loose boards . . .

laid across the rafters, so that boxes can be stored there" and over the next ten years gained two equally nondescript additions and a storage shed.[44] It stood, however, at the center of Wachovia's economy from 1759 until 1772. Because the storekeeper alone was authorized to buy for the *Oeconomy,* many of the people coming to trade in Bethabara had to visit the store first in order to sell the products with which they planned to pay for their purchases. What went on there was supposed to be quick and easy. Spangenberg gave the first storekeeper, Johannes Schaub, specific instructions that "bidding and counter bidding, raising and reducing prices, and such common and worldly practices are not to exist among us. One examines the item which one intends to purchase, to determine that it is good quality. One asks the people who offer anything for sale: 'What do you want for it?' Should one be unable to give them this and make a single counter offer, one stands firm, preferring to let them go away if they are not satisfied." If a sale was arranged customers could take payment in cash or *Zettel,* tickets that passed as currency between the store and various branches of the *Oeconomy,*[45] and proceed to particular craftsmen in order to buy what they wanted. They could also take payment in store goods, however, and because the storekeeper tried to keep on hand a supply of the products available elsewhere in town, and had a monopoly on the sale of imported goods, many customers went no farther. With its combination of purchasing power and inventory, Bethabara's store soon became the major economic link between Moravians and strangers, not only providing a more efficient purchasing and marketing system but also helping to channel outsiders away from the membership-at-large.

The discovery of an export and the establishment of a store in which to collect it did not, however, complete Wachovia's entry into the Atlantic economy. The Brethren still had to find a market through which to sell the former and stock the latter. They had been looking for such a market off and on since 1754, though with no great luck. They had tried Wilmington first. They wanted to make it easier to ship supplies and personnel from Pennsylvania to Wachovia, and Wilmington was the closest port to Bethabara. Through inquiries made in Philadelphia and Wilmington, the Brethren discovered the Maultsby family, Quaker traders with branches in both cities, and sent at least two trial shipments through them between 1754 and 1756. The results were disappointing, though; the trip via Wilmington proved slower and just as expensive as the overland route. Moreover, the Brethren found Wilmington a disappointing market in which to buy imported goods. All they said at first was "everything [was] bad" there, though in later years they explained that prices were too high and the selection of goods was too small.[46]

Next they tried a store at Pine Tree, South Carolina, some one hundred fifty miles south of Bethabara on the Wateree River. There had been a store there since before the Brethren came to Wachovia, but in 1758 a Charles Town company sent Joseph Kershaw to Pine Tree to open an upcountry branch of their firm. The Moravians had learned of this "bigger newer store" by November of that year and initially considered it "the best opportunity for us in trade." So early the next year they sent *Vorsteher* Jacob Lösch "to see for himself whether things there are as we have heard." Lösch found they were not, and Bethabara's elders reluctantly concluded, "trade thither is not for us."[47]

Thus when the Unity pushed Bethabara into the Atlantic economy, the Brethren there were only familiar with three markets through which to make their entry: Pennsylvania, Pine Tree, and Cape Fear. Pennsylvania was a long way off, and Wachovia did not yet produce anything it could exchange there for the goods it wanted. Its tropical industries were failing; Pennsylvania was awash in its own bread and flour; cattle had been considered and rejected; and for reasons that remain a mystery, no one in Pennsylvania expressed much interest in the deerskins that were starting to trickle into Bethabara. Pine Tree, too, was rejected and that left just Cape Fear; so in the fall of 1759 the Brethren began what were supposed to be regular wagon trips to the market there. They took wheat and wheat products, all they really had to offer at the time, to Wilmington and Springhill, a landing on the Cape Fear River near Cross Creek, and traded them for store goods. The Helpers Conference described this trade as "successful" but clearly believed there was room for improvement. They continued, therefore, to look for something better, especially after they began to concentrate on deerskin as an export in the early 1760s. And in 1761 two new possibilities appeared: Petersburg (also called Powlins Point), Virginia, and Charles Town, South Carolina.[48] Extant records provide no clue as to how or when the Brethren learned of Petersburg. The idea of trading with Charles Town almost certainly reached Bethabara with Henry Laurens in January 1761. Laurens was a colonel in the South Carolina militia and according to *The South Carolina Gazette* came to North Carolina during the French and Indian War in search of recruits for Arthur Middleton's regiment. Laurens was also, in the words of Jacob Lösch, "a rich merchant" in Charles Town, and he used this tour of the backcountry to sign up business as well as soldiers. In Bethabara he talked to the elders about what Wachovia's *Oeconomy* could buy and sell in Charles Town and extended to them both his services as a friend and a £200 line of credit. Promises were not enough to win the Moravians' trade, though; the Brethren wanted to see for themselves what each of the new contenders had to offer. Early in 1761 they sent trial shipments to both Charles Town and Petersburg, and as reports from the two came back, officials in Bethabara compared them to one another and to the Cape Fear markets with which they had been trading since 1759.[49]

Results of the competition were mixed. Charles Town merchants had a wider selection of goods to sell, sold them at lower prices, and paid more for the Moravians' deerskins; but the South Carolina market was also farther from Wachovia than either Petersburg or Cape Fear was, which meant higher shipping costs. Petersburg was almost as distant as Charles Town and promised neither prices nor inventories to match it; but Virginia merchants were less particular about the hides they bought and would take deerskins "in the hair and not fit for the Charles Town market." As for Cape Fear, nothing distinguished it except proximity. Wilmington was the closest port to Wachovia, and Springhill was as close as one could transport goods by water; but their merchants paid lower prices for what they bought, charged more for what they sold, and had less to offer than their rivals to the north and south. After weighing them all, the Brethren decided to split their trade between Charles Town and Petersburg, prime deerskins to the former and inferior skins to the latter. Within a year, though, they abandoned the Virginia market completely because prices there were "entirely too poor," and in the fall of 1762 John Ettwein informed his superiors in Bethlehem, "now Charles Town is certainly our marketplace."[50]

And Charles Town remained their chief market through the close of the *Oeconomy.* Twice a year—sometimes more, sometimes less—Moravian wagons left for South Carolina carrying thousands of deerskins, an occasional beaver pelt, and modest quantities of tallow, butter, pottery, and medicinal herbs. Sometimes the carters went only as far as Pine Tree, but usually their destination was Charles Town and the firm of Joseph Nicholson and William Bampfield, the latter of whom *Oeconomy* officials described as "our merchant." This relationship was probably initiated for personal reasons; Henry Laurens was married to Bampfield's cousin and probably steered the Brethren in that direction. Its continuation, however, was pure business; in October of 1766 the Helpers Conference directed Matthew Micksch and Jacob Steiner to enter Charles Town several days ahead of the wagons they were leading to market and to visit merchants other than Bampfield in order to check the prices they were paying for skins and charging for goods. A word from Henry Laurens may have brought the Brethren to Bampfield and Nicholson the first time, but economics brought them back. Returning to Bethabara, Moravian wagons carried glass, pewter, tinware, blankets, clothing, medical supplies, coffee, tea, rice, sugar, wine, rum, pottery glaze, gunpowder, locks for guns, and at least one indentured servant.[51]

Charles Town was not, however, the Moravians' only market after 1762. On at least one occasion they went to Cross Creek for store goods because, as Frederic Marschall reported, "one cannot travel to Charlestown at this season [August] because of the shortage of fodder and fresh water." Moreover, they continued a specialized trade with the Cape Fear through the close of the *Oeconomy*—wheat and flour for salt and shells. The brothers and sisters in Wachovia needed salt to preserve and flavor their food and oyster shells to provide lime for construction and tanning leather. As vital as these items were, however, neither had a very high ratio of value to weight; each sold for a few pence a pound in colonial North Carolina. Because of that, the Moravians chose to buy them from the closer Cape Fear markets, even though prices there were slightly higher, rather than have transported all the way from Charles Town. To pay for them the *Oeconomy* usually sent flour and wheat, which had equally low ratios of value to weight, and sometimes butter, which sold for nine to ten pence per pound, rather than squander deerskin, which at more than two shillings per pound was worth taking to more distant markets in South Carolina. Throughout the 1760s and early 1770s, Wachovia's settlers maintained this traffic in bulky goods between their colony and the Cape Fear towns of Cross Creek, Wilmington, and Brunswick. North Carolina officials tried repeatedly in the 1760s to attract more Moravian business to Cape Fear, but merchants there could not compete with those in Charles Town and the latter remained Wachovia's chief link with the Atlantic economy.[52]

With the discovery of an export, a means of collecting it, and a market in which to sell it, Wachovia's *Oeconomy* had assumed its final form. Through the close of the *Oeconomy,* and for years thereafter, Wachovia's *gemein Ort* existed in comfortable and profitable symbiosis with its hinterland, and economic ties between Moravians and non-Moravians in the system were both wide and strong.

At the center of this economy was Bethabara, its marketing and manufacturing center. During the *Oeconomy's* third phase most of Bethabara's adult male population was occupied in nonfarm activities. A few were administrators or clerics; others worked in construction, especially that of Salem; but most were involved in manufacturing, processing, or retailing. The latter three activities employed more than 60 percent of Bethabara's adult male residents and produced goods and services worth twice as much as those from its farming sector.[53] Manufacturers included tailors, shoemakers, blacksmiths, tinsmiths, gunsmiths, gunstockers, cabinetmakers, weavers, saddlemakers, and potters, all of whom made products for use inside the *Oeconomy* and for sale outside of it. The potter, for example, supplied the communal kitchens, dining rooms, and living rooms of Bethabara with crocks, bowls, pitchers, pipes, tile stoves, and other items while selling enough to those outside the *Oeconomy* to earn a median annual profit of £116, North Carolina, during the decade ending June 1, 1771.[54] Among processors were millers, brewers, distillers, tanners, and at least one of the storekeepers—men who took the bounty of woods and fields and turned it into more finished, more valuable products for internal consumption or external sale. When William Dixon ran the store, for example, he took deerskin in the hair worth about 2 shillings per pound and by dressing them increased their value to approximately 3.5 shillings per pound.[55] Retailing was still divided among a number of individuals. Most sales were through the store or tavern, but some of the Brethren involved in manufacturing or processing, like the potter or miller, also sold directly to consumers.

There were still some farmers in Bethabara during the *Oeconomy's* final phase, but their output and importance declined steadily. Early in the 1760s, when Indian warfare drove other farmers from their fields and militia quartermasters came searching for food, farming was big business in Bethabara. The Brethren grew all the wheat they could during the war years, ground the wheat into flour, and sold the flour either to troops passing through Bethabara or to middlemen who carried it west and resold it to troops fighting the Cherokee Indians. In the three years 1761–63 the *Oeconomy's* median annual wheat harvest was 1,140 bushels and never fell below one thousand; and in 1761 alone it sold over twenty-five tons of flour to the militia and earned some £250, Virginia. Once the Cherokee campaign ended, however, the Brethren in Bethabara went back to doing what they did best and reduced their farming drastically. Between 1764 and 1769 the *Oeconomy's* median wheat harvest was just 548 bushels per year, less than half the wartime high and below, even, the level of a decade earlier. Members of the *Oeconomy* also continued to raise horses, cattle, sheep, and pigs throughout its third phase plus a large vegetable garden and

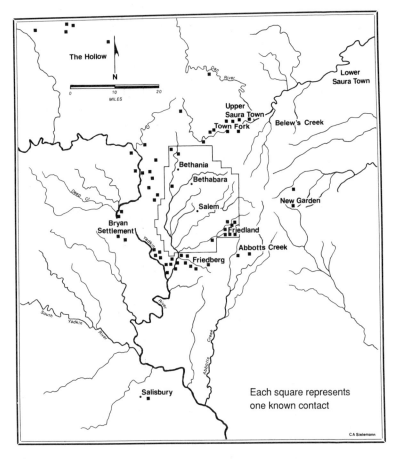

Map 5. Wachovia's Non-Moravian Business Contacts, 1759–1771

orchards containing nearly two thousand fruit trees. But none of these activities grew at anything like the rates of either population or nonfarm profits after 1763.[56]

Paired with Bethabara's manufacturing and marketing complex was an agrarian hinterland that continued to grow smaller and denser during the *Oeconomy's* final phase (Map 5). The population of this hinterland also underwent a fundamental change during this period as church members entered it for the first time. Starting with the establishment of Bethania, in 1759, a small number of Moravian families moved out of the *Oeconomy* and with the church's blessing began to live and work on their own. Most of these families lived in Bethania, though beginning in 1768 a few settled on farms near Bethabara or Salem. All remained members of the church and subject to its supervision and discipline, but they worked for themselves. Some of those in Bethania were part-time craftsmen. All, however, were farmers first, raising food for their families and selling their surpluses in Bethabara. There were also non-Moravian farmers inside the bounds of Wachovia for the first time during these last years of the *Oeconomy.* Some were friends of the church who bought or leased land from the Unity or from the Land und Colonie Etablissement. Others were Palatine Germans given permission in 1769 to settle Wachovia's southeastern corner. There they established the village of Friedland and became a diaspora society (a group of Christians affiliated with the Unity but not a part of it). The largest element of Bethabara's hinterland, though, was still the band of farms just outside Wachovia's borders, especially to the north, west, and south. During the *Oeconomy*'s third stage, links between this region and Bethabara remained strong, while those between the Moravian town and slightly more distant neighborhoods, like New Garden, continued to fade in the light of competing centers such as Hillsboro and Salisbury.

Of course beyond this immediate hinterland the Brethren increased significantly their long-distance business connections during the *Oeconomy*'s last decade. Trade flowed back and forth from Bethabara to Charles Town and Pine Tree, in South Carolina; to Cross Creek, Wilmington, and Brunswick, in North Carolina; and to Petersburg and the New River valley, in Virginia. These links, however, were to discrete places and people, like spokes radiating from the hub of a wheel, rather than a general expansion of the Moravians' hinterland.

During this final phase, as in the two before it, Wachovia's Moravian community relied on outsiders for a variety of useful and essential products. Food was the most essential of these.

During the war years of the early 1760s the Moravians' dependence on non-Moravian food was relatively limited. The *Oeconomy's* farm produced more than enough wheat to meet its needs; mill tolls added to the surplus; and the Brethren depended on strangers only for corn, which was cheaper than wheat and generally used in Wachovia for fodder or distilling. When the *Oeconomy* cut back on wheat production at the close of the Cherokee campaign, though, they cut way back. Between 1762 and 1764 Bethabara's population rose 18 percent, but its wheat harvest fell by 62 percent. The result was a shortfall in 1764 of approximately four hundred bushels, a deficit barely filled with grain the miller took in tolls. In later years the situation was even worse. Harvests remained small and there is no indication that tolls collected at the mill increased significantly (in fact they probably declined as the mill deteriorated physically); population rose, though, and wheat consumption with it, forcing the *Oeconomy* to buy hundreds of bushels of wheat each year simply to feed its members. And that was in addition to the large quantities of corn it bought to feed its livestock and the barley and rye it bought to make into beer and brandy. Some of this came from Moravian residents of Bethania, but most came from non-Moravians living around Wachovia.[57]

The Brethren depended on strangers for more than food, though. Nearly every manufacturer, processor, or retailer in Bethabara and Salem relied to some extent on non-Moravian goods. Some of them could have functioned without those supplies—the potter, for example, could have done without the red lead he imported from Charles Town—but most could not. The store, by now Bethabara's largest moneymaker, was especially dependent. Both the deerskin it used to pay for its inventory and most of that inventory itself came from non-Moravian suppliers. Residents of Wachovia might occasionally kill a deer and bring its hide to the storekeeper, but it was a rare event. Virtually all the skins exported from Bethabara came from non-Moravian hunters who sold them to the storekeeper there. The *Oeconomy's* books show that fact month after month in dreary columns of figures. It was demonstrated most vividly, however, in the fall of 1771. Six months earlier William Tryon had broken the Regulator Movement at Alamance Creek, and in November one of Bethabara's leaders noted that the Moravians' wagon had gone to market "bare of skins the Country having no arms." Without non-Moravian hunters the *Oeconomy* had little to sell. But even empty the wagon had to go to market, because without the goods it brought back from Charles Town many of the shelves in Bethabara's store would be empty and the *Oeconomy* would lose a major source of income.[58]

The store, however, was simply the most dramatic example of the mature *Oeconomy*'s dependence on non-Moravian suppliers. Without external sources Moravian blacksmiths and gunsmiths would have faced long delays and great expense transporting iron and locks from Bethlehem; brewers, distillers, bakers, and tanners would have had far less material with which to work; tavernkeepers would have had nothing to sell; and the construction of Salem would have taken considerably longer due to difficulties acquiring lime and sawn timber. The Brethren could have lived without the things outsiders supplied, but their community would been smaller and poorer for it.[59]

The brothers and sisters in Wachovia also continued to obtain labor in the market around them. They had hired day laborers since 1755, but the practice became more widespread during the *Oeconomy*'s final decade. By late 1762 the number of outsiders working in Bethabara had reached fifteen, a figure equal to 24 percent of the village's adult population, and almost certainly rose even higher when work began on Salem in 1766, though surviving records provide no exact count after 1762 by which to confirm this. Until 1766 at least, when work started on Salem, most of the hired laborers worked in the fields around Bethabara, especially at harvest time. Others watched the *Oeconomy*'s cattle, worked in its tavern and brewery, built an addition to its store, repaired roads, and hauled goods to Charles Town and back. And the *Oeconomy* came to rely heavily on outsiders. In March of 1764, for example, Gottlieb Reuter had complained from Bethabara, "one does not have nearly enough [people] for building and almost all of it must be done by hired laborers." Similarly, when rumors of a smallpox epidemic during the summer of 1759 kept most non-Moravians away from Bethabara members of the Moravian community were hard pressed to bring the harvest in. Brothers and sisters alike helped in the fields; the Helpers Conference went nearly two months without meeting because of the work; and one writer explained, "we would have thus been in great need regarding our harvest if our people had not . . . resolved to test whether they might not be in a position to bear the harvest alone."[60]

Furthermore, it was during the *Oeconomy*'s final decade that the Moravians in Wachovia first employed bound labor, which they also obtained in the market around them. They began hiring slaves from their neighbors in the summer of 1763, and when they eventually began to buy slaves they bought from outsiders too: Sam came from William Ridge of Rowan County; Sue and her daughter Sukey from Peter Copland of Pittsylvania County, Virginia; Sambo from one Edmund Lyne; and Franc from William Gilbert of Rowan County. They also bought a single indentured servant, Robert Denck, from Henry Laurens.[61]

In exchange for what it bought the *Oeconomy* sold its neighbors an even greater variety of goods and services after 1759 than it had before. In addition to the brandy, shoes, leather, pottery, iron ware, medicine, and other items the Brethren themselves produced for sale, the *Oeconomy* also resold much of what it bought in Charles Town: coffee, tea, sugar, gunpowder, tinware, glass, blankets, clothing, and more. Unfortunately, changes in Moravian bookkeeping and the presence of Moravians outside the *Oeconomy* make it almost impossible to measure the volume of cross-boundary trade during these years. As one would expect, though, it was clearly greater than it had been in either of the *Oeconomy*'s first two stages. Before 1759 the highpoint of trade between Brethren and strangers had been approximately £1150, Virginia, in 1758. Every year between 1761 and 1771, however, the buying and reselling of deerskin alone was worth that much.[62]

These final years of the *Oeconomy* also saw the Brethren enter into landlord-tenant relationships with their neighbors. They started small; beginning in 1759 the *Oeconomy* negotiated a number of deals with its neighbors permitting the latter to hunt or keep cattle on Unity land for a modest fee. The following year there were sharecropping agreements between the *Oeconomy* and some of the wartime refugees in Bethabara, and by 1762 the church had begun renting land to non-Moravians. Leaders of the Unity hoped to attract a large number of renters to Wachovia; "otherwise," wrote Frederic Marschall, "there is the chance that this great Tract will not be settled, by Brethren, in fifty years," and if that happened the Unity would earn little on its investment. Tenants were offered 21-year leases with no rent for the first three years, but there were few takers. Between 1762 and 1772 fewer than a dozen outsiders rented Moravian land. The church had slightly better luck selling land to nonmembers, but only slightly . During the *Oeconomy*'s last years it sold land to some two dozen non-Moravians. Leasing and selling land to outsiders, then, was a smaller part of the *Oeconomy* than Wachovia's planners had hoped it would be, but it was another economic bond between Moravians and non-Moravians in North Carolina.[63]

And of course Brethren and strangers remained linked to one another by ties of credit during the *Oeconomy*'s third phase. When Bethabara's store opened in 1759, Spangenberg warned the Brethren, "we can do no business on a credit basis, for it cannot be collected. Even were we not cheated (but we are cheated) we cannot extent ourselves so." Once again, however, tradesmen and leaders of the Moravian colony found that the only alternative to doing business on credit was doing no business at all; so during the 1760s both debts due the Brethren and concern about those debts mounted steadily. By the middle of 1763 customers owed the store £319.16.6., North Carolina, the tavern £224.14.3., and other *Oeconomy* enterprises a further £350—a total of almost £900. Three years later accounts receivable showed a total of £1,600, North Carolina, due from "about 600" outsiders. At this point things were starting to get out of hand, and the following year, 1767, the Helpers Conference announced, "we must arrive at a generally modest course in our

commerce and offer no more credit to people from whom we
have no security they will pay." It proved a hollow threat,
though. When the Helpers made it debts due the store totaled
£1,321; a year later, in 1768, the storekeeper wrote off entirely
£620 in "doubtful debts," but within three years debtors again
owed the store £1,127.[64]

Most of the Moravians' debt to outsiders during these years
was to merchants from whom they purchased store goods. In
1762–63, for example, records show a payment to Bampfield
and Nicholson of nearly £300, North Carolina, an obligation the
store had incurred while building up its inventory in 1761.
Church leaders made very clear their opposition to borrowing
from outsiders. They tolerated it, however, because they still
had little choice. By 1760 the *Oeconomy* was far richer than it had
been in the preceding decade, but there were still times when it
had to borrow from strangers or go without materials essential
to the Moravian colony's growth.[65]

Long before its close, Wachovia's *Oeconomy* had become an
integral part of the regional, provincial, and Atlantic economies
around it. By 1772 the Moravian community stood at the center
of a largely non-Moravian economy stretching from the mountains of Virginia to the streets of Charles Town. There is no
question that involvement in this economy caused occasional
problems for the Brethren. Unchurched day laborers sometimes
brought into Bethabara ideas that its leaders found inappropriate, and the Unity lost hundreds of pounds in unpaid debts.
But those problems were clearly outweighed by the benefits of
Moravian participation in the non-Moravian economy. Wachovia's neighbors helped keep the Brethren alive during their
first years in the colony, and as time passed outsiders helped
the Brethren maintain a standard of living unsurpassed on the
Carolina frontier. The *Oeconomy* returned the favor, though.
Over nineteen years of operation it almost certainly paid into
the local economy as much as it took out. While the Brethren
earned hundreds of pounds each year trading with their neighbors, they plowed every penny of it, and more, back into the
construction of Bethabara, Bethania, and Salem. Salem alone
cost more than £4,000 between 1766 and 1772,[66] and much of

that went to non-Moravian workers and suppliers. The economic ties between Brethren and strangers in North Carolina clearly benefitted both. Few, perhaps, in either group thought they were rich enough in 1772, but what progress they had made since 1753 they had made together.

CHAPTER 6

Law and Politics Moravian Style

Like the faithful of many religions, the Moravians in Wachovia lived under two kings. Their allegiance lay with the King of Kings, but as long as they lived in North Carolina they were also subjects of the British king. As a result, the legal and political ties binding them to the larger community around Wachovia were almost as extensive as the economic ones. Unlike the latter, however, the former were not something the Unity particularly wanted. Many of its leaders considered English legal and political practices unseemly and would have gladly separated themselves from the laws and government of North Carolina if they could have done it without endangering the religious and economic goals that led them to settle there in the first place. They could not, however, and they knew it. Moreover, they also knew they would have to do more than simply obey the laws and pay their taxes. As one church conference explained in 1767, "if we take no part in the election of Assembly-men, Sheriffs, etc., we and our descendants may suffer from the injustice of our neighbors, who can make laws that we must obey. It is more risky to be the subject of a republican state than of a despotic government, as has been made evident in New England."[1]

That conviction forced the Brethren to participate actively in the institutions that made and interpreted the laws of North Carolina and in those that administered the parish, county, and colony in which they lived. As they did in their business dealings, the Moravians tried to channel these legal and political contacts through a limited number of specialists in order to insulate most of the brothers and sisters from potential danger.

But as a community, the Brethren living in Wachovia forged a growing array of links between themselves and the outside world between 1753 and 1772.

The first step was to learn the laws of their new home, which in itself was quite an accomplishment. Most of the Brethren had been born outside the British Empire, and an unknown but certainly large number of them neither read nor spoke the English language.[2] By birth and upbringing most of the brothers and sisters living in Wachovia were Germans, and many of them knew no other language. Moreover, they had grown up in cities and states regulated by German law and legal traditions, which as Laura Becker's work on Reading, Pennsylvania, has emphasized, were strikingly different from English laws and practices during the eighteenth century.[3] No less confusing, though, were variations within the British Empire. Even August Spangenberg, who had spent most of the past twenty years in England and its colonies, confessed that when he first reached North Carolina he found numerous statutes with which he was unfamiliar. They were "not unreasonable [laws]," he wrote, "but if they are not known they might easily be broken."[4]

To reduce the chance of their people breaking laws through ignorance Moravian officials began studying the statutes of North Carolina before they sent a single colonist to the province. When Spangenberg crossed the colony in search of land he was also under instructions to investigate "the Customs, Laws, By Laws and Constitution of North Carolina." While in Edenton he had a chance to study the colony's code, and before leaving town ordered a copy for the Brethren. The book did not reach Bethlehem before the first settlers left for Wachovia, but the men hardly missed it. Within six weeks of reaching Carolina they had appointed Jacob Lösch "[to] acquaint himself with the laws [of the province] and see that we keep them," and within nine months Lösch had managed to borrow a copy of the colony's laws to study. In subsequent years he and others added to Wachovia's legal library. In 1756 they arranged with James Davis, North Carolina's public printer, to send them "the other laws issued since the publication of the lawbook in bound form and to continue doing so whenever laws are adopted from time to time," and somewhere they picked up copies of Wood's *Institutes*, Shaw's *Practikels Justice of the Peace*, and an *Institutes of the Laws of England*.⁵

Fueling this drive for legal literacy were three very practical concerns. First, a thorough knowledge of Carolina law would help deprive enemies of the Brethren of the club with which to threaten them. Experience in Europe and America during the 1730s and 1740s had shown church members that violations of civil law provided an easy opening through which anyone with a grudge against the Unity could attack it. And North Carolina's rapidly expanding population of relatively poor non-Moravians seemed to Moravian officials a likely source of both religious opposition and economic envy. In church eyes, therefore, openly breaking the law might expose Moravian persons or their property to vengeful neighbors; so obedience to the law was essential. When, for example, the press of work in Bethabara prevented the Brethren there from keeping their own Sabbath, Saturday, they still insisted on honoring the legally established Anglican Sabbath, Sunday, "that the World should have nothing against us." Seven years earlier, in 1746, several brothers living in Bethlehem had almost gone to jail for cutting grain on a Sunday in what one Moravian writer described as an example of harassment by jealous neighbors "under the pretense of zeal for law and religion." That sort of trouble would also be possible in North Carolina, and no amount of legal knowledge could provide absolute security against it, but the Brethren could avoid making easy targets of themselves by learning the laws and trying to obey them whenever possible.⁶

This is not to say that Moravians never broke the law. In fact, the second motive behind their interest in North Carolina law was to help them keep up appearances when they did break it. Eighteenth-century Moravians regarded statute law as a human creation that might or might not reflect God's will. Obedience to it, therefore, might or might not be in His best interest. It was the task of church officials to decide through prayer, discussion, and the Lot exactly what God wanted and to balance His demands against those of the state. It the two could be accommodated, and they usually could, there was no problem. If they could not be the Brethren were in a tricky spot. They had to find some way of breaking the law while appearing to obey it.

During the years of the *Oeconomy* the brothers and sisters in Wachovia faced this dilemma most often in regard to the laws defining freemanship in North Carolina and those establishing the Anglican Church. In the case of each, the Brethren knowingly and repeatedly broke the law in order to protect their community and serve their God. The 1741 "Act for Establishing the Church," for example, required vestrymen to declare "I, A. B. do declare, that I will not oppose the Liturgy of the Church of England, as it is by law established." By 1758 Moravian leaders owned copies of the vestry law, had already impaneled one vestry, and certainly knew what it required. Yet in June of that year they instructed potential vestrymen in Wachovia to substitute for the required declaration the statement: "We do conform to the Liturgy of England & to the Liturgy of the Unitas Fratrum." "At least they shall try this," wrote Spangenberg and a committee of elders from Bethlehem, "and if it goes, well and good." Fortunately for the Brethren it went, as did a number of similar episodes of calculated lawbreaking. The Moravians' knowledge of provincial law showed them the precise laws, or parts of laws, they had to break while helping them maintain the appearance of obedience.[7]

The third factor behind Moravian interest in the law was the assistance it could provide in protecting their rights without having to go to court. The Moravians did everything they could to avoid legal showdowns with their neighbors, even when the law was on their side. This was largely a result of their fear that the combative atmosphere of an Anglo-American court would generate resentment toward them that lingered after the trial was over and did more damage in the long run than whatever injury prompted their suit in the first place. In addition, some members of the Unity objected to swearing oaths, though such opposition was not a formal tenet of the church. Under English law, therefore, they were forbidden to give evidence in a criminal case or serve on any jury, which meant the Unity might have to go to trial without all its witnesses and with fewer chances of having members in the jury box to give it a sympathetic hearing.

This too may have contributed to the Moravians' reluctance to take people to court. If all else failed the Brethren would fall back on legal proceedings. In the summer of 1764, for instance, the Helpers Conference decided that "insolent" strangers were getting out of hand in Bethabara's tavern and declared that "one should proceed against them according to the law one time." But that was a last resort. They preferred to use their legal knowledge as a deterrent, to make sure that whatever they did would stand up in court and to show potential adversaries that the law was on their side.[8]

Nowhere was this approach more evident than in the brothers' response to trespassers on their land. In August 1759 leaders in Bethabara met to discuss the problem of non-Moravians hunting and grazing their cattle on Unity land. Participants first heard a summary of "hunting and private property rights" under the laws of North Carolina. Then statute book in hand they proceeded to formulate a policy for admitting to their land those hunters and herdsmen who had negotiated formal agreements with them and for impounding the cattle or persons of those who had not. And minutes of the meeting show that every step of the way they checked the appropriate laws to support their action. Six months later the Brethren posted a notice announcing their new policy to deal with hunters on their land, and Gottlieb Reuter, Wachovia's Forest and Hunting Inspector, wrote in his diary that "because many people around here ignore the border of our land articles from the provincial law book were extracted [and included on the broadside]."[9]

The idea of deterrence also lay behind the Unity's insistence on written agreements that could be produced in court if necessary. Any outsider seeking permission to hunt or to pasture cattle on Moravian land, even if that person was a "good friend" of the church, had to sign a formal agreement and pay something for the privilege, even if it was only a single bushel of corn, in recognition of the Unity's proprietary rights. Members of the Unity too, once they had left the *Oeconomy* and the control its provisions exerted upon them, had to sign written leases because their leaders recognized that with verbal accords "the brothers and sisters . . . take this or that word and interpret it as they want or understand as it most agreeable to them." This, the elders believed, was a result of "human weakness" rather than any desire to defraud the church; nevertheless they had to be ready to defend the Unity's interests in court against any potential challenge.[10]

If such a challenge did arise, or seemed likely to arise, the Brethren first tried to show potential adversaries that the law was on God's side and that it would be pointless to pursue the issue. Thus when a neighbor named James Davis tried to establish a prior claim to part of Wachovia, the Moravians made it very clear to him that they knew their rights and would not back down. In the fall of 1754 Davis had written Bethlehem to explain that five years earlier he had paid Morgan Bryan £12 for a land entry on Muddy Creek, which Bryan filed in February 1749/50. But, continued Davis, he had been too ill to ride to Muddy Creek and defend his claim when August Spangenberg arrived in search of land for the Unity. "If I was able to be there," wrote Davis, "then my little place would have been left out [of the Moravian grant]." Davis closed his letter in the hope that, as "Jesus Christ's sincere fellows & brethren," the Moravians would permit him to buy back the land he had entered nearly five years before. In return Davis received a polite but blunt response from John Okley, a church official in Bethlehem. "If I am rightly informed," wrote Okley,

all entries made in the Land Office cost only a Guinea Sterl. & if the Land be not patented in one Year from the Date are void of course: so that your entry being made (as you confess) in the Year 1749/50 and our Land survey'd in 1753, consequently your Right became Null.

I think the Gentleman, who took ye £12 to make you a title to that Land (to which he himself had no Right) ought in Justice to make proper Restitution & Amends; which I conceive may be readily done by his & your Application to the Office for a Grant of an equivalent Spot of Land in some other Place.

I am truly sorry for your Misfortune & should be very glad if it was in our Power to comply with your Request; but all our Lands in N. Carolina being convey'd to a Gentleman in England in Trust it is utterly impossible for us to gratify you in this request.[11]

Had Davis pursued the matter further the Brethren might have offered to pay all or part of his £12 just to avoid the potential unpleasantness of a court fight. In a similar case eleven years later they did just that. Davis, however, dropped his, and in this instance a demonstration of Moravian familiarity with the law was enough to protect the Unity's rights without involving it in a trial.[12]

The Brethren, however, wanted more than an understanding of North Carolina law and its uses. Their first decade in Pennsylvania had shown the elders that including a Moravian community in a heterogeneous political jurisdiction often led to problems. Their ultimate aim in Carolina, as a result, was to secure separate parish and county or corporate status for Wachovia. Writing in 1759, Spangenberg told a European colleague, "we can, I hope, bring things to the point through the governor and assembly, and the King's Council that we become a separate county, have our own assemblymen, our own justices, our own court house, etc. And that would be very beneficial to our settlement and very appropriate to the *Jünger's* basic idea. Thus might not Wachovia become one of the flourishing parts of Carolina."[13]

The decision to enter that fully into the legal political systems of North Carolina apparently sprang from two factors. First, Unity leaders recognized that residents of Wachovia would also be residents of a parish and county in a crown colony and that a certain degree of contact between the Brethren and the people and officials of those political entities would be inevitable. At the very least, they would have to pay taxes to a sheriff or constable and perform road work directed by the county court, and there was no way of knowing what other sorts of contact might become necessary as Wachovia developed. The Unity, however, wanted to discourage such contact between its general membership and outsiders, and the church's elders thought the creation of separate Moravian political jurisdictions would be a major step in that direction. If, for example, county and congregation were coextensive, it would be impossible to assemble a road crew that included unfamiliar outsiders, and congregation members would never have to deal with a sheriff or justice of the peace who did not share their faith. The Brethren could thus give Caesar his due without endangering their souls.

Second, if the Brethren were part of a heterogeneous parish or county and wanted a voice in government, they would have to win it through competition with their neighbors in what church officials called "elections and votes for and against officials." The mere thought of such tumult filled the elders with disgust. "The natural consequence of republican elections," wrote Frederic Marschall, "is that people interested in office must stand for it long in advance. That creates parties and counter-cabals which in consideration for expected support from one another become blind to all others and seek only to accomplish their [own] affairs." That kind of behavior would almost certainly sour relations between the Brethren and their neighbors and might even destroy the brotherly spirit that Moravians sought to maintain inside their own communities. And to make matters worse, if the Moravians were one small element in a mixed electorate their candidates might well lose, forcing them to live under non-Moravian officials. The establishment of an exclusively Moravian parish and county or incorporated town would guarantee the presence of Moravian local authorities without the disorder or risk of defeat involved in genuine elections. Moreover, in a political jurisdiction coextensive with a Moravian congregation, members would be unlikely to complain if the church employed unorthodox electoral procedures to further its aims. Unity leaders, for instance, considered seeking a municipal charter for Salem with several unusual provisions concerning the election of town officers. They wanted the freemen to choose nine men "through the majority of voices" and then, through the Lot, to have God name three of the nine as selectmen—a proposal that non-Moravians would probably oppose.[14]

During the period 1753–72 the Moravians' only success in obtaining separate jurisdictions came at the parish level. As a crown colony, North Carolina was nominally Anglican and was divided into Anglican parishes, each administered by a twelve-man vestry and two church wardens. Although these vestries served at least one important secular function, the administration of poor relief, their major responsibility was to provide adequate support for an Anglican church and minister in their parishes. When the Brethren arrived in North Carolina, vestries there were still organized under a 1741 law that gave them extraordinary power. Parish officials had the exclusive authority to call or dismiss ministers, were responsible for providing salaries, places to live, and places to preach, and in order to pay for all this were empowered to levy an annual poll tax and enforce its collection. Crown officials, however, were growing increasingly critical of the power granted local officials by North Carolina's Vestry Act of 1741 because such local authority ran counter to a new centralizing trend emerging in the Board of Trade after 1748. In 1754, on the Board's recommendation, the crown disallowed the act and embarked on a campaign to secure a new one giving royal officials the authority to appoint ministers. That touched off an eleven-year battle between North Carolina's lower house and the Board of Trade during which three more vestry acts were passed and disallowed. In the end the two sides gave up and accepted the Orthodox Clergy Act of 1765, which by remaining silent on the matter allowed the governor to claim the authority to fill vacant pulpits while the power to do so remained with the vestries.[15]

With as much power as North Carolina vestries had over the souls and purses of their constituents, it is hardly surprising that the Moravians wanted Wachovia to become a separate parish inhabited exclusively by members and friends of the Unity. Such an arrangement would guarantee Moravian control of the vestry and its decisions without the problems posed by an open election. This desire to make Wachovia a parish was also motivated, initially anyway, by a rare Moravian misunderstanding of English law. Until 1755 Unity leaders mistakenly believed that parliamentary recognition of their faith as an "ancient Protestant Episcopal Church" had put them on equal footing with the English church and that a Moravian parish would be free to elect a Moravian vestry, call a Moravian minister, and maintain a Moravian church without making any provision for their Anglican counterparts. The elders thought, incorrectly, that only if their parish contained a mixed population would it have to maintain English institutions as well as Moravian. Thus they expected the recognition of Wachovia as a separate parish to eliminate both the expense of supporting two establishments and the potential for a disruptive rivalry between them.[16]

So badly did the Brethren want their own parish that less than a year after the first settlers reached Bethabara a conference in Bethlehem decided it was time to petition the government of North Carolina for separate status. At that point Wachovia's population numbered just eleven, too few even to fill a vestry. Nevertheless, early in 1755, Bethlehem officials drafted a petition in which they claimed "[to] value nothing so much as Liberty of Conscience, & a free & unlimited exercise of our most holy Religion" and asked the assembly of North Carolina to establish a parish for the Brethren living there.[17]

The effort was flawed, however, by the Moravians' notion that their parish would not require an Anglican establishment. When the Unity's emissary arrived in New Bern, where the assembly was meeting, he quickly learned that the provincial government could not provide what the Unity wanted. As Spangenberg relayed the story to Zinzendorf, "the legislature protested against that and said we cannot give the Brethren *that*: it is not in our power: it is against the constitution of the land. And suppose we did make the Brethren independent of the English Church through an act, we certainly know that act will be disallowed in England and we will receive a reprimand." Parliamentary recognition, several assemblymen explained, did not free the Brethren from the established church; it simply permitted them to establish a parallel system in addition to the Anglican. Their new parish would still be required to call an English minister, support him, build a church or chapel in which he could preach, and elect vestrymen who promised not to oppose the English liturgy.[18]

Though this was not what the Brethren wanted, there was little they could do but accept it. The alternative was to remain a minority in an Anglican parish with little influence over its affairs, and that they did not want. Thus in October 1755 the government of North Carolina erected Dobbs Parish, named for the new governor, and made its boundaries coextensive with

those of Wachovia and a few adjacent tracts of land belonging
to the Unity.[19]

When Bethlehem learned what had happened the first response there was despair. "Our church matter in Wachovia is
again in crisis," wrote Spangenberg as he and the others tried
to figure out how to protect their church while doing as little
damage as possible to the laws of North Carolina. Their fears
soon proved unfounded, though. Dobbs Parish was Anglican in
name only. Its Moravian residents went through the motions of
administering an Anglican establishment, but the whole thing
was a sham that both the Unity and the provincial government
recognized and perpetuated. The personnel and activities of the
parish appeared to meet the requirements of North Carolina law
but were actually a facade behind which the Moravian Church
operated its real religious establishment.[20]

Of the thirty-eight men known to have served on the Dobbs
Parish vestry between its formation, in 1756 and the *Oeconomy's*
close, in 1772, thirty-six were communicant members of the Moravian Church; the other two were members of a society, affiliated with but not yet members of the Unity. Every known
church warden during that period was also Moravian. Moreover, on at least one occasion not a single member of the vestry
was legally qualified to serve, but no one seems to have cared.
In 1756 the vestrymen, few of whom spoke English, misunderstood the affirmation they were supposed to make. They mistakenly believed that the required promise not to oppose the
Anglican Church was "a formal declaration of a change of their
religion" and refused to sign it. Instead, they affirmed their support of the Unitas Fratrum. Sheriff David Jones, who was responsible for confirming the vestry's fitness to serve and was
not a Moravian, admitted that this did not meet the legal requirement but chose to ignore that fact and qualified the men
anyway. When Unity leaders discovered what Jones had done
they tried to correct the situation, but provincial officials in New
Bern seemed not to care either and told the Brethren not to
worry; so the vestry served a full three-year term though none
of its members were qualified.[21]

In the execution of their duties Dobbs Parish officials provided even stronger evidence that they were simply a tool through which the Moravian Church acted. The vestry never levied a tax to support the Anglican Church because the Unity paid whatever modest expenses the parish incurred. Several duties that fell to vestries elsewhere, such as the administration of poor relief or maintenance of the parish cemetery, were assigned to individual Moravians by conferences of Moravian elders, while the vestry had no apparent voice in the matter. And church wardens seem to have done nothing at all. In June 1757, for example, the outgoing wardens explained that they were not submitting to their successors the legally required account of parish expenses "because the Salary of our present Minister and his Other Entertainment, Likewise the Expenses for many Ecclesiastical Things, and what other expenses are made . . . for that time ex Communi Casa of the United Brethren are payed; therefore we think it be not needful to make some Accounts." [22]

The vestry of Dobbs Parish never even performed the most fundamental duty of an Anglican vestry—the calling of an Anglican minister. That too was done by the Moravian Church and merely announced by the vestry. Early in 1756 Spangenberg wrote the colonists from Bethlehem: "When the first Vestrymen are chosen and the Church Wardens are also in their offices, they will be required to call a minister. I have written to the *Jünger* about this and await his decision who we should take for it. You can only write a call and leave a blank in it where the name must be inserted. It will be written in thereafter when we know the *Jünger's* opinion and everything is agreed on properly." The messenger who carried Spangenberg's letter to Bethabara also took "a draft of a call for a minister in which the name is left blank." As instructed, the vestry signed the document and returned it to Bethlehem. Six months later they received word they had called Jacob Rogers to the pulpit. When Rogers resigned his post, in 1762, it was apparently Spangenberg who decided that for the time being the vestry should invite an Anglican preacher into the parish four times a year (the minimum required by law) rather than appoint another resident minister.

And when the parish did receive a new incumbent, Richard Utley, he was chosen and dispatched by Unity officials meeting in Europe.[23]

Not surprisingly, neither Rogers nor Utley was licensed by the Bishop of London, despite the fact that by early 1756, if not before, Moravian leaders knew that such a license was required by North Carolina law. The Unity simply sent Moravian clerics and called them English. Jacob Rogers was a Moravian minister, but he was neither ordained in nor licensed by the Anglican Church, and everyone seems to have known it. On arriving in North Carolina, Rogers met with Governor Dobbs and Chief Justice Hasell and made no effort to hide his deficiency. "Now at almost my first appearance," Rogers told Spangenberg, "the Chief Justice asked me if I had a license from the Bishop of London, to wch. I was oblig'd to answer no. At wch. he seem'd to be a little startled, but did not make much of it . . . th. Governor did not come to say anything of the matter to me, being willing it should be passed over." The provincial government was equally willing to overlook the fact that Rogers's successor, Richard Utley, had no more standing in the Anglican Church than Rogers did. In spite of that, both men bore the title English Minister of Dobbs Parish, and both performed Anglican services during their tenure.[24]

In many ways, then, Dobbs Parish was a fraud designed to serve the needs of the Unity. Its vestry contained no Anglicans; its minister was a Moravian; and decisions affecting it were actually made by leaders of the Moravian Church. Yet for all that, it was a functioning parish that did as good a job providing the public services required of it as any other in North Carolina, and better than most west of the Fall Line. The Anglican Church was never very strong in North Carolina. As late as 1765 Governor Tryon reported there were just six English ministers and ten church buildings in the entire colony. The established church was especially weak in the west, though. There were Anglicans in the backcountry—hundreds if not thousands of them—but they were outnumbered by Presbyterians, Baptists, and German sectarians.[25] These dissenters frequently gained control of frontier vestries and effectively disestablished the established church. By refusing to take the requisite oath, and thus disqualifying themselves as vestrymen, non-Anglicans left their parishes with no body authorized to call a minister or build a church. This happened repeatedly in Rowan, Guilford, and Mecklenburg counties during the 1760s and left Anglicans throughout the backcountry feeling, in the words of one petition from St. Luke's Parish, in Rowan County, that "we can never expect the regular and enlivening beams of the Holy Gospel to shine upon us."[26]

Dobbs Parish never built a church or chapel, but none of its western counterparts did either. It never built a glebe for its minister, but only one parish did in colonial North Carolina, and Dobbs, at least, provided food and housing for its incumbent. The Moravian parish also provided charity for the poor and a public cemetery. Its most important service, though, was in bringing a minister to the region. Although neither Rogers nor Utley was a proper Anglican and neither scrupled to seek converts for the Unity while preaching for the parish, they did preach in English, and Rogers at least used the Anglican liturgy. There was no apparent pattern to their preaching until early in the 1770s, when Utley settled into a routine of holding English services once a month. Until then they seem to have scheduled services according to the wishes of their neighbors, riding from time to time to one of the settlements outside Wachovia and holding services in a private home. They also performed baptisms and funerals, though weddings they left to the local magistrate, also a Moravian. Not everyone was satisfied with the Dobbs Parish ministers; some people thought they should baptize more freely and not worry so much about the morality or immorality of candidates. On the whole though, Anglicans around Wachovia seem to have been pleased with their Moravian parish.[27]

Leaders of the Unity also hoped that Wachovia's residents would gain control over the secular arm of their local government by obtaining county or corporate status for themselves. Such an arrangement would eliminate the need for brothers and sisters to mix indiscriminately with the outsiders while performing their civic duties. It would also give them control over the

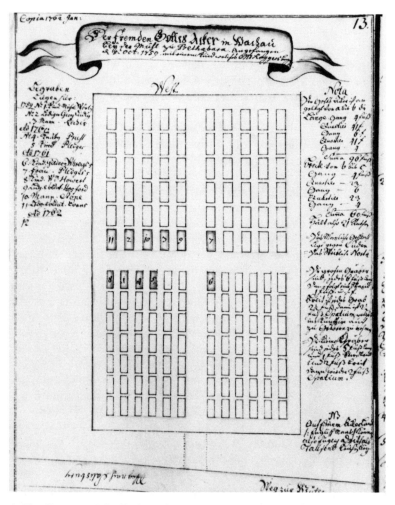

6. The Strangers' God's Acre, begun near Bethabara's mill in 1759, eventually became the Dobbs Parish Cemetery. Although Dobbs Parish was Anglican in name only, its Moravian vestrymen took seriously their obligation to provide public services, including Christian burial, for parish residents. (Used with permission of the Archives of the Moravian Church in America—Northern Province)

most visible and influential organ of government in their daily lives, the county court or municipal commissioners, without having to compete for it in genuine elections. That would give church officials significant temporal powers. They would enjoy police power over non-Moravian visitors, the right to levy and collect taxes, the right to determine the location of roads, ferries, and taverns, and the right to send representatives to the provincial assembly.

During the years of the *Oeconomy* the Brethren never really pushed for Wachovia to become a county. There were simply too many problems with the idea. In the first place, there were practical concerns. Making Wachovia a separate civil jurisdiction would add to the already greater than anticipated expense of settling the colony. Because so many of its residents were members of the *Oeconomy*, which paid their taxes, the Moravian Church would end up footing most of the bill to erect a courthouse and jail for the new county. Moreover, Wachovia's population during these first two decades was so small, fewer than two hundred taxables by 1772, that the church feared it might not contain enough qualified men to serve as justices of the peace or to fill other important posts in a county administration. Second, there were troubling theological complications with county status. Because Brethren who scrupled to swear an oath were forbidden to serve on juries, would the new county have enough jurors to operate a Court of Pleas and Quarter Sessions? And if it did, would Moravian justices and jurors be able to perform their duties in good conscience? As Spangenberg pointed out in 1753: "we must hold trials in criminal cases according to the law as it there [North Carolina] exists, and must pronounce sentence, not, as in Germany, according to justice and right, but according to the law." Spangenberg was afraid that good Moravians could not be good magistrates and warned "that if we undertake what does not accord with our general [spiritual] circumstances it will only do us harm."[28]

Corporate status, on the other hand, seemed much more practical. What the Brethren had in mind was a royal charter for Wachovia's *gemein Ort* and the Unity-owned buffer around it with specific provisions granting them a seat in the general assembly, authorizing them to establish a market and promulgate for it regulations "according to which everyone has to act," and providing the town's selectmen with powers inside the corporation's boundaries equal to those of justices of the peace. The last of these provisions would spare the Brethren the crises of conscience about which Spangenberg worried by enabling the selectmen to convene a magistrates' court. Such courts did not employ juries and could not consider criminal cases; so they presented no problems for affirming Brethren. And because their jurisdiction was limited to relatively small matters— breaches of the peace generally—it was unlikely that a Moravian magistrate would ever face a situation in which the letter of the law contradicted his own sense of justice and appropriate punishment.[29]

From time to time, therefore, Unity leaders discussed the possibility of incorporating Wachovia's *gemein Ort*. At first they refused to endorse the idea on the grounds that no one living there was qualified to administer such a corporation. The naming of Frederic Marschall to be Wachovia's *Oeconomus* solved that problem, and shortly before Marschall's departure for Bethabara a Unity conference adopted his proposal for the rights and powers to be requested in any petition for incorporation. But then the Lord intervened, declaring through the Lot that it was still not time to seek a charter.[30] That was in 1767, and the question of incorporating Salem did not come again until after the American Revolution. Throughout the period under study here Wachovia remained part of a mixed county—Rowan until 1770 and Surry after that.[31]

The failure to gain separate civil status for Wachovia, however, did not deny the Moravians all the benefits that such status would have brought. The colony's residents still managed to influence county affairs and protect their interests through Moravian justices sitting on the county court. County courts were the most important institution of local government in colonial North Carolina and probably the single most influential government agency of any type in the daily lives of eighteenth-century North Carolinians. Each county was administered by a county court made up of justices of the peace appointed by the governor. The court met four times a year to try noncapital offenses and civil actions involving amounts not in excess of £20. They levied taxes, supervised the administration of estates, regulated land transactions, ordered road work, and licensed mills and taverns in their jurisdiction.[32] The importance of justices and county courts in North Carolina was not lost on Wachovia's planners. Before a single colonist left Bethlehem, Spangenberg wrote a memo suggesting that the first party include "several trustworthy and qualified Englishmen . . . [to serve] as justices." It was a dispute over taxes, however, that prompted the Unity to act on Spangenberg's suggestion. In 1756 the vestry of St. Luke's Parish, also in Rowan County and a Presbyterian stronghold, refused to levy a tax to support its Anglican establishment. The county court, therefore, intervened and taxed everyone in the county, including the residents of Dobbs Parish, to cover St. Luke's expenses. The brothers in Wachovia promptly wrote their superiors that "we must pay even as many taxes as when we were not a distinct parish" and complained that they had to have a member on the county bench to protect themselves from such treatment in the future. The elders in Bethlehem agreed and sent a request to Governor Dobbs of North Carolina asking that he appoint Jacob Lösch to the Rowan County Court. Dobbs had no objections; so in 1757 Lösch was included in a new Commission of the Peace and *Dedimus* for Rowan County and in October 1758 appeared in court to qualify for his new post.[33]

For the next thirteen years Wachovia's Moravian community was represented by a single member on the county bench. Lösch performed that duty until 1769, when he returned to Pennsylvania and Jacob Bonn succeeded him. After Surry County was created, in 1770, Bonn moved to its bench and was joined there by Jacobus van der Merk and Charles Holder, bringing the number of Moravian justices to three. Even with the three members, though, the Brethren certainly never dominated the court. They attended usually just two of the court's four sessions in any given year (never attending more than three) and apparently missed 1762 altogether; most often a lone Moravian sat down with two to seven non-Moravians. But

Lösch and the others were not there to dominate the court. Church leaders considered their justices valuable not for anything they could do on the bench but for their ability to monitor the actions of its non-Moravian majority. Just three months after Jacob Lösch was qualified for a seat, Spangenberg explained that the importance of his presence would lay in the fact that "justices from each county regulate tax matters together, and thus he can prevent, merely by being there, that injustice happens to our settlement." In the years following Lösch's appointment there were no more complaints from Wachovia like that voiced in 1756, and while it is impossible to prove that the court's good behavior was due to the presence of a Moravian member, the Brethren certainly believed it was.[34]

Moravian justices also rendered valuable service to the church through their presence in Bethabara. As His Majesty's Justices of the Peace, they were the only significant representatives of provincial and crown authority in Wachovia. Inside the Moravian congregations this was relatively unimportant because problems there were invariably handled by church officials. Just once between 1753 and 1772 did Bethabara's elders use a magistrate's authority against one of their own. Rather, the value of a Moravian justice in Bethabara lay in his authority over non-Moravians in the colony. Under North Carolina law a single justice did not have extensive police powers, but he did have enough to maintain civil order. Sitting as a magistrate's court Lösch or Bonn could hear debt cases involving sums of less than twenty shillings, had jurisdiction over such offenses as public drunkenness, profanity, breaking the Sabbath, and the disposition of unmarked cattle, could issue warrants for the arrest and possible detention until trial of accused criminals, and could issue attachments on the estates of debtors reported to be preparing for flight from the province. Such a court was perfectly suited to the needs of the Moravian community. While magistrates could only try debt cases involving sums under a pound, on the last known list of the Moravians' debtors (dated 1760) two-thirds of the individuals named owed less than that. And though a lone justice had no authority to handle major criminal cases, all the Brethren wanted was the ability to try petty offenses like the illmannered behavior of tavern patrons who overindulged; anything bigger had too many religious complications for them.[35] Unfortunately, magistrates' courts did not keep records of their activities. Consequently, one cannot say precisely how often or in exactly what ways Moravian justices of the peace employed their authority to protect their community. Congregation records, however, reveal several examples that are no doubt typical. In the fall of 1766, for instance, a customer in the tavern refused to pay his bill and assaulted the tavernkeeper. Justice Lösch quickly responded by arresting the man and sending him under guard to the county jail in Salisbury. This and similar episodes show that Moravian magistrates played an important role in the protection of Wachovia's Moravian community. Further evidence of this comes from the community's response to the threatened loss of its magistrate. When, in 1762, it seemed that Jacob Lösch would return to Bethlehem, officials in Wachovia expressed horror at the thought of losing him and asked their superiors "how can we manage without a justice here, [as] we live among the discarded refuse of Ireland and America . . . and have a strong settlement behind us in the Hollow [Mt. Airy] of loud disorderly people and a large band of thieves." Moravian settlers in Wachovia clearly shared the opinion of Spangenberg, who wrote in 1757 that "merely to have a justice at some place prevents many evil things from happening." And this opinion seems to have been correct. Wachovia's justices of the peace were an essential factor in the Moravians' ability to function in a heterogeneous society.[36]

Moravian justices served more than their own church community, though. They were the king's justices and served the king's subjects whether inside or outside of the Moravian church. While sitting with the court in Salisbury they ruled on whatever cases came before them and participated in a myriad of administrative decisions. There is no evidence they ever withdrew from a matter before the court, and no charges of favoritism or incompetence against them specifically have survived.[37] As individual magistrates living in Bethabara, Lösch and Bonn also served their non-Moravian neighbors. They performed marriages for them, administered the estates of those who died intestate, held coroner's inquests into suspicious deaths, alerted the public to Indian threats and known criminals in the area, organized posses, and with their constables transferred prisoners and runaway slaves through their own jurisdiction and into the hands of authorities in the next. Justices Lösch and Bonn, then, helped bind the Moravian community to its neighbors as well as protect it from them.[38]

The Brethren also managed, in spite of Wachovia's having neither county nor town status, to perform their duties as citizens without exposing too many members to non-Moravian officials or citizens. In one regard, that of jury duty, the Brethren were spared by act of Parliament from mixing with outsiders; members needed only affirm rather than swear, and they were free from service on juries. A more important factor, however, in the Moravians' ability to fulfill their civic responsibilities in relative isolation was their success at having transferred to Dobbs Parish control over matters that were usually handled by county officials in North Carolina.

The militia was one such matter. Although Parliament had released Unity members from compulsory military service, the Brethren were not pacifists. When the French and Indian War spread to North Carolina they distinguished between offensive and defensive warfare and participated in the latter. The Brethren refused "to follow after our Enemies, to take away their lives," but they recognized a need to defend themselves and their neighbors against what they labeled "the murdering Indians." Thus they willingly fortified Bethabara and its mill as places of refuge for Moravian and non-Moravian alike, enlarged their arsenal, and prepared to fight. The problem was that North Carolina's militia was organized by counties, and as part of the Rowan County contingent the Brethren would almost certainly be placed under non-Moravian officers who might not understand or honor the distinction they made between offensive and defensive operations. Furthermore, membership in the county militia entailed participation in its musters. That was an idea that appalled Moravian leaders. They had seen five Rowan companies drill outside Bethabara in 1754, and "after the Muster," wrote Bethabara's diarist, "the men were so full of whiskey that they fought each other until they were covered with blood."[39]

To get around these problems Moravian leaders asked Governor Dobbs to grant them an arrangement in North Carolina similar to that they enjoyed in Pennsylvania. They wanted to raise a watch exclusively from Dobbs Parish and place it under the governor's direct command. It took two requests to make clear what they wanted, but eventually the Brethren got what they asked for. "Our Watch-Master stands under no colonel," Spangenberg wrote in 1759, "rather directly beneath the governor and does not engage himself to be used offensively with his people, rather only defensively against the murderers near our homes." This "Independent Company," as it was called, served the Moravians' purposes admirably. It permitted them to defend themselves without compromising their beliefs. At the same time it allowed them to protect their neighbors, dozens of whom spent weeks at a time with the Brethren during the French and Indian War, and thus counter rumors that the Unity was pro-French. And they were able to do it all without joining the ungodly in Rowan's militia.[40]

Through a similar agreement, the Moravian residents of Wachovia also managed to fulfill their road building duties and get the roads they wanted while avoiding extensive contact with outsiders. County courts in North Carolina regularly ordered the construction and maintenance of roads and bridges they deemed necessary or desirable and compelled residents to serve on juries to lay them out and on construction crews to build them. As early as 1754, Edward Hughes, then a friend of the Brethren and a Rowan County justice, arranged for them to do their share of road work by themselves. A decade later the county court formalized this arrangement by acting favorably on the Moravians' petition for "a road-master of our own, selected from among us." The court's timing could not have been better. Two years later the Brethren began building Salem and wanted to connect their *gemein Ort* to the rest of North Carolina. During the late 1760s they petitioned the court for roads between Salem and Salisbury, Cross Creek, Town Fork, Belew's

Creek, Abbotts Creek, and the Shallow Ford of the Yadkin. With their own road master and crews the Moravians were able to build the portions of these roads inside Wachovia by themselves and link up with the sections outside Wachovia that had been built by non-Moravians. Both groups benefitted from improved transportation, and members of the Unity did not have to mix with outsiders to get it. The church kept this arrangement at least through 1769—records that year stated explicitly that the county court had made road work within Dobbs Parish a responsibility of parish residents—and probably through the close of the *Oeconomy*. It did not mean that Moravians and non-Moravians never worked together; church elders sometimes hired outsiders to help the Brethren build or repair roads and bridges inside Dobbs Parish. In those instances, however, the nonmembers were chosen by Moravian officials, supervised by them, and could be dismissed immediately if problems arose.[41]

The Brethren also appear to have frequently, if not always, paid their taxes without subjecting individual brothers and sisters to visits from non-Moravian sheriffs and constables. Where the *Oeconomy* existed its directors paid lump sums to cover the county and provincial levies for its members. Elsewhere congregational officials appointed a member or two to collect taxes from the rest and turn them in to the proper county authorities. "It is best that we handle all such matters as a community," declared one conference in 1772, "as we wish to keep on friendly terms with the officials of the land and yet avoid letting them become too well acquainted with our affairs."[42]

Nor did the Moravians' failure to gain county or corporate status prevent them from participating in North Carolina politics at the provincial level. Though Wachovia never gained the privilege of sending its own representative to the general assembly, and though the only Moravian to stand for election before 1772 lost, the Brethren still followed closely what the legislature did and sought to influence its decisions.

Their most visible attempts to affect provincial politics, though by no means their most successful, came as voters. Voting created a number of problems for the Brethren. They considered campaigns and elections inherently disruptive events.

Moreover, to vote one had to go a polling place and expose one-self to raucous, drunken behavior like that Charles Sydnor described so vividly in Virginia elections. Neither of these proved terribly worrisome to Unity officials, though. The former they accepted as a regrettable but inevitable part of Anglo-American politics, and the latter they managed to avoid by sending one or two contact specialists to the polls with proxy votes for the rest of the brothers. The real problem was that North Carolina law required that a man be "in actual possession of an Estate real for his own life" to vote. That restriction was probably intended to insure that voters were economically independent and, thus, free of influence that might affect their judgment. But such independence was precisely what the Unity sought to deny its members. It wanted them to vote in the church's interest, not their own. Furthermore, possession of a freehold would remove a man from Wachovia's communal *Oeconomy*, one of the principal mechanisms for maintaining his commitment to the Moravian community.[43]

To escape this dilemma the church tried to provide its members with the appearance of freehold status but not the substance. Initially at least, they did this by giving some of Wachovia's settlers documents that identified them as freeholders but did not actually convey any land to them. Early in 1756, for example, officials in Bethlehem informed the Wachovia Brethren that David Nitschman had written a letter stating that he had given fifty acres of land to each of twenty men in the colony. The letter alone was not a legal conveyance, and there was no reference to an actual deed. The elders simply explained that " 'Father' David Nitschman's letter serves as credentials for our freemen," and that "if necessary this letter can be produced." Evidently, they hoped the twenty could simply claim freeman's status without anyone challenging their right to do so. In a similar fashion, in 1758 Spangenberg granted fifty-acre leaseholds for life to each of five Brethren leaving Bethlehem to settle in Bethabara, though there is no evidence that the leases were ever entered in North Carolina.[44]

This technique seems to have worked well, however by 1764 some church leaders were worried their luck was running out.

Frederic Marschall, for one, pointed out that "putting twelve Brethren in possession of fifty acres each pro forma, may answer for a time in an unorganized land, but so soon as things are brought into better order, or some one finds it to his interest to challenge our vote, there will be difficulties." In response to such concerns, a 1767 church conference spent several days looking for a way to make Wachovia's residents freeholders without reducing church influence over their actions but finally concluded that under existing law there was no way to do it. They decided, therefore, to ask North Carolina's government for a new law—"an Act under which a citizen of Salem worth £50 will be rated as a Freeholder and allowed to vote" in spite of the fact that he held his land through an annual lease or had no land at all. Nothing came of the proposal, and through the close of the *Oeconomy* the Unity made do with its ersatz freeholders.[45]

Despite their lack of legal standing, Moravian voters were relatively active in North Carolina elections. Between their arrival in 1753 and the close of the *Oeconomy* the Brethren had eleven opportunities to vote for members of the general assembly. They definitely voted in four elections—1757, 1760, 1761, and 1771. Each time a few Brethren went to the polls with proxy votes for the rest. On another occasion, 1764, they tried to vote but said the crowd was so large their votecarrier could not get through. In five other cases—1754, twice in 1762, 1766, and 1770—the records fail to show conclusively whether they voted or not. Only once, in 1769, did they definitely abstain, a step they apparently took to avoid choosing sides "between the so-called Regulators and the others."[46]

Perhaps the most interesting point about Moravian voting, though, is the fact that no one ever seems to have challenged it. In 1760 the North Carolina assembly passed "an Act to Regulate Elections" in which sheriffs were instructed to appoint poll watchers to insure that none voted but those who met the economic and residential requirements. The Moravians certainly never hid the facts that they lived under a communal economy and the church owned their land, and the 1760s were a decade of rising political conflict in western North Carolina. Yet no government official, no defeated candidate, and no rival voter ever questioned the Moravians' right to participate in provincial elections. Indeed, on at least two occasions outsiders actively encouraged them to participate. Edward Underhill wrote to Bethabara's elders in 1757 offering himself as a candidate in the upcoming assembly election and promising "always [to] exert myself in strenuously aiming to support you in the free Exercise of your Holy Religion, free from being under the Restraint of Complying to any Laws, but what shall be calculated for your immediate Protection and Happiness and will heartily strive to preserve you all the Indulgences you wish or propose." (Underhill's letter was in vain, though; Moravian votes went to Hugh Waddell.) Fourteen years later, in the spring of 1771, Bethabara's diarist reported that "many neighbors" came to the Brethren and asked that one or more of them stand for election from Surry County "as many believed that they would be able to serve this land."[47]

It is possible that the Moravians' act tricked their neighbors into believing they were legally qualified to vote. It is just as likely, though, that the neighbors knew better but did not care. Throughout the 1750s there had been problems securing proper titles to land in Lord Granville's district, and in 1763 the proprietor's North Carolina office had closed for good. As a result, untold numbers of backcountry settlers were unable to get legal titles to their land; so none of them could legally vote either. In that situation it may have been that no one cared to enforce the electoral laws because everyone would suffer if they did.[48]

For all that, it is doubtful that the Moravians, even though they voted as a block, had a significant impact on elections in either Rowan or Surry County. While Wachovia remained in Rowan its residents were too few to affect any but the closest contest. In 1759, after a precipitous decline following the start of the French and Indian War, Rowan County still had an estimated eight hundred taxables, but just fifty-nine were Moravian and barely half of those voted the following April. Things improved somewhat when Surry County was established, in 1770, but not enough to give the Brethren control of county elections. Surry recorded 687 heads of household in 1771; of that number sixty-one lived in or around Bethabara and Bethania, and even if one includes the men in Salem, which was still part of Rowan County until 1773, the Brethren had only ninety-seven heads of household, or 14 percent of Surry's 1771 total. That this was not enough is clear from the fact that one of the brothers stood for election from Surry County in 1771 and lost.[49]

Voting was not the only way to affect provincial politics, though. During the years of the *Oeconomy* the Brethren had far more success through lobbyists and letters than they did through elections. This was the politics they knew best. Zinzendorf and other church leaders had learned long ago the value of a well-placed friend. Their relations in the Danish court of Christian VI had opened the way for much of their missionary work in Europe, Africa, and the Americas; their discussions with the Georgia trustees resulted in an invitation to settle in that colony; and the friendship of Lord Granville, General James Oglethorpe, and others had won Parliamentary recognition for the Unity in spite of opposition from some of the king's ministers. In North Carolina, as they had in Europe, the Brethren used both low-key efforts to establish and maintain friendly relations with leading figures in the provincial government and occasional bursts of intense activity aimed at winning particular concessions.[50]

As early as 1752 the Moravians had begun thinking of ways to influence North Carolina officials. In September of that year, just two months after the death of North Carolina's governor, Gabriel Johnston, Spangenberg wrote in his diary: "Many regret his [Johnston's] death and speak of him as a fine man. Be that as it may, the sending of a new Governor will give a good opportunity for My Lord Granville, if he pleases, to give instructions [to the new governor] about our matters." Spangenberg went on to mention three specific privileges that the new executive could help the Brethren secure from the assembly, though there is no evidence that he or other Unity officials ever acted on the suggestion. But Moravian lobbying of North Carolina politicians had certainly begun by late 1754, and once the process started it continued without interruption.[51]

For a handful of ranking Brethren—Christian Henrich

Rauch, Jacob Lösch, John Ettwein, Frederic Marschall, Abraham von Gammern, Richard Utley, Johann Muschbach, and Traugott Bagge—part of their job was to cultivate key officials in North Carolina. Meetings between the Brethren and colonial officials were held in a number of places. Some were in New Bern, when the governor or assembly was there; others in Salisbury, when the chief justice was sitting with the superior court; still others were in Wachovia, when government figures as ranking as the governor came to see the Moravian town. Whenever they took place, the meetings were an important opportunity for the Brethren to demonstrate their loyalty to His Majesty's government. When Governor Tryon came to Bethabara, for example, once in 1767 and again in 1771, there were ceremonies to welcome him, a formal presentation of gifts, declarations of fealty, feasts, toasts, and serenades in the visitors' honor. There was also plenty of time for leaders of the Moravian congregation to explain their needs and views to Tryon, and they made the most of the opportunity.[52]

Meetings such as these were part of a continual but relatively quiet process by which the Brethren sought "to promote our good relations with the Government." There were also times, however, when the Unity wanted a particular concession from provincial authorities, and in those instances church leaders were much more aggressive in their lobbying. The finest example of this was the 1754–55 campaign to achieve parish status for Wachovia. It began in August of 1754, when officials in Bethlehem sent Peter Böhler, a bishop in the Moravian Church, with a petition to the governor and assembly of North Carolina asking them to make Wachovia a separate parish. On the way south Böhler learned that because the new governor, Arthur Dobbs, had not yet arrived, the assembly was not expected to meet until the following spring. Rather than waste a trip Böhler went on to New Bern and met James Hasell, chief justice of the province, and Francis Corbin, Granville's agent in the colony. He discussed the parish matter with them and identified two other officials he thought the Unity should contact: Samuel Swann, former speaker of the lower house, and Reading Blount, who was likely to be a member of the new assembly. Böhler then returned to Pennsylvania and prepared reports of his journey for various Unity officials.[53]

The following April Bethlehem tried again. This time they sent David Nitschman and Christian Thomas Benzien with instructions to call on Chief Justice Hasell, Speaker Swann, and Matthew Rowan, President of the Council, in order to solicit their ideas regarding the best way to submit the Unity's petition. As Böhler had done the year before, Nitschman and Benzien went via Bethabara, where they had planned to wait until the legislature convened. They did not wait idly, though. Both men rode to Salisbury and had a "satisfactory interview" with the chief justice, and Benzien returned two months later to meet Governor Dobbs. By then Nitschman had gone back to Bethlehem, but in August Benzien finally left for New Bern, stopping on the way to spend a week at the home of the chief justice before he and Hasell set off for the assembly.[54]

Arriving in New Bern, Benzien and Hasell met with Robert Jones, Jr., a delegate from Northhampton County and a leading member in the 1755 session of the assembly. Jones, in turn, enlisted the help of Samuel Swann, not the speaker this time but still a powerful member, and of Thomas Barker, representative from Edenton, treasurer of the northern counties, and a leader of the Albemarle faction in its long battle with the Cape Fear delegates over representation in the assembly. During the next several weeks this brain trust explained to Benzien how the Brethren had misunderstood North Carolina's Vestry Act, rewrote the bill Benzien wanted to submit so it conformed to North Carolina law, and plotted how best to circumvent the expected opposition of John Starkey, treasurer for the southern counties, a leader of the Cape Fear faction, and, in Benzien's words, leader of "a set of Low People" in the assembly. It does not appear that anyone thought Starkey might oppose the creation of a Moravian parish out of any particular animosity toward the Brethren. More likely, Jones and Barker, as spokesmen for the Albemarle counties, simply expected automatic opposition from the Cape Fear group to anything they suggested.[55]

Benzien's advisors took their time. They were determined to

keep the Unity's bill off the floor "until they had cooled somewhat several assemblymen who were very keenly opposed to
it." At last, two weeks into the session, Jones introduced the
measure into the House. His preparations quickly paid off. The
bill first came before House and Council on October 9; by the
eleventh it had passed both chambers; and on the fifteenth it
was submitted to the governor for his approval. Benzien's work
was still not done, though. Before returning to Pennsylvania,
he called again on Governor Dobbs to present him with a map
of Wachovia—a gift from the Brethren to thank Dobbs for services rendered and to pave the way for continued good relations.[56]

Between 1753 and 1772 Wachovia's Moravian community became steadily more involved in the legal and political institutions of North Carolina. The Lord asked only that church members give Caesar his due, that they pay his taxes and obey most
of his laws. The Brethren went beyond that, however, and
joined the caesars. As parish and county officials, men like Jacob
Lösch were certainly valuable to their church. They spoke for
the Unity in North Carolina's unadorned corridors of power and
mediated between its members and a world they considered
dangerous to their souls. But these men also served the larger
community of which Wachovia was a part. During the 1750s and
1760s Euroamerican society was trying to emerge from the wilderness of western North Carolina. As historians have often
noted, the process was far from easy, and government officials
themselves were frequently part of the problem. Yet one has
only to read the minutes of a county court or the diary of a
Moravian congregation to see how much these officials did to
organize frontier society. Through their efforts roads were built,
property sales and inheritance were regularized, white men
were organized to kill red ones and enslave black ones, and
some of the more blatant crimes against white persons and
property were punished. And in the region surrounding Wachovia, Moravian vestrymen and justices played an important
role in this process.

CHAPTER 7

Getting on with the Neighbors

There is a certain irony to all the Moravians' dealings with their neighbors in North Carolina. The Brethren clearly looked with thinly veiled contempt on many of the people around them; in the privacy of their own meetings and records the brothers and sisters frequently described their fellow Carolinians as "rabble," as "the discarded refuse of Ireland and America," and in other unflattering terms.[1] Yet they seldom showed this contempt openly. In fact they regularly tried to please and impress many of the people they most despised by listening to what they said, trying to anticipate what they would think, and adjusting their own behavior in a deliberate effort to improve their image in non-Moravian eyes. This irony is easy to explain, though. Zinzendorf's followers may not have liked many of their neighbors, but they knew they had to live with them and do business with them. That meant they had to be civil to one another, at least. The Brethren, therefore, made a deliberate effort to maintain good relations with the strangers around them.

The men and women who planned Wachovia identified three things that might endanger the good relations they hoped to maintain—religion, money, and politics. They were probably most worried about the first, though, because eighteenth-century Moravians felt they and their ancestors had suffered for their faith since the fifteenth century. Their prophet, John Hus, had endured a martyr's death in 1415; Catholic armies had nearly destroyed the Ancient Unity during the Counter Reformation; and members of the Renewed Unity believed they had been the victims of verbal, legal, economic, and physical persecution since the church's renewal in 1727. Why, they asked, should things be any different in North Carolina? It too had an established faith, the adherents of which might resent and persecute the Brethren in spite of Parliament's declaration that the Renewed Unity was "an ancient Protestant Episcopal Church." If the establishment did respect Moravian rights, though, it might expose the brothers and sisters to even greater danger. Thousands of North Carolinians belonged to dissenting faiths, like the Presbyterians and Baptists, who enjoyed no special status in the colony and often came under attack from the Anglicans. If the Brethren appeared to receive preferential treatment how would these other dissenters react? Would they vent their frustrations with the established church on the more vulnerable Moravians?[2]

Money threatened almost as many problems as religion. The church leaders who planned Wachovia were clearly worried that the contrast between Moravian and non-Moravian levels of economic success in North Carolina might generate animosity toward the Brethren. When Spangenberg toured the colony in 1752 he was hardly impressed by either the degree of economic development he found or the industry of the people he met. Carolinians were poor and, it seemed to Spangenberg, likely to stay that way. Yet the church was planning to send into the poorest section of this poor colony a small party with cash, equipment, abundant supplies, and instructions to prosper quickly. Spangenberg, at least, saw great danger in this. The very prosperity he and others wished for Wachovia would simply remind others in North Carolina of their own poverty and would "stirr up their Envy against the Brethren." That, he wrote, "will perhaps bring Sufferings upon them."[3]

Last among the anticipated sources of conflict between Brethren and strangers was politics. Though they said little about it explicitly, the elders planning Wachovia clearly recognized that politics would be one arena in which those with religious or economic grudges against the Brethren would try to settle them. They hoped to insulate the settlers in Wachovia from some of that conflict by securing political jurisdictions coextensive with the boundaries of the Moravian community. The elders must have known, however, that even if they got what they wanted and Wachovia became a separate township or county, its representatives would still have to compete in the general assembly with those from towns and counties. Political conflict, they knew, was the Anglo-American way.

In addition to the religious, economic, and political problems that Unity leaders foresaw while planning Wachovia, Moravian settlers found two other sources of trouble once they got to Carolina. First came the French and Indian War. Wars had often caused problems for the Brethren because of the latter's refusal to participate in them as fully as their neighbors thought they should. During the War of Jenkin's Ear (1739–42) English settlers in Georgia had questioned the Moravians' loyalty when they refused to join the war against Spain. As that conflict grew into King George's War (1740–48), New York authorities had suspected the Brethren of secret ties to the French. The outbreak of the French and Indian War, soon after the Brethren reached Wachovia seemed to presage a new round of accusations. Five months after the fighting began *The North Carolina Gazette* printed "A Letter from Canada" in which the author, identified only as "a French Officer," described the Brethren as "our Good Friends . . . [who] refused to take up arms against us." This, the Moravians believed, was a forgery intended "to stir up invidium and Odium" toward them, and they worried that more would follow.[4]

The other unexpected threat came from the Regulator Movement. Regulators first appeared in 1766 in Orange County, where they demanded the removal of local officials they claimed were extorting illegal fees and taxes from them. The idea soon spread to other frontier counties, including Rowan, and triggered a popular campaign "for regulating publik Grievances & abuses of Power." At first the Regulators focused their anger on allegedly corrupt county officials—seizing or impeding tax collectors, blocking efforts to impound property for nonpayment of taxes, and in a few spectacular instances shutting down the courts. Gradually, however, their resentment moved east, toward the provincial authorities they claimed supported unscrupulous local officials and sanctioned their crimes. During the late 1760s and early 1770s the Regulators grew increasingly frustrated with the assembly and governor for their refusal to redress western grievances and for their use of the militia to maintain order. Finally Governor Tryon felt compelled to assert his authority and in the spring of 1771 led militia units from the Cape Fear region into the backcountry to restore order. On May 16, Tryon's little army met a larger body of Regulators along Alamance Creek. In the battle that followed the governor's victory was quick and complete, and in the days and weeks that followed he used both hangings and pardons to end the uprising, though bitter memories lingered for years.[5]

The great fear in Wachovia during all this was that supporters of the Regulators would resent the Moravians' loyalty to county officials and to the government in New Bern. Publicly, the Brethren justified their obedience on religious grounds, claiming they were required to accept the governments that God placed over them. But practical concerns were just as important. As a small and vulnerable minority, the Moravians relied heavily on laws and governments to protect them against the popular will, and only if they were convinced that a change in government was inevitable would they shift their allegiance. In the long run this policy served them well during the Regulator years because Tryon was able to crush the insurrection and remembered his friends in Wachovia. In the short run, however, the Brethren felt very exposed and worried that their neighbors' criticism of the government would turn to criticism of those who supported it, including them.

The Moravian response to these dangers, real or perceived, was a deliberate campaign to monitor and improve relations between themselves and their neighbors. They understood clearly that no amount of government support would be enough if the populace around Wachovia turned on its residents; so they set out to win their neighbors over—or at least keep them neutral. Superficially at least, some of the practices employed in this campaign seem to contradict one another. Sometimes the Brethren chose to say little about themselves and lay low, while at other times members went out of their way to explain their actions to outsiders. Sometimes the church demanded that members obey the laws of North Carolina and at other times insisted that they ignore those same laws. But the motive behind these actions was always the same: Unity leaders wanted to improve the church's reputation among nonmembers. Throughout the years 1753–72 Moravian elders carefully watched relations between their community and the rest of North Carolina and did their best to manipulate the latter's perceptions of the former. And they picked the targets of their manipulation quite deliberately. The degree to which the Moravians were concerned with maintaining the respect and friendship of an individual seems to have been directly proportional to that individual's position in county or provincial government or geographic proximity to Wachovia. The greater one's authority over the Brethren or the closer one lived to them, the harder they tried to win and maintain one's friendship.

The Moravians' simplest technique was secrecy. They hid whatever they thought might anger or frighten people and hoped the latter could not get upset by what they did not know. Church leaders hid the fact, for instance, that Lord Granville had given them six years instead of the usual three in which to clear three percent of their land. Because word of the arrangement "might occasion Dissatisfaction in the said Earl Granville's present Tenants in N. Carolina," they and the proprietor kept quiet in order to keep the peace. The Brethren also chose to remain silent in 1755 when a letter allegedly written to a French officer by a Canadian appeared in *The North Carolina Gazette* and described them as allies of the French. Moravian leaders were certain the letter was a fake, "a satanical invention of a certain man" they did not name. They concluded, however, that anything they said would simply keep alive an issue they wanted to fade as quickly as possible; so Christian Henrich Rauch, then acting as Wachovia's executive, told congregation members that if anyone spoke to them about the matter they should "keep quiet and not answer back." Similarly, at the height of the Regulator disturbances the Brethren tried to lay low. Wagons bound for Charles Town left Bethania in two small groups rather than a single large one in an effort "to make the shipment less conspicuous."[6]

This desire to maintain a low profile was probably a factor in the Moravians' decision to bar outsiders from most of their religious services. Restricting admission to members was primarily a means of reinforcing a sense of community among the Brethren, but the elders also seem to have thought it might reduce the risk of doctrinal disputes with their neighbors by denying the latter any certain knowledge of what went on in Unity services. Thus the first settlers in Wachovia closed most of their services by outsiders. By the early 1760s however, church leaders had decided that such a policy created more problems than it solved. A growing number of non-Moravians had started to wonder just what went on in those closed meetings, and the Brethren, in turn, grew concerned that curiosity about them might turn to violence against them.

In an effort to ease their neighbors' anxiety, therefore, officials in Bethabara took steps to educate them about Unity beliefs and practices. "We assembled early in the *gemein Saal*," the Bethabara diarist wrote at Easter, 1762;

> the minister began with the salutation 'Der Herr ist auf erstanden!' and then in English 'Christ is arisen in indeed!' The congregation sang: 'Welcome among they flock of grace,' etc. Then an explanation was given in English to the strangers present, telling them the ground and reason for our procession to the graveyard and our liturgy there; for certain remarkable reports have been spread about it, for instance that we open the graves and wake the dead with our trumpets! . . . Instead of German preaching a sermon was read, and that was followed by the reading of a sermon in English on the text: 'Because I live ye shall live also.'[7]

The Brethren had permitted outsiders to attend some of their services in the past, but they had done so reluctantly in an attempt to be good hosts or to accommodate Christians who had not heard a preacher in months, if not years. Now, however, their motive was different. Easter services were opened specifically to dispel some of the mystery surrounding Unity practices and disarm potential critics.

Moreover, two months later John Ettwein explained to Henry Laurens another element in the Unity's publicity campaign.

Ettwein told his merchant friend, "it is our Rule never to refuse Admitance to any Magistrat that wants to be present [at any Moravian service]." Unity officials had no intention of opening all their services to the "rabble" around them; as Ettwein expressed it, "we believe that the Church of Christ should have mysteries and don't approve of the now common Way that all the Pearls are thrown before the Swine & Dogs." Justices of the peace were a different matter, though. If the Moravians could win their trust and support they could rely on them to check the spread of inflammatory rumors among their constituents. Four years later Ettwein showed the same willingness to educate the right people when he visited Governor and Lady Tryon in New Bern. During the three days he spent with the first family, Ettwein did his best to answer their questions about Wachovia, its residents, and their religion. And before leaving, he begged the governor "that if he heard anything doubtful about us he would kindly let his secretary write and ask us . . . for while many give us more praise than we deserve, there are always those who speak evil without cause." To Ettwein and the rest of Wachovia's elders there was a time for secrecy and a time for candor, but both served the same end—to improve the Unity's image in the eyes of outsiders.[8]

The Brethren demonstrated a similar concern with perceptions when dealing with the legal and moral codes of the province in which they lived. As the preceding chapter emphasized, planners and residents of Wachovia recognized the need to understand the laws of North Carolina and, for the most part, to obey them "that the World should have nothing against us." Thus they honored the Anglican Sabbath while working on their own; they knew the Lord would understand, though their neighbors might not.[9] This same concern with what others might think showed clearly in the fall of 1765 when Wachovia's leaders tried to clean up the mess left by August Schubert's departure from the colony. Schubert's prolonged feud with his superiors in Bethabara not only polarized the Moravian community but spawned rumors among non-Moravians concerning the reason for expulsion, including one report that it was because his superiors had discovered "he was guilty of fornication with a non-Moravian woman." Through the summer and fall of 1765, Frederic Marschall, Wachovia's official but absent *Oeconomus,* and John Ettwein, his resident deputy in the colony, wrote back and forth trying to decide what to do about congregation members who had been barred from communion for supporting Schubert. In the course of this exchange Marschall reminded Ettwein that the affair was already too well-known and that "the more publicity the matter has gained, the more necessary it will become that before any of them is ever readmitted [to communion] the loyalty of the people must be won again, so that no day laborer [i.e., hired non-Moravian] in the place could say evil matters are winked at."[10]

On those occasions when the Brethren deliberately broke the law they were even more concerned about the response of outsiders and tried hard to maintain at least the appearance of obedience. This was certainly clear in the case of Dobbs Parish. Though Dobbs had no Anglican population, no Anglican church or chapel, a minister chosen and ordained by the Moravian Church and unlicensed by the Bishop of London, and a vestry made up of twelve Moravian laymen, it acted like an Anglican parish. Its minister was called the English minister—he preached often enough to fulfill his legal obligation, baptized, married, or buried those who needed his services, and kept parish records of his activities—and its vestry met from time to time to elect church wardens and to decide that no parish levy was necessary because the parish had spent no money. And through it all, the brothers and sisters understood perfectly that the performance was largely for the benefit of their neighbors. When, for example, Jacob Rogers arrived in Wachovia to assume his duties as Dobbs' first incumbent, he brought with him several pages of instructions from church leaders in Bethlehem. Among the provisions were two that clearly show the Moravians' appreciation of Rogers' public role:

> 15) It must not be forgotten that the Parish is for the eyes of all men, and care should be taken that no evil doer comes in to distress and annoy the people of the Lord.
> 16) For the same reason Br. Rogers must carry himself with the decorum of a Minister; and our Brethren and sisters in Wachovia must

be careful in their intercourse with him, especially in the presence of strangers,—for instance, they should not use the familiar *thou* in addressing him.[11]

Dobbs Parish was just one of several examples, though, and in each of the others Unity officials showed a similar concern for public opinion among Wachovia's neighbors and a determination to mask illegal actions behind an illusion of legality.

The Brethren were equally wary of exercising their rights under the laws of North Carolina. Nowhere is this more evident than in the infrequency with which they took debtors to court. The mercantile economy that emerged around Wachovia in the 1750s and 1760s ran on credit. Much of it was supplied by Moravian shopkeepers, and by the middle of the 1760s hundreds of outsiders owed them a total in excess of £1500. Given the Unity's weak financial condition, it could scarcely afford the losses incurred when debtors fled to avoid payment or simply refused to meet their obligations. But Bethabara's elders decided that the good will of their neighbors was worth even more. In November of 1766 Mattheus Schropp, the colony's *Vice-Oeconomus* and *Vorsteher*, told his superiors in Bethlehem that it would be a mistake to take legal action against defaulting strangers "for to deal with people according to the law is unseemly for us from one point of view, and from another would bring about a great opposition to us, considering that we have 600 debtors." In the end Schropp prevailed, and the *Oeconomy* wrote off hundreds of pounds in bad debts rather than risk angering its neighbors.[12]

Conversely, on at least one of the rare occasions that the Moravians did bring charges against an outsider they did so because other outsiders urged them to. In 1762 Bethabara's congregational diarist mentioned that Gottlieb Fockel had gone to Salisbury "to appear against the thief who stole our horses last fall, as the people who had the horses demanded that we prosecute them."[13]

The Brethren were just as careful in politics as they were in law; sometimes they exercised their rights and sometimes they refrained, but they always tried to imagine how others would see what they did. For example, the only election from which they definitely abstained was held in July of 1769. By that time the Regulators' anger was rising, and church leaders decided they could not risk crossing them by voting against their candidates. The elders justified their nonparticipation on the grounds that Wachovia's Moravian residents were not freeholders; the Unity owned by their land, and, thus, they could not vote legally. That had been the case since the colony's establishment, though, and it had never stopped them from voting before. Nor did it stop them after the suppression of the Regulators; just two months of Tryon's victory at Alamance the Brethren returned to the polls, even though the Unity still owned their land. Clearly, the real motive behind the Moravians' decision to sit out the election of 1769 was their fear of being caught up in what one of their diarists called "friction between the so-called Regulators and the others." The question of freehold status was simply a convenient excuse.[14]

Church members were also sensitive to outside opinion concerning the possibility of a Moravian in the colonial assembly. As detailed in the preceding chapter, Unity leaders discussed whether and how to secure a seat for Wachovia in the lower house throughout the colony's first fifteen years. By the end of that discussion both proponents and opponents of the idea had invoked non-Moravian opinion to support their cause. When, in 1767, members of the Unity Vorsteher Collegium debated the wisdom of requesting a corporate charter for Salem, and with it a seat in the North Carolina assembly, advocates of incorporation claimed that the Unity's reluctance to seek a charter seemed suspicious to the government of North Carolina and that the Brethren needed to participate fully in provincial politics in order to dispel "mistrust" of them. "Even if we only use our right [to send a representative] when we need it," argued one Collegium member, "and do not mix in party matters, we will not be open to the charge of exclusiveness, and its dangers." The Brethren resident in North Carolina had precisely the opposite view, but they too used public opinion to justify it. Just a month after the Unity Vorsteher Collegium considered the question of a Moravian assemblyman, Governor Tryon paid a visit to Bethabara and suggested that the Brethren really should have someone in the assembly. Jacob Lösch, however, downplayed the idea, explaining to Tryon "that we are afraid it might cause envy and ill-will against us" to have one.[15]

Moreover, when a Moravian finally did stand for election to the assembly he did so on the grounds that the neighbors demanded it. Late in June, 1771 the Bethabara diarist wrote that "yesterday and today many neighbors came and urgently begged Br. Bagge and Br. Marschall that they, or one of them, would run for office as Assemblyman, as many believed that they would be able to serve this land." The next day congregation members from all over Wachovia met to consider the request, and, as Frederic Marschall told his superiors, "the brothers and sisters were unanimous that we could not deprive the neighbors of their wish." Marschall, however, declined to run because he was not a freeholder; so Traugott Bagge became the first resident of Wachovia to stand for election to the provincial assembly. In spite of the fact that Brother Bagge lost, his running at all demonstrates again the Moravians' concern for the opinions of their neighbors.[16]

Even in their diaspora work the Brethren were influenced by their concern for the opinions of their neighbors. Moravians had not come to Carolina in search of converts. Zinzendorf, in fact, was distinctly opposed to Wachovia's becoming "a preaching place." Christians living near the colony had other ideas, though; they were so happy to have a minister handy, any minister, that they flocked into Bethabara to hear sermons preached there. When word of this reached Pennsylvania, officials there were not pleased. "That is not the *Jünger*'s inclination," they declared. But when the issue came up at a conference in the fall of 1755, Zinzendorf's intention gave way to conditions in North Carolina. Christian Seidel, who later became Wachovia's *Ordinarius*, pointed out that it would be hard to stop the people coming to Bethabara "because far and wide there is no word of God [in the backcountry]." His colleagues reluctantly agreed and instructed the colonists not to encourage such visits but not to prevent them either. "The neighbors can come and warm themselves by the fire of the congregation, but a congregation must not become a preaching place," they declared. Consequently, for the next four years Wachovia's leaders allowed non-Moravians to hear sermons but refused to accept converts and turned down the many requests they received for a Moravian minister to preach in neighboring settlements.[17]

Eventually those barriers began coming down too, and once again Moravian sensitivity to non-Moravian opinion was one factor contributing to the change. In June of 1759, Spangenberg arrived in Bethabara on an episcopal visit that lasted nearly a year. While there, authorized the establishment of Wachovia's first society, a step toward accepting converts, and dispatched the first Moravian minister to preach to a non-Moravian community in the region. The fact that Spangenberg, personally, was a more aggressive proselytizer than Zinzendorf during the 1750s was undoubtedly an important factor in his decision to launch a North Carolina diaspora. But Spangenberg also knew that Bethabara's neighbors wanted to hear God's word and felt that denying their request cast the Unity in a bad light. In an earlier letter to Cornelius van Laer he had discussed the possible construction of a missionary church in Wachovia in response to non-Moravian demands and concluded: "I hope we can bring the thing to pass soon, because it would give the whole country, and especially our government, a good impression . . . as it is not good for a country that religion be neglected." And in the years that followed, when Spangenberg succeeded Zinzendorf as the Unity's dominant figure, Moravian itinerants responded to their neighbors' calls and covered a steadily expanding circuit, a circuit that by 1772 extended sixty miles beyond Wachovia's borders.[18]

But the Moravians' greatest concern was with their image as businessmen. Both temporal and spiritual interests required the Brethren to be above reproach in the marketplace. Every year hundreds of outsiders came to Moravian shops to buy and sell, and every transaction involved the possibility that a customer would feel cheated. Early modern Americans and Europeans frequently resorted to violence against merchants suspected of exploitation, and Unity leaders knew that accusations of cheating could quickly bring a mob down on Bethabara. Even without violence, though, dissatisfied customers would threaten

Wachovia's success because the Unity depended so heavily on trade with outsiders for the money necessary to support and enlarge its colony. If those outsiders took their business elsewhere, Wachovia would quickly wither and leave the church even more deeply in debt than it had been when it started the colony. Just as important as these temporal concerns, however, were the spiritual. Accusations of sharp trading, even if unaccompanied by an angry mob or a sudden drop in revenues, would call into question the Moravians' commitment to their Christian duty. Spangenberg had explained in 1754 that by settling Wachovia and establishing plantations there "we shall not only, with God's blessing, be able to assist one another, but also to help all the Country round about us; [a] great part of which lays quite barren." Three years later he urged the brothers and sisters in Bethabara to remember, "in all your business doings be guided by the aim that the Lord may gain honor by it and your neighbors be served as much as yourselves." The Brethren could hardly interpret the grumbling of dissatisfied customers as a sign that they had served either their God or their neighbors. For a variety of reasons then it was essential to the Moravians that outsiders perceive them as honest traders.[19]

To enhance their image church leaders took great care in choosing the men and women who served in Bethabara's tavern, mill, and shops. These merchants and craftsmen were among the Unity's most important contact specialists and were highly visible symbols of the community they served. Visitors arriving in Bethabara or Salem might see most of the town's residents before they left, but in most cases the miller, tavernkeeper, or storekeeper was the only one with whom they had any real contact. In the minds of those visitors, recollections of a single member might become impressions of the entire Unitas Fratrum, a fact not lost on church leaders. Because of it they tried to select contact specialists whose behavior would reflect well on the Unity. In the spring of 1760, for example, a trio of Bethabara's elders wrote Bethlehem to complain about two of the *Oeconomy's* craftsmen. George Schmid, its blacksmith, "makes us little joy and honor with his profession," they wrote, while Thomas Hoffman, Bethabara's tanner, had given them "no end of trouble." "Therefore," they concluded, "if you could or would also think how better to provide for both those branches, it would be very agreeable to us, because they have many connections with the world and can contribute a great deal to our good or bad name in the region."[20]

Choosing carefully the right men and women to represent them, Moravian leaders also laid down "principles . . . for the conduct of our commerce and trades" in an effort to insure that the actions of those individuals reflected well on their community. Chief among these principles were those by which the Brethren set prices and profits; Moravian entrepreneurs had to satisfy God, their customers, and their competition. In general, church elders believed that the best way to please everyone was to operate according to the notion of a just price, one that reflected the intrinsic value of a product or service plus "a small profit by way of compensation." Thus they refused to increase the price at which they sold an item simply because rising demand would allow them to; in the midst of a poor harvest, for example, they continued to sell bread and flour at "their usual price." Nor would the Brethren pay more for an item just because the seller happened to be poor; "should one want to show kindness to someone because he is poor," said the storekeeper's instructions, "one is to pay him the just price for his goods, and no more, and then he [the storekeeper] is to have an interview with the *Vorsteher* to draw his attention to this individual so that help may be given him."[21]

But Moravian adherence to a just price was flexible. Officials in Bethabara regularly adjusted their prices to avoid upsetting other merchants in the area. Because many of their costs were lower than those of their competitors, the Brethren should have been able to charge less for products in their store than rivals did in theirs. Instead they set prices above a genuinely just level and did so deliberately to protect themselves from the anger of non-Moravian businesses. As Spangenberg explained in 1759: "to offer in Bethabara goods which we order from Philadelphia at prices below those charged in Wilmington cannot well be done and could make enemies among people engaged in business. The same holds good regarding the purchase price of items; one has to conform to some small extent to what is currently charged in the area, in cases where this applies." To carry out this policy, traders in Bethabara and Salem were "to learn what the prices are which they [other merchants in province] set for the purchase or sale of one item or another" and to offer or take "whatever is customary locally, but not the highest nor yet the lowest, but the median."[22]

The Brethren who operated Wachovia's shops were also instructed to avoid any appearance of cheating. When the Bethabara store opened, in 1759, Spangenberg told its keeper that he must never try to foist damaged merchandise on his customers. "Should anything become defective," he explained, "it must be sold to the people as such." And in 1757 the Helpers Conference decided that "because Mr. Shepherd always brings his own half-bushel for a measure out of mistrust of us, we must register with the Inspector of Measures at the next court." Such directives were, no doubt, partly motivated by the Moravians' concept of Christian behavior, but they also reflect a distinct sensitivity to the opinions of outsiders.[23]

This concern with the attitudes of their neighbors was also one of the reasons that Unity officials did not want the colonists extending credit to strangers. As early as 1756, Bishop Spangenberg wrote Jacob Lösch, the colony's *Vorsteher*, "I also want to ask you not to get involved in credit." "It cannot work," he warned. "And afterward, the last anger of people is as bad as the first. Rather send people away if they are too poor to pay. Or take what they have [in trade]. I mean corn, cattle, [illegible], flax, and so forth." Of course Lösch and his fellow pioneers had already gone against Spangenberg's advice, and just as the bishop had predicted they eventually found it impossible to collect on many of the debts due them because they worried that the aggressive measures necessary to force payments out of people would incite their "last anger."[24]

Identifying potential sources of conflict and describing what the Brethren did about them is the easy part. The hard part is determining if those steps were necessary or effective. There is little non-Moravian evidence addressing either question. Most of what has survived are second or thirdhand reports filtered through Moravian intermediaries, and while such evidence says a great deal about Moravian perceptions of the world, it says considerably less about whether or not those perceptions were accurate. Unfortunately, secondhand testimony is often all we have; so it will have to do.

Among the five sources of conflict identified earlier in this chapter, the French and Indian War seems to have been the least threatening. As late as 1763 the Brethren reported that a rumor was circulating of active Moravian support for the Indians against white settlers. Such reports were rare, though, and do not seem to have bothered the Brethren very much. Evidently, Bethabara's role in the defense of Rowan County during the war years served its inhabitants well. The Moravians offered shelter to hundreds of strangers for weeks at a time and took steps to defend the refugees as well as themselves if necessary. Presumably, the fact that so many outsiders saw the Brethren in this role reduced the likelihood that non-Moravians would take seriously the allegations of Moravian aid to hostile Indians.[25]

Religion, fortunately, led to much less trouble than anyone expected. It did cause people to talk but little came of it. For nearly a decade after their arrival, the Brethren wrote that their neighbors were either supportive or entirely indifferent to what they did theologically. They began to notice a change, however, early in the 1760s. In 1762 the Bethabara diarist claimed that "people near and far are beginning to watch us more closely than hitherto," and a number of comments from outside the Moravian community suggest that orthodox outsiders did not like all they saw. Henry Laurens wrote in 1762 that people in Charles Town "hold the same prejudices against your Religious tenets that Men in general who are not of your perswasion do in other parts of the world." A few years later Charles Woodmason, also in South Carolina, included the Moravians among the "Motley Sects" taking root on the southern frontier and wrote that "they have all things (save women) in Common." Closer to home, J. F. D. Smyth reported in 1772 that in North Carolina it was "much and universally credited" among non-Moravians that Unity elders "enjoy their women in common" and that one result of raising Moravian children in choirs was

that "all personal attachments and parental love and regard are
. . . diligently checked, discouraged, diminished, and , in great
degree, annihilated." While a year earlier Theodorus Drage, the
rector of adjacent St. Luke's Parish, wrote back to London that
the carving of Surry County out of Rowan was a plot hatched
by persons unnamed "that the Dissenters, separate Baptists,
and Moravians should be stronger or have an equal Interest
with the church of England with the view if possible to prevent
any [Anglican] clergymen from being received."[26]

Reverend Drage notwithstanding, however, dissenters in
and around Wachovia were not natural allies. Some of the
Quakers nearby, for instance, considered the Brethren as wrong
as any other non-Quaker faith. According to the Bethabara diarist one Friend attended the Moravians' Easter service in 1762
and declared it "fanciful and heathenish, since no man knew
the exact day on which Christ arose." As for the Presbyterians,
Frederic Marschall claimed in 1771 that a Presbyterian neighbor
"seemed a bit jealous" when the latter complained that "the
Brethren were the only ones to have a separate parish while
they, the Presbyterians, had none though they were more numerous in North Carolina." According to Marschall, the complaint "did not seem to be really seriously intended." It came,
however, in the midst of a dispute over whether Wachovia
would remain in Rowan County or become part of newly created Surry County, and the man who voiced it was a Surry
County commissioner; so it seems just as likely that the resentment was genuine and that the speaker was simply trying to
cover it in an effort to avoid antagonizing the Brethren until the
general assembly had decided in which county they belonged.[27]

Even with their admirers the Brethren had religious differences from time to time. Soon after the first settlers reached
Wachovia their neighbors began asking to share in the benefits
of Christianity. In particular they wanted to hear sermons and
have their children baptized, and requests for both soon came
into Bethabara from the region around it. In the years that followed the number of these inquiries rose and came to include
many from people seeking to form societies affiliated with the

Unity or to join the Unity itself. And although the Brethren acceded to some of the requests, especially after 1759, they never satisfied the demand.

None of these religious issues ever got out of hand, though. In spite of clearly resentful individuals like Theodorus Drage, the Anglican establishment in North Carolina was quite content to coexist with the Brethren. And although some Baptists closed their meetings to itinerant Moravian preachers in the early 1770s, the multitude of dissenters in colonial Rowan and Surry counties generally got along quite well.[28]

Economics turned out to be a much greater source of friction between Wachovia and its neighbors than religion was. There were occasional disputes over trade, such as Mr. Shepard's suspicion of the Moravians' half-bushel measure, but competition for land was the big problem. For more than a decade after they settled in Wachovia the Brethren had to deal with rival claimants to various parts of that tract. They had to contend even longer with outsiders asserting prior claims to other bits of land the Unity owned around Wachovia, as late as 1765 in the case of a tract on Town Fork Creek and 1771 in that of two tracts between Wachovia and the Yadkin. Outsiders also accused the Brethren of engrossing land. In addition to what it had in and adjacent to Wachovia, the Unity owned more than eight thousand acres at Mulberry Fields, on the upper reaches of the Yadkin. Throughout the 1760s a number of men squatting on this land approached officials in Bethabara about buying small parcels along the river. The church refused to sell bottomland, though, unless purchasers took the upland too, which the squatters refused. Some of the resentment this caused became clear in the mid-1770s, when the Moravians advertised their intention to sell the land at Mulberry Fields in one large block. According to Traugott Bagge, Wachovia's storekeeper at the time, one of the advertisements announcing this sale fell into the hands of some men who took it and "had their sport with it." They took it to "a place where there were three stumps," claimed Bagge; "these men fixed the advertisement to one of the stumps, and then in a drunken frolic said among themselves, let this stump tell that stump, and that stump tell yon stump, and yon stump tell that stump the contents of this Advertisement."[29]

But the most dangerous problems between the Moravian community and its neighbors came in politics, though it is hard to distinguish between political actions and the economic motives that often lay behind them. The most celebrated instance of this is undoubtedly the clash between Regulators and Brethren in late 1770 and early 1771. Unfortunately, there is no surviving testimony from the Regulators themselves as to their grievances against Wachovia. All we have are Moravian accounts of what prompted the disturbances, and the only specific issues they mention were economic in origin. In November of 1770 a party of Regulators threatened a member of the Friedberg society when he complained about their driving hogs across his land and into Wachovia without his permission or that of the Brethren. In March of 1771 another group of Regulators came to Bethabara seeking redress for an alleged land fraud perpetrated by Jacob Lösch. And a month later many of the same men accused Bethabara's miller, Jacob Kapp, of taking an illegal double toll from one of his customers. Presumably, the Regulators were also angry at the Brethren for dutifully paying their taxes and otherwise supporting what the demonstrators regarded as a corrupt government, but Moravian sources relate no specific complaints to that effect.[30]

A less well-known issue, the creation of new counties out of Rowan, resulted in political conflict that was less violent than with the Regulation but apparently just as bitter. Non-Moravian resentment first appeared in 1765 in a letter written by John Frohock, then representing Rowan County in the general assembly. Frohock included Moravians among those "Designing People who has no regard to the Community or how many poor people Suffer as their own ends be accomplished" through the partition of the county. In his anger, though, Frohock failed to explain just what he thought the Moravians' "Private & Sinister ends" were in seeking to divide Rowan, and as the alleged plot went no further that year nothing more is known about his fears. Six years later, when the idea of dividing Rowan finally bore fruit, the central question was clear: would the Moravian settlements, and the taxpayers in them, stay part of the old county or become part of the new?[31]

There is no evidence whatsoever that Moravian officials influenced the initial decision to split Rowan into two counties, and where their community ended up was of secondary importance to the Brethren. All they really cared about was keeping their entire tract in one county or the other and preserving its status as a separate parish. When Surry County was laid out, in 1771, the Surry-Rowan line cut Wachovia in half, and though most of its residents were in the Surry half, only the Rowan portion retained the privileges of Dobbs Parish. To rectify this, Moravian leaders immediately began lobbying the provincial government to adjust the boundary and restore their community's physical and legal integrity. This, in turn, worried Surry County officials. It mattered a great deal to them where Wachovia lay. If the assembly reassigned Surry's Moravians to Rowan it would deprive the new county of what its leaders regarded as a significant portion of its population and, as the Bethabara diarist reported, "leave Surry County too weak." The issue remained in dispute for almost two years, threatening relations between the Brethren and officials of both counties involved. Officially, it came to an end in 1773, when an act of the legislature enlarged Surry County to include all of Wachovia and restored Dobbs Parish to its former condition. But according to Moravian officials the decision left a lingering resentment toward them among some Rowan officials.[32]

There were, then, a number of disputes between the Brethren and their neighbors in colonial North Carolina, and at least one, the Regulator Movement, reached the point of bringing armed and angry men to Bethabara. But such incidents were few in number and never actually turned violent. And given what other historians have said about the incidence of mobs serving an extralegal function in the redress of popular grievances, the Moravians' lot was no worse than that of many creditors and large landowners in early America and better than some.[33] These confrontations loom large in the edited *Records of*

the Moravians in North Carolina. Seen in the full context of the
unexpurgated source, though, they are brief episodes punctuat-
ing an essentially peaceful relationship between the Moravian
community in Wachovia and the non-Moravian population
around it.

Conclusion

The southern backcountry was no more a melting pot than most other parts of early America were. Whether it was the Dutch in New York, the Quakers in Pennsylvania, or the Moravians in North Carolina, the colonial frontier was not a place in which cultural, linguistic, and confessional differences quickly disappeared into a new, homogeneous, American population. Rather, it was a region in which distinctive, suspicious, and sometimes hostile local communities eyed one another, learned to tolerate one another, and gradually accepted intercourse with one another. It was, in the words of John Roche, "an open society dotted with closed enclaves."[1]

Each of these enclaves had discernable boundaries, boundaries visible to its own residents even if modern historians sometimes have trouble finding them. The existence of such boundaries and of mechanisms for reaffirming them are not unique to any time or place in human history but seem to fill some deeply felt need by the members of almost any society to distinguish between us and them. Historians, anthropologists, and sociologists have found them among ancient Greeks, in remote peoples of southeast Asia, central Africa, and arctic Europe, and between gangs of teenage blacks, whites, and hispanics in modern American cities. Whenever and wherever human beings have created societies they have also tried to define who belonged to them and who did not. But the boundaries between groups are neither impenetrable nor inflexible. They are, from the start, semipermeable barriers through which or across which certain forms of peaceful contact with other groups invariably take place. Leaving aside warfare, cross-boundary contact generally begins with those forms that seem beneficial to both sides and least likely to effect a change in either group's identity. From there, the process may gradually move to increasingly more intimate forms of contact, and as that happens old boundaries frequently fade and are replaced by new ones separating a new us from them.[2]

The history of Wachovia's Moravian community between 1753 and 1772 shows clearly the start of this process on the southern frontier. The Brethren regarded themselves as distinct from, and usually superior to, most of their neighbors, and many of the latter felt the same way about them. No one, therefore, had any intention of removing all the barriers between themselves and their neighbors, yet some forms of cross-boundary contact began almost at once. Trade came almost immediately after settlement. It was useful and at times essential to all the different peoples of Rowan County that they buy from and sell to one another. Moreover, trade involved only limited contact with outsiders; it did not take long to negotiate an exchange, and it could often be done through contact specialists. Political relations also came early in the region's history. Here too contact promised immediate and tangible benefits to all parties. Some might benefit more than others, but all were better off participating than they would be if they refused. And here too it was possible to conduct most of the cross-boundary contact through specialists on the county court or in other organs of government without involving the rest of the community.

Closer forms of contact involving other members of the Moravian community came more slowly, if at all, during these first nineteen years. With the start of the French and Indian War, outsiders were permitted to stay as long-term visitors, and beginning in 1759, selected non-Moravians were allowed to settle in some parts of the community in the expectation that they would probably become Moravians before long. There was, however, little social intercourse between Moravians and non-Moravians before 1772. The Brethren sometimes referred to a particular outsider as "our friend" and entertained that individual if he or she came to Wachovia, but such relationships seem

to have been largely utilitarian. Only higher congregation officials made reciprocal visits, and there is little evidence that such
calls were ever purely social. And marriage outside the Moravian community remained absolutely forbidden to any member
regardless of rank or any temporal benefit that such an alliance
might bring.

The experience of Wachovia's Moravian community does
more, however, than demonstrate the presence of boundaries
and contact across them on the colonial southern frontier. It also
suggests how the frontier environment may have affected
boundary maintenance and the growth of pluralism in America.
First, it suggests that the supply of land on the frontier was an
important factor in the ease or difficulty with which different
groups accepted one another. An abundance of land not only
removed a major source of economic conflict between different
groups but meant they could separate themselves physically
and conduct their earliest relations with one another by means
of contact specialists crossing the no-man's land between them.
Then, as the comings and goings of these specialists led to increased understanding and decreased suspicion, it was possible
for the buffers between communities to shrink and bring them
into peaceful juxtaposition.[3]

William TeBrake has recently suggested this may have happened on the frontiers of Carolingian Europe,[4] and it certainly
seems to have happened on the frontier of colonial North Carolina. Different groups settled there in discrete enclaves distinguished by language, religion, and culture and separated from
one another by miles of undeveloped woodland. These communities were close enough to one another to trade regularly
and cooperate in the construction of roads and the administration of justice, but they were far enough apart to impede cross-
boundary socializing and marriage. Gradually, as communities
in the backcountry grew both larger and more familiar with one
another, the woodland barriers between them shrank, and the
people on either side grew closer without feeling unduly threatened. Then they could begin crossing national and denomina-
tional lines to marry, and the babel of foreign tongues could
begin fading into English. If, however, this coming together oc-

curred too rapidly because the supply of land was inadequate to keep still unfamiliar groups apart, the result could be less harmonious. This may explain why English settlers in rural Pennsylvania, for example, seem to have lived peacefully with their German neighbors at precisely the same time that Benjamin Franklin, living in the closer quarters of Philadelphia, was asking "why should the Palatine boors be suffered to swarm into our settlements, and, by herding together, establish their language and manners, to the exclusion of ours?"[5]

The colonial southern frontier may also have promoted peaceful cross-boundary contact between various Euro-American groups by presenting a greater threat to them collectively than they did to one another. The most dramatic threat, of course, came from the Cherokees and other Indians living to the west. Although the Europeans did concede that individual Indians might sometimes be admirable men or women, the stereotype among whites on the southern frontier was, in one Moravians' words, of "murdering Indians." Fear of these "savages" exerted a powerful influence on settlers in early America. According to Michael Zuckerman, it was crucial not only to the fabrication of their individual identity—individual colonists defining their civility by comparing it to the savagery around them—but also to the growth of associations among individuals, and it clearly drove Europeans elsewhere in America to associate, even if only temporarily, with people from different religious and ethnic groups. Rival French and English planters on the island of St. Christopher, for example, had joined forces to surprise and slaughter the Carib Indians in 1624 and then had gone back to fighting one another, when the Carib were out of the way. In North Carolina, much the same thing happened during the French and Indian War. The Moravians, concerned they might not have enough men to defend both Bethabara and Bethania, admitted non-Moravians to the latter when they established it in 1759, and by the time the war ended the experiment had worked well enough to convince the Brethren to continue it.[6]

But Indians were not the only danger prompting Europeans to cooperate on the colonial southern frontier. The forest itself was also a threat. In this age of shrinking resources and environmental awareness it is easy to forget that immigrants living in the shadow of the American wilderness often considered it a monster to be tamed rather than a treasure to be preserved. That fear had manifested itself since William Bradford described the "hideous and desolate wilderness" around Plymouth early in the seventeenth century. A century later, Moravian officials in Bethlehem wrote in 1753 that the journey to Wachovia would take the Brethren through five hundred miles teeming with "bears, wolves, panthers, and other beasts" and described Wachovia itself as a wilderness. After Charles Latrobe toured the Illinois frontier during the early 1830s he wrote, "a life in the woods teaches many lessons, and this among the rest, that you must both give assistance to your neighbors and receive it in return without either gruding or pouting," and the Moravians had discovered the same thing on the Carolina frontier. They had neither given nor received as much help as some of their contemporaries, perhaps—declining, for example, to attend a house-raising on the grounds that "more time is spent drinking brandy than in working." But they did establish and employ a number of other reciprocal relations with their neighbors almost from the day of their arrival.[7]

The process that began in 1753 continued long after 1772. Over the next eighty-five years the Moravians remained a distinctive element in North Carolina society while gradually permitting more and more contact between individual members and the world around them. Until well into the nineteenth century the Moravian Church continued to think of Wachovia as a refuge in which God's people could live their lives and raise their children in an environment free of ungodly influences; so the boundary faded slowly. In business, for example, the church wanted its members to make money in the marketplace but not to act or think like the other traders there. When the *Oeconomy* ended the elders tried to do this through yearlong leases negotiated with nominally independent craftsmen. Under this new regime most economic activities in the Moravian community were operated by individual Brethren who did business with anyone they chose, paid their own expenses, and kept their own profits. It was hardly free enterprise; the church tried to keep out what its leaders considered unbrotherly competition and unseemly riches by refusing to allow in Wachovia more than one master in any particular craft and by regulating the prices they could charge for their goods and services. The effort proved almost impossible, however, because of the elders' reluctance to cancel the leases of those who violated their commands. In 1856 they finally gave up and ended the lease system, and after that there was little to distinguish Moravian businessmen from their neighbors.[8]

In government and politics, too, cross-boundary contact continued after 1772 and came to involve individual Brethren more directly. Members of the Moravian community continued to vote in provincial and then state elections, except for a three-year hiatus during the American Revolution when politics again seemed too dangerous for them, and they continued to hold posts in county government. In addition they began in 1778 to participate more fully at the state level. In that year they sent the first Moravian to North Carolina's general assembly and continued sending men to the legislature quite frequently in the years that followed. Moreover, the Brethren gave every indication of being quite at home in politics. During the eighteenth century the community participated enthusiastically in loosely aligned interest groups, and as party politics took root and flourished in North Carolina early in the next century, Brethren too lined up behind state and national organizations. Perhaps the most visible symbol, however, of the Moravians' complete entry into civic affairs in North Carolina was their role in the military. During the Revolution they declined either to serve in the armed forces or to provide substitutes for Brethren who were drafted, preferring to pay fines for their refusal. By the end of the eighteenth century they had begun to hire and equip substitutes when necessary, and in 1831, when the assembly ended their exemption from militia service, Moravian men flocked to join the county regiment.[9]

The years after 1772 also saw the gradual elimination of church restrictions on settlement in Wachovia by non-Moravians. This took time, however, and the elders continued to control immigration into some parts of the tract, such as the *gemein Ort*, until the 1850s. They did this through their continuing control of the land. The church still owned the land on which Salem was built and let it on annual leases only. With that and their use of restrictive covenants when selling land in Bethabara, Bethania, and their immediate environs, Unity officials were often able to keep out or put out those who seemed likely to threaten the spiritual values they hoped to preserve. It remained possible for approved outsiders to join the Brethren— indeed under Spangenberg and his successors the church established societies and accepted converts more willingly than it had in Wachovia's early years—but all of these individuals were screened by the elders. Not until lease system came to an end did the church relinquish its control over migration into Wachovia.

By the middle of the nineteenth century, even marriage to an outsider, the most intimate form of cross-boundary contact, was permissible. The precise time of this change is unclear but it seems to have come quietly between 1820 and 1856. Until 1818 proposed marriages still required the approval of both the Lot and the elders, and marriage outside the faith was forbidden. There were instances in which use of the Lot was waived, just as there had been before 1772, and there were a growing number of brothers and sisters who tried to marry in secret, but the norm remained divine and ministerial consent and a union in the faith, and those who refused to obey the rules could still be expelled. In 1818 a Unity Synod finally ended the Lot's role in family formation, though it clearly affirmed the requirement that congregation officials give their consent and implied that members of the church still had to choose mates from within its ranks. During the next twenty years, though, both rules seem to have been quietly abandoned.[10]

By the eve of the Civil War much of Wachovia's distinctiveness had disappeared. The Moravian Church was a voluntary organization like most other churches in America. Salem was a busy market town almost indistinguishable from its non-Moravian neighbor Winston. On the streets one heard English with a southern accent, and German was seldom heard except in the homes of older brothers and sisters. And when north and south went to war in 1861, dozens of young men marched out of Salem to fight for the Confederacy, while four hundred miles to the north their Brethren in Bethlehem donned blue and marched out to meet them.

Notes

Introduction

1. Richard J. Hooker, ed., *The Carolina Backcountry on the Eve of the Revolution: The Journal and Other Writings of Charles Woodmason, Anglican Itinerant* (Chapel Hill: Univ. of North Carolina Press, 1953), 6–7. The most recent discussion of the scope and nature of migration to the late colonial southern frontier is in Bernard Bailyn, *Voyagers to the West: A Passage in the Peopling of America on the Eve of the Revolution* (New York: Knopf, 1986), especially 7–28, 430–572.

2. A. Roger Ekirch, *"Poor Carolina": Politics and Society in Colonial North Carolina, 1726–1776* (Chapel Hill: Univ. of North Carolina Press, 1981); James P. Whittenburg, "Planters, Merchants, and Lawyers: Social Change and the Origins of the North Carolina Regulation," *William and Mary Quarterly*, 3rd ser., 34 (1977): 215–38, and "Colonial North Carolina's 'Burnt-over District': The Pattern of Backcountry Settlement," paper presented to the Southern Historical Association, 1986; Marvin L. Michael Kay, "The North Carolina Regulation, 1766–1776," in Alfred F. Young, ed., *The American Revolution: Explorations in the History of American Radicalism* (DeKalb: Northern Illinois Univ. Press, 1976), 71–123; Rachel N. Klein, "Ordering the Backcountry: The South Carolina Regulation," *William and Mary Quarterly*, 3rd ser., 38 (1981): 661–80; Rhys Isaac, "Evangelical Revolt: The Nature of the Baptists' Challenge to the Traditional Order in Virginia, 1765 to 1775," *William and Mary Quarterly*, 3rd ser., 31 (1974): 345–68; Ronald Hoffman, Thad W. Tate, and Peter J. Albert, eds., *An Uncivil War: The Southern Backcountry during the American Revolution* (Charlottesville: Univ. Press of Virginia, 1985). Albert H. Tillson, Jr., "The Localist Roots of Backcountry Loyalism: An Examination of Popular Political Culture in Virginia's New River Valley," *Journal of Southern History* 54 (1988): 387–404.

3. Richard Beeman, *The Evolution of the Southern Backcountry: A Case Study of Lunenburg County, Virginia, 1746–1832* (Philadelphia: Univ. of Pennsylvania Press, 1984); H. Roy Merrens, *Colonial North Carolina in the Eighteenth Century* (Chapel Hill: Univ. of North Carolina Press, 1964); Robert D. Mitchell, *Commercialism and Frontier: Perspectives on the Early Shenandoah Valley* (Charlottesville: Univ. Press of Virginia, 1977).

4. Carl Bridenbaugh, *Myths and Realities* (Baton Rouge: Louisiana State Univ. Press, 1952; New York: Atheneum, 1963).

5. Michael Zuckerman, ed., *Friends and Neighbors: Group Life in America's First Plural Society* (Philadelphia: Temple Univ. Press, 1982), 22.

6. Fredrik Barth, ed., *Ethnic Groups and Boundaries* (Boston: Little, Brown, 1969), 16.

7. Mitchell, *Commercialism and Frontier*; Beeman, *Evolution of the Southern Backcountry.*

8. A tiny portion of the material in one Moravian archives has been translated, edited, and published over the years as Adelaide Fries, Kenneth G. Hamilton, Douglas L. Rights, and Minnie J. Smith, eds., *Records of the Moravians in North Carolina*, 11 vols. to date (Raleigh: North Carolina Historical Commission, 1922–69). Those volumes, however, only hint at the vast quantity of material contained in church archives in Winston-Salem, North Carolina, and Bethlehem, Pennsylvania, and in the manuscript division of the Library of Congress.

9. Rosabeth Moss Kanter, *Commitment and Community* (Cambridge: Harvard Univ. Press, 1972).

10. Merrens, *Colonial North Carolina*, 62.

11. Clarence S. Brigham, *History and Bibliography of American Newspapers, 1690–1820*, 2 vols. (Worcester, Mass.: American Antiquarian Society, 1947), 2: 758–82.

12. Jerry L. Surratt, in his work, *Gottlieb Schober of Salem: Discipleship and Ecumenical Vision in an Early Moravian Town* (Macon, Ga.: Mercer Univ. Press, 1983), has begun the process of explaining Salem's decline.

CHAPTER 1

The Road to Carolina

1. Fries et al., *Records*, 1: 73–74; Jonas Paulus Weissens Vorschlag an die Strassburger Brüder wegen North Carolina, Dec. 21, 1753, Library of Congress, Manuscript Division, Moravian Church Records (hereinafter cited as LC-MC), R.14.Ba.Nr.2b: 89–93. The collection now identified as Moravian Church Records in the Library of Congress was, until recently, known as European Photostats, Germany, Herrnhut,

Archiv der Brüder Unitat, and I identified it as such in my earlier publications. The letters and numbers used within the collection to identify specific boxes and bundles, however, have not changed.

2. Fries et al., *Records*, 1: 73.

3. Adelaide L. Fries, *Customs and Practices of the Moravian Church*, 3rd ed. (Winston-Salem, N.C.: Board of Christian Education and Evangelism, 1973), 7–20; Gillian L. Gollin, *Moravians in Two Worlds* (New York: Columbia Univ. Press, 1967), 4–5; Jacob John Sessler, *Communal Pietism Among Early American Moravians* (New York: Henry Holt, 1933; New York: AMS Press, 1971), 1–6; Joseph M. Levering, *A History of Bethlehem, Pennsylvania, 1741–1892* (Bethlehem: Times Pub., 1903), 9–15; Amedeo Molnar, "Die Böhmische Brüderunität. Abriss Ihrer Geschichte," in Mari P. van Buijtenen, Cornelis Dekker, and Huib Leeuwenberg, eds., *Unitas Fratrum* (Utrecht: Rijksarchief in Utrecht, 1975), 15–34; Adolf Vacovsky, "History of the 'hidden seed' (1620–1722)," in van Buijtenen, Dekker, and Leeuwenberg, *Unitas Fratrum*, 35–54.

4. Dale Brown, *Understanding Pietism* (Grand Rapids, Mich.: William B. Eerdmans Pub., 1978), 21–2; Peter C. Erb, ed., *Pietists: Selected Writings*, Classics of Western Spirituality (New York: Paulist Press, 1983), 1–11; Mary Fulbrook, *Piety and Politics: Religion and the Rise of Absolutism in England, Württemberg and Prussia* (Cambridge: Cambridge Univ. Press, 1983), 19–44.

5. J. Taylor Hamilton and Kenneth G. Hamilton, *History of the Moravian Church* (Winston-Salem, N.C.: Interprovincial Board of Christian Education, Moravian Church in America, 1967), 13–22; Werner Kessler, "Die Evangelische Brüdergemeine im Deutschen Raum von der Entstehung Herrnhuts an bis heute," in van Buijtenen, Dekker, and Leeuwenberg, *Unitas Fratrum*, 55–92.

6. Gollin, *Moravians*, 5; Hamilton and Hamilton, *History*, 23–33; Fries, *Customs*, 60–64; F. Ernest Stoeffler, *German Pietism During the Eighteenth Century* (Leiden: E. J. Brill, 1973), 133–34.

7. Hamilton and Hamilton, *History*, 154; Spener's *Pia Desideria*, in Erb, *Pietists*, 48; Zinzendorf's *Der Deutsche Socrates*, in Erb, *Pietists*, 291; and Zinzendorf's *Sixteen Discourses on the Redemption of Man by the Death of Christ Preached at Berlin* (London: 1740), 45–46. See also, Stoeffler, *German Pietism*, 142–45; and David S. Lovejoy, *Religious Enthusiasm in the New World* (Cambridge: Harvard Univ. Press, 1985), 162–64.

8. Sessler, *Communal Pietism*, 6–9; Hamilton and Hamilton, *History*, 60–67; John R. Weinlick, "Colonial Moravians, Their Status Among the Churches," *Pennsylvania History* 26 (1959): 213–25. See also, Lovejoy, *Religious Enthusiasm*, 162–64.

9. The following discussion of Moravian beliefs and practices is based largely on: Fries, *Customs;* Hamilton and Hamilton, *History,* 154–59; Sessler, *Communal Pietism;* Stoeffler, *German Pietism,* 131–67; Zinzendorf, *Sixteen Discourses;* Zinzendorf, *Nine Public Lectures on Important Subjects in Religion Preached in Fetter Lane Chapel in London in the Year 1746,* trans. and ed. George W. Forell (Iowa City: Univ. of Iowa Press, 1973); David A. Schattschneider, "The Missionary Theologies of Zinzendorf and Spangenberg," *Transactions of the Moravian Historical Society* 22 (1975): 213–33.

10. Stoeffler, *German Pietism,* 146; Hamilton and Hamilton, *History,* 72–75.

11. Stoeffler, *German Pietism,* 156; Sessler, *Communal Pietism,* 24.

12. Hamilton and Hamilton, *History,* 71.

13. Erb, *Pietists,* 32–33.

14. Georg Neisser, *A History of the Beginnings of Moravian Work in America,* trans. William N. Schwarze and Samuel H. Gapp (Bethlehem, Pa.: Moravian Archives, 1955), 144–45; Sessler, *Communal Pietism,* 93–105; Gollin, *Moravians,* 67–89.

15. "Rev. John Wesley's Journal" in *The Works of the Rev. John Wesley,* 10 vols. (New York: J. and J. Harper, 1826–27), 1: 224; Sessler, *Communal Pietism,* 99, 106–37.

16. Sessler, *Communal Pietism,* 108–11; Walter Blankenburg, "Die Musik der Brüdergemeine in Europa," in van Buijtenen, Dekker, and Leeuwenberg *Unitas Fratrum,* 351–86, especially 360–67.

17. Hamilton and Hamilton, *History,* 39, 179; Jerry L. Surratt, "The Role of Dissent in Community Evolution among Moravians in Salem, 1772–1860," *North Carolina Historical Review* 52 (1975): 235–55; Gollin, *Moravians,* 50–63.

18. Zinzendorf, *Nine Lectures,* 76; Hamilton and Hamilton, *History,* 34–145; van Buijtenen, Dekker, and Leeuwenberg, *Unitas Fratrum;* Christopher Edwin Hendricks, "The Planning and Development of Two Moravian Congregation Towns: Salem, North Carolina and Gracehill, Northern Ireland," (M.A. thesis, The College of William and Mary in Virginia, 1987), 13–14.

19. Schattschneider, "Missionary Theologies"; Stoeffler, *German Pietism,* 156–57, 162–65; John R. Weinlick, *Count Zinzendorf* (Nashville, Tenn.: Abingdon Press, 1956), 213–14; Clifford W. Towlson, *Moravian and Methodist* (London: Epworth Press, 1957), 118–73.

20. Sessler, *Communal Pietism,* 156–81.

21. Towlson, *Moravian and Methodist,* 27–38; Weinlick, *Zinzendorf,* 192, 213–14; Stoeffler, *German Pietism,* 162–64; Sessler, *Communal Pie-*

tism, 178–79; J. T. Hamilton, "The Recognition of the Unitas Fratrum as an Old Episcopal Church by the Parliament of Great Britain in 1749," *Transactions of the Moravian Historical Society*, Special Series, 2 (1925), part 2; Lovejoy, *Religious Enthusiasm*, 206–14; Alan Heimert and Perry Miller, eds., *The Great Awakening* (Indianapolis: Bobbs-Merrill, 1967), xxx–lii; Hamilton and Hamilton, *History*, 76-81, 121–22.

22. Hamilton, "Recognition"; Hamilton and Hamilton, *History*, 140; Historischer Bericht vom Anfang und Fortganze der Brüder Etablissements in der Wachau, 1752–1772 (hereinafter cited as Historischer Bericht), LC-MC, R.14.Ba.Nr.2a: 19–42; William S. Powell, *The Carolina Charter of 1663* (Raleigh: State Dept. of Archives and History, 1954), 65–67; E. Merton Coulter, "The Granville District," *James Sprunt Historical Publications* 13 (1913), 1: 33–56.

23. Hamilton and Hamilton, *History*, 100–6; Sessler, *Communal Pietism*, 177; Kessler, "Evangelische Brüdergemeine," 63–65.

24. Spangenberg to White, The intended State of the Brethrens Settlement in Wachovia in North Carolina, Jan. 17, 1754, LC-MC, R.14.Ba.Nr.2b: 117; Spangenberg to van Laer, Jan. 22, 1754, LC-MC, R.14.Ba.Nr.2b: 124–27.

25. The notion that Wachovia was established, in part, because of a missionary impulse among Moravian leaders seems to date from the late eighteenth century, when August Spangenberg led the Unity's emergence as a separate church. This process evidently involved a certain degree of rewriting Moravian history, including the church's motive for settling where it did in North Carolina. For example, in 1794 someone, probably Frederic W. Marschall, produced "An Account of the Rise and Progress of the United Brethren's Settlement in North Carolina" that is now in the Archives of the Moravian Church in America-Southern Province, in Winston-Salem, North Carolina (hereinafter cited as MA-SP). The archives' catalogue describes this work as a translation of the 1772 Historischer Bericht cited in note 22 above, but several parts of the Marschall version are entirely different from the earlier document. Some of the most marked changes are in the explanation of why the Unity accepted Granville's offer of land in Carolina. The 1772 account says that it was because Granville "had already proved to be a friend of our people on several occasions" and that the Unity intended "that it should become an entire land in which people who belonged to the Brethren lived." The 1794 version, on the other hand, includes neither of those statements and claims that the church accepted the land "in hopes to come nigh the Indian nations, to preach the Gospel to them"—a motive never mentioned in 1772.

26. Schattschneider, "Missionary Theologies."

27. Gollin, *Moravians*, 45, 236.

28. Conferenz über den Wachauischen Plan gehalten in Bethl[ehem], Sept. 22, 1755, LC-MC, R.14.Ba.Nr.2b: 596–601 and Archives of the Moravian Church in America-Northern Province, Bethlehem, Pa. (hereinafter cited as MA-NP), Wachovia II, folder 2, item 2–5 (quote from MA-NP copy). See also, Historischer Bericht, LC-MC, R.14.Ba.Nr.2a: 19–42; Wegen Carolina. Den Jünger an Spangenberg, n. d., LC-MC, R.14.Ba.Nr.2b: 55–56; Fragen wegen Nord Carolina von J. P. W. [J. P. Weiss] an den Ord. Frr. [Zinzendorf], April 1755, MA–NP, Wachovia II, folder 2, item 1–23.

29. Wegen Carolina. Den Jünger an Spangenberg, n.d., LC-MC, R.14.Ba.Nr.2b: 55–56.

30. Merrens, *Colonial North Carolina*, 53–81; James T. Lemon, *The Best Poor Man's Country: A Geographical Study of Early Southeastern Pennsylvania* (Baltimore: Johns Hopkins Univ. Press, 1972; New York: Norton, 1976), 42–70; Mitchell, *Commercialism and Frontier*, 16–58; Robert W. Ramsey, *Carolina Cradle: Settlement of the Northwest Carolina Frontier, 1747–1762* (Chapel Hill: Univ. of North Carolina Press, 1964), 10–62.

31. Ben J. Wattenberg, ed., *The Statistical History of the United States from Colonial Times to the Present* (New York: Basic Books, 1976), Series Z 15; Merrens, *Colonial North Carolina*, 32–49.

32. Granville to Corbin and Innes, May 14, 1750, LC-MC, R.14.Ba.Nr.1: 3–4; Preliminary Proposals to a Grant of land in North Carolina from the Earl of Granville to ye Present Lord Advocate of the Unitas Fratrum, [1750], LC-MC, R.14.Ba.Nr.1: 12–14; Hutton to Spangenberg, n. d., LC-MC, R.14.Ba.Nr.2b: 11–12; Indorsement on the Interim Instrument in my Ld Granville's Hand, n. d., MA-NP, Wachovia II, folder 1, item 4–8; Levin T. Reichel, *The Moravians in North Carolina* (Philadelphia: Lippincott, 1857), 15.

33. Hamilton and Hamilton, *History*, 82–85; Schattschneider, "Missionary Theologies"; Neisser, *History*, 68–69.

34. Copies of Spangenberg's diary and letters about this trip are in both LC-MC and in MA-SP; they can also be found in an edited translation in Fries et al., *Records*, 1: 30–62.

35. "Der Nord Carolina Land und Colonie Etablissement," Fries et al., *Records*, 1: 65–67; Fries et al., *Records*, 1: 62n.

36. David L. Corbitt, *The Formation of North Carolina Counties, 1663–1943* (Raleigh: State Dept. of Archives and History, 1950), 185; *Handbook of North Carolina.* (Raleigh: State Board of Agriculture, 1893), 135; Spangenberg's Report to Zinzendorf, Fries et al., *Records*, 1: 59–60; Wachau

or Dobbs Parish, Fries et al., *Records*, 2: 557–85; Ohnmassgebliches Project zur besezung des Districts in North Carolina, Sept. 12, 1753, MA-NP, Wachovia II, folder 1, item 2–36; Spangenberg to White, The intended State of the Brethrens Settlement in Wachovia in North Carolina, Jan. 17, 1754, LC-MC, R.14.Ba.Nr.2b: 117.

37. North Carolina. A Table of the Number of Taxables in this Province from the Year 1748 . . . to the Year 1770, in William K. Boyd, ed., *Some Eighteenth Century Tracts Concerning North Carolina* (Raleigh: North Carolina Historical Commission, 1927; Spartanburg, S.C.: The Reprint Co., 1973), 416 (multiplier of 3.5 used to convert taxables to residents on the basis of Merrens, *Colonial North Carolina*, 194–97); Adelaide L. Fries, Stuart Thurman Wright, and J. Edwin Hendricks, *Forsyth: The History of a County on the March*, revised edition (Chapel Hill: Univ. of North Carolina Press, 1976), 4–5, 9, 24–28; Ramsey, *Carolina Cradle*, 30–37; Bethabara diary, Fries, et al., *Records*, 1: 78–83; [map of] Wachovia or Dobbs Parish in Rowan County North Carolina, Oct. 15, 1767, copy (neg. S 976) in photograph collection of Old Salem Inc., Winston-Salem, N.C. of original in Archiv der Brüder Unitat, Herrnhut, GDR; [undated map of Wachovia], LC-MC, R.14.Ba.Nr.2b: 233–34; Friis to Spangenberg, April 30, 1755, LC-MC, R.14.Ba.Nr.2b: 475–81.

38. Catherine Phillips, *Memoirs of the Life of Catherine Phillips* (Philadelphia: Budd & Bartram, 1798), 84.

39. Fries, Wright, and Hendricks, *Forsyth*, 4–5, 9; Jethro Rumple, *A History of Rowan County, North Carolina* (Salisbury, N.C.: J. J. Bruner, 1881; Baltimore: Baltimore Regional Pub. Co., 1974), 38–39; Douglas L. Rights, "The Trading Path to the Indians," *North Carolina Historical Review* 8 (1931): 403–26; Spangenberg diary, Fries, et al., *Records*, 1: 30–62; Ekirch, "*Poor Carolina*," especially 174; James S. Brawley, *Rowan County: A Brief History* (Raleigh: North Carolina Dept. of Cultural Resources, 1974), 3, 144; Merrens, *Colonial North Carolina*, 54–55, 194–98; Ramsey, *Carolina Cradle*, 46, 135–36, 186–87, 193; Seth B. Hinshaw, *The North Carolina Quaker Experience* (Davidson, N.C.: Briar Patch Press, 1983), 23–24; Phillips, *Memoirs*, 75–85.

40. Ekirch, "*Poor Carolina*," 130–31; Höger to Weiss, Dec. 26, 1754, LC-MC, R.14.Ba.Nr.2b: 375–78; Spangenberg diary, Fries et al., *Records*, 1: 30–62; Lösch to Lawatsch, April 24, 1754, LC-MC, R.14.Ba.Nr.2b: 204–205; Nathanael [Seidel] to Johannes [von Watteville], March 19, 1754, LC-MC, R.14.Ba.Nr.2b: 175–78.

41. Entwurf zu dem Settlement der Brüder in North Carolina, [Oct. 1753], LC-MC, R.14.Ba.Nr.2a: 7–14; Daniel B. Thorp, "The City That Never Was: Count von Zinzendorf's Original Plan for Salem," *North*

Carolina Historical Review 61 (1984): 36–58; Wegen Carolina. Den Jünger an Spangenberg, n.d., LC-MC, R.14.Ba.Nr.2b: 55–56; Nathanael [Seidel] to Johannes [von Watteville], March 19, 1754, LC-MC, R.14.Ba.Nr.2b: 175–78; Spangenberg, Weiss, and Hutton to Kosenbaum, Jan. 9, 1754, LC-MC, R.14.Ba.Nr.2b: 109–12; Copy der Instructions vor die Directores des North Carolinischen Settlements, Dec. 18, 1753, LC-MC, R.14.Ba.Nr.2b: 84–85; Ueberschlag der Kosten von North-Carolina, Oct. 18, 1753, LC-MC, R.14.Ba.Nr.2b: 66–71; Spangenberg to van Laer, Jan. 27, 1759, LC-MC, R.14.Ba.Nr.2c: 265–72; Bethabara diary, Fries et al., *Records*, 1: 79–80. For a fuller discussion of the Unity's plans for Wachovia, see Daniel B. Thorp, "Moravian Colonization of Wachovia, 1753–1772: The Maintenance of Community in Late Colonial North Carolina" (Ph.D. dissertation, The Johns Hopkins Univ., 1982), 42–73.

42. Historischer Bericht, LC-MC, R.14.Ba.Nr.2a.: 19–42.

43. Merrens, *Colonial North Carolina*, 5, 111–19, 196–97.

44. Bethabara diary, Fries et al., *Records*, 1: 79–80.

CHAPTER 2

The Chosen People

1. For a fuller description of Wachovia's other residents, see Thorp, "Moravian Colonization," 104–21.

2. 2ten Gemein Rath gehalten von Br. Jacob Lösch, April 12, 1758, LC-MC, R.14.Ba.Nr.2c: 245–46; Journal Beym Land Messen in Wachau . . . , [1760], LC-MC, R.14.Ba.Nr.2c.: 462–77; [minutes of a conference held in Bethabara], May 20, 1763, MA-NP, Wachovia III, folder 3, item 4; Carolinische Conferenz im Directorial Collegio, July 26, 1763, MA-NP, Wachovia VI, Papiere die Wachau betreffend 1762–64, item 1; Unity Vorsteher Collegium to Elders Conference in Bethabara, Aug. 31, 1765, MA-SP; Bethabara diary extracts, Fries et al., *Records*, 1: 439–40.

3. Peter Böhler to die Conferenz in der Wachau, Oct. 25, 1762, MA-SP; Spangenberg to the Conference in Bethabara, Jan. 21, 1761, MA-SP, trans. K. G. Hamilton; Unity Vorsteher Collegium to Elders Conference in Bethabara, August 31, 1765, MA-SP, trans. E. Marx; memoirs of Daniel Schnepf and Susanna Maria Schnepf, nee Dressel, MA-SP.

4. Ettwein to Henry Laurens, June 24, 1762, in Phillip M. Hamer, George C. Rogers, Jr., David R. Chesnutt, C. James Taylor, and Peggy J. Clark, eds., *The Papers of Henry Laurens*, 11 vols. to date (Columbia: Univ. of South Carolina Press, 1968–), 3: 101–5; Fries, *Customs*, 7.

5. [Unity Directory] to the Elders Conferences in the Congregations, June 28, 1768, MA-SP, trans. E. Marx; Mattheus [Hehl] to the Elders Conference in Bethabara, April 30, 1767, MA-SP, trans. E. Marx; [Spangenberg to My Dearly Beloved Brethren and Sisters], June 16, 1760, MA-SP. For examples of individuals being rejected, see Böhler to Spangenberg, Oct. 23, 1753, LC-MC, R.14.Ba.Nr.2b: 73–74; Ettwein to Schropps, Graffs, Lorenz [Bagge], etc., March 14, 1767, MA-SP; Mattheus [Hehl] to the Elders Conference in Bethabara, April 30, 1767, MA-SP.

6. Spangenberg to Johannes [von Watteville], Oct. 21, 1759, LC-MC, R.14.Ba.Nr.2c: 386–87. For a more detailed discussion of life in Wachovia's Oeconomy, see Thorp, "Moravian Colonization," 320–57.

7. Entwurf zu dem Settlement der Brüder in North-Carolina, [Oct. 1753], LC-MC, R.14.Ba.Nr.2a: 7–14; Fragen wegen Nord Carolina von J. P. W. [J. P. Weiss] an der Ord. Frr. [Zinzendorf], April 1755, MA-NP, Wachovia II, folder 2, item 1–23; Extract einiger Briefe von Brüdern in North Carolina an Br. Joseph [a name used within the Unity by August Spangenberg], Nov. 18, 1754, LC-MC, R.14.Ba.Nr.2b: 356–59.

8. Spangenberg, Weiss, and Hutton to Kosenbaum, Jan. 9, 1754, LC-MC, R.14.Ba.Nr.2b: 109–12.

9. Spangenberg to the Wachovia Brethren, Sept. 16, 1755, LC-MC, R.14.Ba.Nr.2b: 591–93; Spangenberg, Weiss, and Hutton to Kosenbaum, Jan. 9, 1754, LC-MC, R.14.Ba.Nr.2b: 109–12; Entwurf zu dem Settlement der Brüder in North-Carolina, [Oct. 1753], LC-MC, R.14.Ba.Nr.2a: 7–14.

10. For the demographics of other southern frontiers soon after settlement began, see Darrett B. and Anita H. Rutman, "'More True and Perfect Lists': The Reconstruction of Censuses for Middlesex County, Virginia, 1668–1704," Virginia Magazine of History and Biography 88 (1980): 37–74; Irene W. D. Hecht, "The Virginia Muster of 1624/25 as a Source for Demographic History," William and Mary Quarterly, 3rd ser., 30 (1973): 65–92; Mitchell, Commercialism and Frontier, 59–132; Kaylene Hughes, "Populating the Back Country: The Demographic and Social Characteristics of the South Carolina Frontier, 1730–1760" (Ph.D. dissertation, Florida State Univ., 1985), 1–103.

11. Spangenberg to [?], May 21, 1754, in Beylage zur XXVIIten Woche des Jünger Haus Diarii, LC-MC, R.14.Ba.Nr.2b: 218–19; For a fuller discussion of this shift in the Unity's economic goals for Wachovia, see chapter 5.

12. Spangenberg to the Brethren and Sisters [at Bethabara], [Dec. 6, 1756], MA-SP.

13. For a fuller discussion of the Unity's desire to give Wachovia greater autonomy, see chapter 4.

14. Spangenberg to the Brothers in Wachovia, June 29, 1755, LC-MC, R.14.Ba.Nr.2b: 509–15 and in MA-SP, trans. K. G. Hamilton; Sessler, *Communal Pietism*, 175; Gollin, *Moravians*, 110–13, 122–23; Wegen Carolina. Den Jünger an Spangenberg, n.d., LC-MC, R.14.Ba.Nr.2b: 55–56.

15. [Spangenberg to von Watteville], July 2, 1759, LC-MC, R.14.Ba.Nr.2c: 306–7; Ettwein to die Conferenz in Bethabara, Feb. 28, 1761, LC-MC, R.14.Ba.Nr.2c: 539–40; Kurze Nachricht von Bethania, Sept. 21, 1759, LC-MC, R.14.Ba. Nr.2c: 314–19; Daniel B. Thorp, "Assimilation in North Carolina's Moravian Community," *Journal of Southern History* 52 (1986): 20–42.

16. Protocoll der Engen Conferenz, June 20, 1759, MA-SP; Kurze Nachricht von Bethania, Sept. 21, 1759, LC-MC, R.14.Ba.Nr.2c: 314–19; [letter from Martin Hauser and others], July 1, 1759, LC-MC, R.14.Ba.Nr.2c: 305.

17. Protocoll der Engen Conferenz, April 22, 1760, MA-SP.

18. For a more thorough discussion of stable populations in Europe and the colonial American South, see E. A. Wrigley and R. S. Schofield, *The Population History of England, 1541–1871* (Cambridge: Harvard Univ. Press, 1981); Darrett B. and Anita H. Rutman, *A Place in Time: Middlesex County, Virginia, 1650–1750* (New York: Norton, 1984); and Alan Kulikoff, *Tobacco and Slaves: The Development of Southern Cultures in the Chesapeake, 1680–1800* (Chapel Hill: Univ. of North Carolina Press, 1986).

19. Rutman and Rutman, "'More True and Perfect Lists,'" especially 55; Mitchell, *Commercialism and Frontier*, fig. 19, 103. Hughes ("Populating the Back Country," 52) shows an adult sex ratio of 184 : 100 in Purrysburg, S.C. when settlement began there but offers no estimate for later years.

20. Rutman and Rutman, "'More True and Perfect Lists,'" 55; Mitchell, *Commercialism and Frontier*, fig. 19, 103.

21. For details concerning the choice of Salem's site, see Thorp, "Moravian Colonization," 76–82.

22. In Middlesex County, Va., for example, the sex ratio among unmarried adults in 1699 was still 518 : 100 (Rutman and Rutman, "'More True and Perfect Lists,'" 55).

23. Gollin, *Moravians*, 255, n.6; Christian Degn, *Die Schimmelmanns im Atlantischen Dreieckshandel: Gewinn und Gewissen* (Neumünster: D. Wachholtz, 1974), 47.

24. Count Zinzendorf's Farewell Letter wrote to the Negroes in St. Thos. when he departed from them, Feb. 15, 1739, MA-NP, West Indies Miscellaneous Letters: 1739–1769; Winthrop D. Jordan, *White Over Black: American Attitudes Toward the Negro, 1550–1812* (Chapel Hill: Univ. of North Carolina Press, 1968), 17–19, 54; David Brion Davis, *The Problem of Slavery in Western Culture* (Ithaca, N.Y.: Cornell Univ. Press, 1966), 63–64.

25. Count Zinzendorf's Farewell Letter. One of the clearest and most accessible examples of the Moravian attitude toward Africans and slavery during the eighteenth century is C. G. A. Oldendorp, *History of the Mission of the Evangelical Brethren on the Caribbean Islands of St. Thomas, St. Croix, and St. John*, ed. and trans. Arnold R. Highfield and Vladimir Barac (Ann Arbor, Mich.: Karoma Pub., 1987), 159–265.

26. Degn, *Schimmelmanns*, 43; Jan Marinus van der Linde, "Herrnhuter im Karibischen Raum," in van Buijtenen, Dekker, and Leeuwenberg, *Unitas Fratrum*, 241–60; Hamilton and Hamilton, *History*, 43; Count Zinzendorf's Farewell Letter.

27. Spangenberg to Weiss, Oct. 13, 1755, LC-MC, R.14.Ba.Nr.2b: 608–10; Spangenberg to van Laer, Jan. 27, 1759, LC-MC, R.14.Ba.Nr.2c: 265–72; [J. P. Weiss], mein Gedanken über br. Spangenbergs Vortrag wegen der Wachau, May 13, 1763, LC-MC, R.14.Ba.Nr.2d: 157–66.

28. [Untitled document], Nov. 1753, LC-MC, R.14.Ba.Nr.27: 103; Susan Lenius, "Slavery and the Moravian Church in North Carolina" (honors thesis in history, Moravian College, Bethlehem, Pa., 1974), 108.

29. Daniel B. Thorp, "Chattel with a Soul: The Autobiography of a Moravian Slave," *Pennsylvania Magazine of History and Biography*, 112 (1988): 433–51.

30. Concerning the financial barrier, see Bericht an das Unit. Diener Department, Aug. 3, 1770, MA-SP, Reports to the Unity (there is a translated extract of this document in Fries et al., *Records*, 1: 614). Concerning the racial barrier, see the Bericht cited above; letters of Peter Böhler and George Schulius, LC-MC, R.14.A.Nr.9: 35–60; Degn, *Schimmelmanns*, 54; Ettwein to Laurens, March 2, 1763, Hamer et al., *Papers of Henry Laurens*, 3: 355–57.

31. Ettwein to Laurens. Christian Oldendorp reacted in much the same way when he visited Moravian missionaries in the Danish Antilles between 1767 and 1769. In his *History of the Mission* Oldendorp wrote: "Since the native *Whites*, or *Creoles*, have been accustomed from childhood onward to be served by slaves, as well as to give those same slaves orders, they, therefore, become aware quite early of their external superiority over those poor creatures. From there, the transition to

pride and a domineering character is quick and easy. Neither does the example which they witness on all sides in the treatment of slaves by others lead to the development of humanitarian sentiments." Oldendorp, *History of the Mission*, 157).

32. Bethabara diary extracts, Fries et al., *Records*, 1: 274; Spangenberg to Zinzendorf, Nov. 15, 1757, LC-MC, R.14.Ba.Nr.2c: 202–8; Wegen Carolina, Oct. 10, 1758, LC-MC, R.14.Ba.Nr.2d: 37–38; Spangenberg to Ettwein, Jan. 20, 1761, LC-MC, R.14.Ba.Nr.2c: 241–46; Carolinische Conferenz in Directorial Collegio, July 26, 1763, MA-NP, Wachovia VI, Papiere die Wachau betreffend 1762–64, item 1; [loose sheet labeled A.1 filed with Report to U.V. Coll.], April 14, 1768, MA-SP, Reports to the Unity; Protocoll der Helfers Conferenz, Oct. 1, 1764, April 14, 1766, April 11 and 28, 1767, MA-SP.

33. Protocoll der Helfers Conferenz, Aug. 14, 1769, MA-SP; Wachovia Memorabilia, Fries et al., *Records*, 1: 385. Sam was first hired sometime between March 31 and June 24, 1766 to replace another slave who had been transferred from the cattle yard to the tavern (Protocoll der Helfers Conferenz, April 1, 1765, March 31 and June 24, 1766, MA-SP). He first appears in the records simply as Billy Rich's [William Ridge's] slave, but by October 1766 he is referred to by name (Protocoll der Helfers Conferenz, Oct. 19, 1766, MA-SP).

34. Bill of sale for Sam dated Aug. 9, 1769 in MA-SP, Bills of Sale; Graff to Ettwein, n.d., MA-NP, Wachovia III, folder 5, item 9; Salem and Bethabara diary extracts, Fries et al., *Records*, 1: 445–46, 2: 678, 821; bills of sale dated March 28, 1771 (Franc), Aug. 24, 1771 (Sambo), and Oct. 12, 1771 (Sue and Sukey), MA-SP, Bills of Sale.

CHAPTER 3
The Church Family

1. Sessler, *Communal Pietism*, 117, 175; Gollin, *Moravians*, 14, 110–13.

2. Henry H. Meyer, *Child Nature and Nurture According to Nicholaus Ludwig von Zinzendorf* (New York: Abingdon Press, 1928), 137; der Gemein Rath [in Bethabara], Sept. 14, 1756, LC-MC, R.14.Ba.Nr.2c: 147–48; [Spangenberg] to [?], Sept. 14, 1759, LC-MC, R.14.Ba.Nr.2c: 345–46.

3. Protocoll der Helfers Conferenz, Nov. 4, 1766, MA-SP; Gollin, *Moravians*, 68–70, 110–11.

4. Sessler, *Communal Pietism*, 93–97.

5. Gollin, *Moravians*, 67–89; Hamilton and Hamilton, *History*, 19, 32.

Sessler (*Communal Pietism*, 106–20) provides the best account of how bands and choirs reflect stages in the life of Christ.

6. Hamilton and Hamilton, *History*, 94–106; Gollin, *Moravians*, 67–109; Sessler, *Communal Pietism*, 94–99.

7. Gollin, *Moravians*, 81–82.

8. Spangenberg to Weiss, Nov. 18, 1754, LC-MC, R.14.Ba.Nr.2b: 292–93; Thorp, "City", 42–50; Fragen wegen Nord Carolina von J. P. W. [J. P. Weiss] an der Ord. Frr. [Zinzendorf], April 1755, MA-NP, Wachovia II, folder 2, item 1–23.

9. Gollin, *Moravians*, 111–12.

10. Protocoll der Helfers Conferenz, Jan. 20, 1767, MA-SP; Bethabara diary extracts, Fries et al., *Records*, 1: 357.

11. Chapter 2 above; Spangenberg to Ettwein, Jan. 20, 1761, LC-MC, R.14.Ba.Nr.2c: 541–46; Bischoff, Hofman, and Ettwein to die Conferenz in Bethlehem, [April 26, 1760], LC-MC, R.14.Ba.Nr.2c: 488–89.

12. "The Doctor," Fries et al., *Records*, 1: 216–23. The only other marriage that seems to have been initiated by the couple involved was that of Peter Hauser and Margaret Elizabeth Spönhauer in 1762 (Ettwein to the Conference in Bethlehem, Jan. 18, 1762, LC-MC, R.14.Ba.Nr.2c: 576–80).

13. Protocoll der Helfers Conferenz, Aug. 20, 1764, Jan. 24 and 28, 1765, Feb. 12, 1765, MA-SP; Memorabilia of Wachovia, 1765, Fries et al., *Records*, 1: 295–97.

14. Card of Anna Johanna Barbara Beroth, nee Lösch, MA-SP, Memoir Index; "The Doctor," Fries, et al., *Records*, 1: 216–23; Bischoff, Hofman, and Ettwein to die Conferenz in Bethlehem, [April 26, 1760], LC-MC, R.14.Ba.Nr.2c: 488–89

15. Spangenberg to die Conferenz in Wachau, Dec. 6, 1756, LC-MC, R.14.Ba.Nr.2c: 151–53; Spangenberg to the Brethren and Sisters [in Bethabara], [Dec. 6, 1756], MA-SP, trans. K. G. Hamilton; Spangenberg to Marschall, July 29, 1770, MA-SP, U. E. C. to Wachovia; Ettwein to die Conferenz in Bethlehem, Jan. 18, 1762, LC-MC, R.14.Ba.Nr.2c: 576–80.

16. Gollin, *Moravians*, 110–13; Robert W. Woosley, Jr., "The Ethics of the Moravians in Wachovia," (M.A. thesis, Southeastern Baptist Theological Seminary, 1956), 35; Fragen wegen Nord Carolina von J. P. W. [J. P. Weiss] an der Ord. Frr. [Zinzendorf], April 1755, MA-NP, Wachovia II, folder 2, item 1–23. Dr. Haupert raised the possibility of these divorces-by-transfer in a personal conversation and hopes to find conclusive evidence supporting his theory through further research. Until

then it is impossible to say with certainty whether or not the church in Zinzendorf's day sanctioned divorce.

17. Meyer, *Child Nature*, 102–42.

18. Thorp, "Moravian Colonization," 94–101; Spangenberg to White, The intended State of the Brethrens Settlement in Wachovia in North Carolina, Jan. 17, 1754, LC-MC, R.14.Ba.Nr.2b: 117.

19. Protocoll of Bethania Committee Minutes, Feb. 4, 1764, MA-SP; Protocoll der Wöchentlicher Conferenz, Dec. 7, 1762, MA-SP; Bethabara Accounts, June 1, 1764–May 31, 1765, MA-NP, Wachovia VI, Papiere die Wachau betreffend 1762–1764; Spangenberg to die Conferenz in Bethabara, Jan. 21, 1761, LC-MC, R.14.Ba.Nr.2c: 539–40 and copy in MA-SP. For a fuller account of material life in the *Oeconomy*, see Thorp, "Moravian Colonization," 320–58.

20. Spangenberg to the Society for Establishing the Colony of the Brethren on Wachovia in North Carolina, April 11, 1756, LC-MC, R.14.Ba.Nr.2c: 58–64; Spangenberg to the Brethren and Sisters [at Bethabara], [Dec. 6, 1756], MA-SP, trans. K. G. Hamilton; Spangenberg to die Conferenz in Bethabara, Dec. 6, 1756, LC-MC, R.14.Ba.Nr.2c: 151–53; Mack to Zinzendorf, Feb. 26, 1757, LC-MC, R.14.Ba.Nr.2c: 162–67; Spangenberg to Marschall, July 29, 1770, MA-SP, U. E. C. to Wachovia; Mobillien Inventaria des Diaconats von der Wachau . . . , 1766, MA-SP.

21. Remarks concerning the Laying Out of the new Congregation Town in the center of Wachovia, Fries et al., *Records*, 1: 313–15.

22. Meyer, *Child Nature*, 123; Bischoff, Hofman, and Ettwein to die Conferenz in Bethlehem, [April 26, 1760], LC-MC, R.14.Ba.Nr.2c: 488–89; Graff to Nathanael [Seidel], June 25, 1762, MA-NP, Wachovia III, folder 1, item 1–7.

23. For a detailed discussion of Moravian educational theory, see Meyer, *Child Nature;* and Mabel Haller, *Early Moravian Education in Pennsylvania* (Nazareth, Pa.: Moravian Historical Society, 1953).

24. Protocoll der Engen Conferenz, Feb. 14, April 18 and 21, 1760, MA-SP; memorabilia, Fries et al., *Records*, 2: 658–66; Marschall to Ettwein, July 31, 1765, MA-SP, trans. K. G. Hamilton; Haller, *Education*, 229, 290, 298–99; Bethabara diary extracts, Fries et al., *Records*, 1: 377; Rundt to Ettwein, Jan. 22, 1761, MA-SP.

25. Meyer, *Child Nature*, 160–72.

26. Protocoll der Helfers Conferenz, Nov. 19, 1764, Jan. 2 and Feb. 12, 1765, MA-SP. A similar process occurred between October and December of 1766.

27. Protocoll der Helfers Conferenz, Jan. 2, 1765 and Oct. 13, 1766, MA-SP; Schropp to [?]. Nov. 20, 1766, MA-SP, trans. E. Marx.

28. Protocoll der Helfers Conferenz, Aug. 19 and 24, 1767, MA-SP; Schober to Marschall, March 21, 1773, MA-SP.

29. Protocoll der Helfers Conferenz, Jan. 23, 1769, MA-SP.

30. Protocoll der Helfers Conferenz, Jan. 2 and Dec. 15, 1766, Jan. 11, 1768, MA-SP; Protocoll of Bethania Committee Minutes, Jan. 13, 1767, MA-SP; Bethabara diary extracts, Fries et al., *Records,* 1: 331; memorabilia, Fries et al., *Records,* 1: 430–37; Salem diary extracts, Fries et al., *Records,* 1: 444.

31. Ettwein to Rodgers, Oct. 8, 1761, LC-MC, R.14.Ba.Nr.2c: 565–66; "The Doctor," Fries et al., *Records,* 1: 216–23; Bethabara diary extracts, Fries et al., *Records,* 1: 286.

32. Ettwein to Rodgers, Oct. 8, 1761, LC-MC, R.14.Ba.Nr.2c: 565–66; Ettwein to die Conferenz in Bethlehem, Nov. 21, 1761, LC-MC, R.14.Ba.Nr.2c: 570–72; [catalogue of residents in Wachovia], Sept. 10, 1762, MA-NP, Wachovia III, folder 1, item 2–2; Protocoll der Wöchentlicher Conferenz, Oct. 17, 1763, MA-SP; Marshall's Reports to U. E. C., [translated extracts], April 9, 1770, Fries et al., *Records,* 2: 612–15; Salem diary extracts, Fries et al., *Records,* 2: 668, 672, 675; An das Department der Helfer im U. Aelt. Collegio, Sept. 2, 1771, MA-SP, Reports to the Unity.

33. If one includes remarriages, the median age for men remains 36 while that for women rises to 28.5. The sole teenage bride was Margaret Elizabeth Spönhauer, who wed at age 16.

34. Memorabilia, Fries et al., *Records,* 1: 319–23.

35. Principia das ledigen Brüder Chöres, 1775, MA-SP.

36. Conferenz über den Wachauischen Plan gehalten in Bethl[ehem], Sept. 22, 1755, LC-MC, R.14.Ba.Nr.2b: 596–601 and MA-NP, Wachovia II, folder 2, item 2–5; Ettwein to Spangenberg, Jan. 18, 1762, LC-MC, R.14.Ba.Nr.2c: 581–82; "Church Services," Fries et al., *Records,* 1: 418–24; Protocoll der Engen Conferenz, Sept. 6, 1759, MA-SP; Classen, Gesellschaften und Besuche der Led. Brr. u. Knaben in Salem, [1765–88], MA-SP, 2–3; Bethabara diary, Fries et al., *Records,* 1: 84.

37. Protocoll der Wöchentlicher Conferenz, Aug. 9, 1762, MA-SP.

38. [Unity Directory] to the Elders Conferences of the Congregations, June 28, 1768, MA-SP, trans. E. Marx. See also Böhler to Ettwein, April 16, 1762, MA-SP; L. Bagge to Nathanael [Seidel], Nov. 21, 1766, MA-NP, Wachovia III, folder 2, item 1–78.

39. Kanter, *Commitment and Community.*

40. Arthur L. Stinchcombe, "Social Structures and Organizations," in *Handbook of Organizations*, ed. James G. March (Chicago: Rand McNally, 1965), 142–91; Remarks concerning the Laying Out of the new Congregation Town in the center of Wachovia, Fries et al., *Records*, 1: 313–15.

CHAPTER 4
"Under Their Own Laws and Ordinances"

1. Memo No. 10 dem Jünger [from Spangenberg], May 2, 1753, LC-MC, R.14.Ba.Nr.2b: 49–50; [Spangenberg] an die Conferenz in Bethlehem, Aug. 9, 1753, LC-MC, R.14.Ba.Nr.2b: 58; Ohnmassgebliches Project zur besezung des Districts in North Caroline, Sept. 12, 1753, MA-NP, Wachovia II, folder 1, item 2–36.

2. Wegen Carolina. Den Jünger an Spangenberg, n.d., LC-MC, R.14.Ba.Nr.2b: 55–56; Puncte, zum Statuten, oder general Revers, von die Geschwister die auf dem district land in North Carolina die Wachau genannt wohnen zum Unterschrieben, n.d., LC-MC, R.14.Ba.Nr.2d: 105–8; Bethabara diary extracts, Fries, et al., *Records*, 1: 243; Conferenz über den Wachauischen Plan gehalten in Bethl[ehem], Sept. 22, 1755, LC-MC, R.14.Ba.Nr.2b: 596–601 and MA-NP, Wachovia II, folder 2, item 2–5; Der Gemein Rath . . . am 14ten Sept. 56, LC-MC, R.14.Ba.Nr.2c: 147–48.

3. The 6 conferences I consider to have been most important in Wachovia during these years were: Helfers Conferenz, Enge Conferenz, Wöchentlicher Conferenz, Aeltesten Conferenz, Privat und Chor Conferenz, and Diacony Conferenz. The records of these bodies seldom include membership lists as such, but they do sometimes identify the men and women present at a particular meeting and this provides a means of determining both their membership and leadership.

4. Gollin, *Moravians*, 35, 43, 111; Conf. des Directorii zu Zeyst, Aug. 31, 1767, MA-SP, Conferences-Decisions of the U. E. C. concerning Salem 1763, 1765, 1767; Salem diary extracts, Fries et al., *Records*, 2: 673–74.

5. Reichel, *Moravians in North Carolina*, 165; Spangenberg to Weiss, Oct. 13, 1755, LC-MC, R.14.Ba.Nr.2b: 608–10; Br. Mattheoi [Hehl] relation von seine Reise nach u. von Wachau, Oct. 20, 1756, LC-MC, R.14.Ba.Nr.2c: 168–73; Ettwein to Nathanael [Seidel], Sept. 12, 1762, MA-NP, Wachovia III, folder 1, item 1–12; Spangenberg to die Conf. in Bethabara, April 17, 1762, LC-MC, R.14.Ba.Nr.2c: 592–600; Protocoll

der Wöchentlicher Conferenz, June 10, 1762, MA-SP; Marschall to Ettwein, July 31, 1765, MA-SP, trans. K. G. Hamilton.

6. Den Gem[ein] Rath in Wachau, Nov. 1, 1756, LC-MC, R.14.Ba.Nr.2c: 149–50; Böhler to Spangenberg, Oct. 2, 1754, LC-MC, R.14.Ba.Nr.2b: 263–66; Lösch to Spangenberg, May 31, 1755, LC-MC, R.14.Ba.Nr.2b: 506–8.

7. Conferenz über den Wachauischen Plan gehalten in Bethl[ehem], Sept. 22, 1755, LC-MC, R.14.Ba.Nr.2b: 596–601 and MA-NP, Wachovia II, folder 2, item 2–5; Spangenberg to the Brethren in Wachovia, Sept. 23, 1755, MA-SP, trans. K. G. Hamilton.

8. Protocol der Helfers Conferenz, Nov. 6, 1755 and Sept. 18, 1756, MA-SP; Bethabara diary extracts, Fries et al., *Records*, 1: 140; memorabilia, Fries et al., *Records*, 1: 154–57.

9. Den Gem[ein] Rath in Wachau, Nov. 1, 1756, LC-MC, R.14.Ba.Nr.2c: 149–50.

10. Conferenz über den Wachauischen Plan gehalten in Bethl[ehem], Sept. 22, 1755, LC-MC, R.14.Ba.Nr.2b: 596–601 and MA-NP, Wachovia II, folder 2, item 2–5. For a more complete discussion of the Lot and its use, see Gollin, *Moravians*, 50–63; "The Lot," Fries et al., *Records*, 2: 555–56; Surratt, "Dissent," 236.

11. Conferenz über den Wachauischen Plan gehalten in Bethl[ehem], Sept. 22, 1755, LC-MC, R.14.Ba.Nr.2b: 596–601 and MA-NP, Wachovia II, folder 2, item 2–5; [minutes of a conference in Bethlehem], June 20, 1758, LC-MC, R.14.Ba.Nr.2c: 250–51.

12. The two marriages sanctioned without the Lot were those of Jacob Blum to A. Maria Born and August Schubert to Anna Elizabeth Kraus. In both cases it seems that the elders and the concerned parties had discussed the proposed matches thoroughly, and the Personal and Choir Conference concluded "We mean, therefore, not to require the Lot first." Privat und Chor Conferenz, Nov. 6, 1764, MA-SP.

13. Spangenberg to the Brethren and Sisters [at Bethabara], [Dec. 6, 1756], MA-SP. trans. K. G. Hamilton; Bethabara Diary, Nov. 25, 1757, MA-SP; Protocoll der Helfers Conferenz, Jan. 9, 1757, MA-SP.

14. Br. Mattheoi [Hehl] relation von seine Reise nach u. von Wachau, Oct. 20, 1756, LC-MC, R.14.Ba.Nr.2c: 168–73; Conferenz über den Wachauischen Plan gehalten in Bethl[ehem], Sept. 22, 1755, LC-MC, R.14.Ba.Nr.2b: 596–601 and MA-NP, Wachovia II, folder 2, item 2–5.

15. Gollin, *Moravians*, 25–49; Levering, *History of Bethlehem*, 263–64.

16. Weiss to Fischer, June 25, 1754, LC-MC, R.14.Ba.Nr.2b: 321–23.

17. Ohnmassgebliches Project zur Besezung des Districts in North

Caroline, Sept. 12, 1753, MA-NP, Wachovia II, folder 1, item 2–36; Weiss to Fischer, June 25, 1764, LC-MC, R.14.Ba.Nr.2b: 321–23; Conferenz über den Wachauischen Plan gehalten in Bethl[ehem], Sept. 22, 1755, LC-MC, R.14.Ba.Nr.2b: 596–601 and MA-NP, Wachovia II, folder 2, item 2–5; Bericht des Directorii an das U. V. Coll. wegen der Amer. Conferenzen gehalten . . . in Zeist, [March 30–April 27, 1767], MA-SP, Conferences-Decisions of U. E. C. concerning Salem 1763, 1765, 1767, translated extract in Fries et al., *Records*, 2: 596–99.

18. Carolinische Conferenz in Directorial Collegio, July 26, 1763, MA-NP, Wachovia VI, Papiere die Wachau betreffend 1762–64, item 1; Spangenberg to the Conference at Bethabara, July 28, 1763, MA-SP, trans. K. G. Hamilton.

19. "Glossary," Fries et al., *Records*, 1: 495–96; Marschall to Ettwein, Aug. 19, 1764, MA-SP, trans. K. G. Hamilton.

20. Bethabara diary extract, Fries et al., *Records*, 1: 236; Hamilton and Hamilton, *History*, 167–68.

21. Conferenz über den Wachauischen Plan gehalten in Bethl[ehem], Sept. 22, 1755, LC-MC, R.14.Ba.Nr.2b: 596–601 and MA-NP, Wachovia II, folder 2, item 2–5; Der Gemein Rath welcher von Br. Mattheo [Hehl] mit den Brüdern in Wachau gehalten werden, Sept. 14, 1756, LC-MC, R.14.Ba.Nr.2c: 147–48; Spangenberg to die Conferenz in Wachau, Dec. 6, 1756, LC-MC, R.14.Ba.Nr.2c: 151–53.

22. Bericht des Directorii an das U.V. Coll. wegen der Amer. Conferenzen gehalten . . . in Zeist, [March 30–April 27, 1767], MA-SP, Conferences-Decisions of U.E.C. concerning Salem 1763, 1765, 1767, translated extract in Fries et al., *Records*, 2: 596–99; Hamilton and Hamilton, *History*, 167–70; memorabilia, Fries et al., *Records*, 1: 396–401.

23. Br. Mattheoi [Hehl] relation von seine Reise nach u. von Wachau, Oct. 20, 1756, LC-MC, R.14.Ba.Nr.2c: 168–73; Bethabara diary extracts, Fries et al., *Records*, 1: 273; Protocoll der Helfers Conferenz, Sept. 30, 1765 and July 23, 1764, MA-SP.

24. Leaders in 1764 were those men and women sitting on both the Helpers Conference and the Personal and Choir Conference. Protocoll der Helfers Conferenz, 1764, MA-SP; Privat und Chor Conferenz, 1764, MA-SP.

25. Protocoll der Helfers Conferenz, 1764, MA-SP.

26 [Marschall] to U. Vorsth. Collegium, April 10, 1769, MA-SP, Reports to the Unity Vorsteher Collegium, translation from extract in Fries et al., *Records*, 2: 607.

27. Protocoll of Bethania Committee Minutes, 1764, MA-SP; Protocoll der Wöchentlicher Conferenz, Aug. 16, 1762, MA-SP.

28. Protocoll der Helfers Conferenz, Dec. 3, 1764, MA-SP. For a fuller discussion of the Inspector of the Forests, see Coleman A. Doggett, "The Moravian Foresters," *Journal of Forest History* 31 (1987), 19–24; William Hinman, "Philip Gottlieb Reuter, First Surveyor of Wachovia," (M.A. thesis, Wake Forest Univ., 1985).

29. Privat und Chor Conferenz, 1764, MA-SP.

30. Privat und Chor Conferenz, Feb. 11, 1764, MA-SP; Protocoll der Wöchentlicher Conferenz, Feb. 3, 1763, MA-SP.

31. Ettwein to Br. R., April 6, 1761, MA-SP, trans. K. G. Hamilton; Spangenberg to Ettwein, April 17, 1762, Fries et al., *Records*, 2: 549–50.

32. Protocoll der Helfers Conferenz, Dec. 18, 1764, MA-SP.

33. Ettwein to Laurens, June 24, 1762, in Hamer et al., *Papers of Henry Laurens*, 3: 101–5; Protocoll der Wöchentlicher Conferenz, Feb. 3, 1763, MA-SP.

34. Protocoll der Wöchentlicher Conferenz, Sept. 13, 1762, MA-SP.

35. [Lease of Jacobus van der Merk], July 11, 1763, MA-NP, Wachovia VI, Papiere die Wachau betreffend 1762–64; [lease of Heinrich Biefel], Sept. 10, 1759, LC-MC, R.14.Ba.Nr.2c: 347–49; [extracts from the notes of Frederic Marschall concerning several Unity conferences], 1767, Fries et al., *Records*, 2: 596–600.

36. The 10 who were expelled between 1753 and 1772 were: George Lösch, sometime in 1758–59; Nicholas Anspach, 1760; Henrich Feldhausen, 1762; August Schubert, 1765; Andrew Betz, 1767; an unnamed single brother, 1768; John Lanius, 1769; and three unnamed men in 1771. Explanations were offered in the cases of Lösch (Spangenberg to My Dearly Beloved Brethren and Sisters, July 16, 1760, MA-SP, trans. K. G. Hamilton), Schubert (Ettwein to Marschall, [May 1765], MA-SP, trans. K. G. Hamilton), Lanius (Wachovia diary extracts, Fries et al., *Records*, 1: 386–87 and Historischer Bericht, LC-MC, R.14.Ba.Nr.2a: 19–42), Feldhausen, (Bethabara diary extracts, Fries et al., *Records*, 1: 247), and Betz (Protocoll der Helfers Conferenz, Jan. 20, 1767, MA-SP). In other cases the specific offense was not mentioned.

37. Hoffman to Nathanael [Seidel], Oct. 9, 1763, MA-NP, Wachovia III, folder 1, item 1–34; Protocoll der Wöchentlicher Conferenz, July 19 and Sept. 13, 1762, Feb. 3, 1763, MA-SP.

38. Privat und Chor Conferenz, Nov. 6 and 7, 1764, MA-SP; Graff to Seidel, Dec. 31, 1764, MA-NP, Wachovia III, folder 2, item 1–57.

39. Ettwein to Marschall, [May 1765], MA-SP, trans. K. G. Hamilton.

40. Ettwein to Marschall, [May 1765], MA-SP, trans. K. G. Hamilton; Ettwein to Marschall, [Nov. 1765], MA-SP, trans. K. G. Hamilton.

41. Ettwein to Marschall, [May 1765], MA-SP, trans. K. G. Hamilton; Bethabara diary extracts, Fries et al., *Records*, 1: 302; Marschall to Ettwein, July 31, 1765, MA-SP, trans. K. G. Hamilton; Protocoll der Helfers Conferenz, May 26, 1765, MA-SP; [editorial comment], Fries et al., *Records*, 1: 303.

CHAPTER 5
Moravians in the Marketplace

1. Philip D. Curtin, *Cross-Cultural Trade in World History*, (Cambridge: Cambridge Univ. Press, 1984); Bethabara diary, Fries et al., *Records*, 1: 80.

2. Gollin, *Moravians*, 148.

3. Historischer Bericht, LC-MC, R.14.Ba.Nr.2a: 19–42. Other examples of this sort of routinization appear in: Curtin, *Cross-Cultural Trade*; Kanter, *Commitment and Community*; James H. Merrell, "Natives in a New World: The Catawba Indians of Carolina, 1650–1800" (Ph.D. dissertation, The Johns Hopkins University, 1982); S. N. Eisenstadt, "The Place of Elites and Primary Groups in the Absorption of New Immigrants in Israel," *American Journal of Sociology* 57 (1951): 222–31.

4. Vorschlage wegen einer Corporation in Salem, April 7, 1767, LC-MC, R.14.A.Nr.44: 22–27.

5. Jo Conrad Butner, "A New Town in Wachovia," in *The Three Forks of Muddy Creek*, ed. Frances Griffin (Winston-Salem, N.C.: Old Salem, Inc., 1978) 5: 1–11; Unity Vorsteher Collegium to Elders Conference in Bethabara, Aug. 31, 1765, MA-SP, trans. E. Marx; J. F. D. Smyth, *A Tour in the United States of America*, 2 vols. (London: G. Robinson, J. Robson, and J. Stewell, 1784), 1: 214 (the internal evidence of Smyth's work suggests that he visited Wachovia in 1772 despite the later publication date of his account).

6. Frances Griffin, "Fremdendiener," in *The Old Salem Gleaner*, 25 (Summer-Fall, 1981): 2; Protocoll der Helfers Conferenz, April 25 and May 16, 1768, April 17, 1769, MA-SP; [letter from Spangenberg dated May 21, 1754] in Beylage zur XXXVIIten Woche des Jünger-Haus Diarii 1754, LC-MC, R.14.Ba.Nr.2b: 218–19; Bethabara Diary, Feb. 8 and 9, 1754, MA-SP.

7. For Brother Joh. Schaub at the Opening of the Brethren's Store in Bethabara, July 9, 1759, MA-SP, trans. K. G. Hamilton; Hunter James, *Old Salem: Official Guidebook* (Winston-Salem, N.C.: Old Salem, Inc., 1971), 88; Spangenberg to die Conferenz in Bethabara, April 17, 1762, LC-MC, R.14.Ba.Nr.2c: 592–600.

8. Lösch to Spangenberg, Dec. 18, 1753, LC-MC, R.14.Ba.Nr.2b: 76; Höger to Weiss, Dec. 26, 1754, LC-MC, R.14.Ba.Nr.2b: 375–78; Lösch to Lawatsch, April 24, 1754, LC-MC, R.14.Ba.Nr.2b: 204–5; Spangenberg diary extracts, Fries et al., *Records*, 1: 30–62; Spangenberg to Hutton, Marschall, and Cossart, Nov. 18, 1754, LC-MC, R.14.Ba.Nr.2b: 290–91; Ohnmassgebliches Project zur Besezung des Districts in North Caroline, Sept. 12, 1753, MA-NP, Wachovia II, folder 1, item 2–36; Spangenberg to [the Brethren in Bethabara], June 29, 1755, MA-SP, trans. K. G. Hamilton.

9. Friis to Spangenberg, April 30, 1755, LC-MC, R.14.Ba.Nr.2b: 475–81; Wachau or Dobbs Parish, Fries et al., *Records*, 2: 557–87; Benziens Relation seiner Reise nach Wachau . . . , Nov. 21, 1755, LC-MC, R.14.Ba.Nr.2b: 619–30; [statement of income and expenses, Oct. 8, 1753–Nov. 10, 1755], LC-MC, R.14.Ba.Nr.2c: 40–57; Bethabara Diary, Dec. 26, 1753, MA-SP; memorabilia, 1756, Fries et al., *Records*, 1: 157–61.

10. Lösch to Böhler, April 27, 1754, LC-MC, R.14.Ba.Nr.2b: 211–13; Benzien to Hess, Dec. 13, 1754, LC-MC, R.14.Ba.Nr.2b: 329–32; Spangenberg to the Society for Establishing the Colony of the Brethren on Wachovia in North Carolina, April 11, 1756, LC-MC, R.14.Ba.Nr.2c: 58–64; Lösch to Lawatsch, April 24, 1754, LC-MC, R.14.Ba.Nr.2b: 204–5; Spangenberg to Lösch, May 3, 1756, LC-MC, R.14.Ba.Nr.2c: 84–87.

11. Ohnmassgebliches Project zur Besezung des Districts in North Caroline, Sept. 12, 1753, MA-NP, Wachovia II, folder 1, item 2–36; [list of the first settlers], Notebook of F. W. Marshall, MA-SP, translated extract in Fries, et al., *Records*, 2: 73–74.

12. Spangenberg to van Laer, June 27, 1754, R. 14. Ba.Nr.2b: 222–23; Spangenberg to Benzien, Oct. 22, 1754, LC-MC, R.14. Ba.Nr.2b: 276–79; Bathabara diary extracts, Fries et al., *Records*, 1: 149; Bethabara Diary, April 5 and 15, 1757, MA-SP; Spangenberg to Lösch, May 3, 1756, LC-MC, R.14 Ba. Nr.2c: 84–87.

13. Friis to Spangenberg, April 30, 1755, LC-MC, R.14.Ba.Nr.2c: 475–81; [statement of income and expenses, Oct. 8, 1753–Nov. 10, 1755], LC-MC, R.14.Ba.Nr.2c: 40–57; [statement of income and expenses, Nov. 10, 1755–Feb. 26, 1756], LC-MC, R.14.Ba.Nr.2c: 67–72.

14. Bethabara diary extracts and memorabilia, Fries et al., *Records*, 1: 105, 108, 121 (1754 figures estimated from count for May to Nov.); Spangenberg to Benzien, Sept. 22, 1754, LC-MC, R.14.Ba.Nr.2b: 276–79; Spangenberg to Weiss, Sept. 3, 1754, LC-MC, R.14.Ba.Nr.2b: 240–47; Spangenberg to Weiss, Nov. 27, 1754, LC-MC, R.14.Ba.Nr.2b: 296–97; [statement of income and expenses Oct. 8, 1753–Nov. 10, 1755], LC-

MC, R.14.Ba.Nr.2c: 40–57; [statement of income and expenses, Nov. 10, 1755–Feb. 26, 1756], LC-MC, R.14.Ba.Nr.2c: 67–72.

15. [Statement of income and expenses, Oct. 8, 1753–Nov. 10, 1755], LC-MC, R.14.Ba.Nr.2c: 40–57; [statement of income and expenses, Nov. 10, 1755–Feb. 26, 1756], LC-MC, R.14.Ba.Nr.2c: 67–72.

16. The names of business contacts came from a wide variety of sources. Identification of their homes came chiefly from: Fries et al., *Records*, passim; [map of the land between the Yadkin River and the Virginia line], 1762, copy (neg. S 969) in photograph collection of Old Salem, Inc., Winston-Salem, N.C. of original in Archiv der Brüder Unitat, Herrnhut, GDR.; [map of] Wachovia or Dobbs Parish in Rowan County North Carolina, Oct. 15, 1767, copy (neg. S 976) in Old Salem, Inc., Winston-Salem, N.C. of original in Archiv der Brüder Unitat, Herrnhut, GDR.; Ramsey, *Carolina Cradle*, passim.

17. Bethabara diary, Fries et al., *Records*, 1: 85–87; Bethabara Diary, Sept. 27, 1754, MA-SP; [letter from Spangenberg dated May 21, 1754] in Beylage zur XXVIIten Woche des Jünger-Haus Diarii 1754, LC-MC, R.14.Ba.Nr.2b: 218–19; Extract eines Briefs von Br. Grube aus Wachau in North Carolina, an die Brüder Gottlob [Königsdorfer], Nathanael [Seidel], und [Christian] Seidel, March 1, 1754, LC-MC, R.14.Ba.Nr.2b: 157–59; Protocoll der Helfers Conferenz, Oct. 12, 1756, MA-SP.

18. Spangenberg to Lösch, June 29, 1755, LC-MC, R.14.Ba.Nr.2b: 516–18; Conferenz über den Wachauischen Plan gehalten in Bethl[ehem], Sept. 22, 1755, LC-MC, R.14.Ba.Nr.2b: 596–601 and MA-NP, Wachovia II, folder 2, item 2–5; Spangenberg to Lösch, May 3, 1756, LC-MC, R.14.Ba.Nr.2c: 84–87.

19. Bethabara diary, Fries et al., *Records*, 1: 82. They did refuse credit to at least one man, though, on the grounds that "we did not know him and he had been able to show nothing about himself" (Bethabara Diary, April 12, 1756, MA-SP).

20. Petrus [Böhler] an Spangenberg wegen North-Carolina, Oct. 23, 1753, LC-MC, R.14.Ba.Nr.2b: 73–74; Lösch to Böhler, April 27, 1754, LC-MC, R.14.Ba.Nr.2b:: 211–13; Lösch to Christian Seydel, Jan. 26, 1754, LC-MC, R.14.Ba.Nr.2b: 403; [untitled list of debts], [Aug. 1756], LC-MC, R.14.Ba.Nr.2c: 133.

21. Bethabara diary extracts, Fries et al., *Records*, 1: 139; [statement of income and expenses, Oct. 8, 1753–Nov. 10, 1755], LC-MC, R.14.Ba.Nr.2c: 40–57; [statement of income and expenses, Nov. 10, 1755–Feb. 26, 1756], LC-MC, R.14.Ba.Nr.2c: 67–72; W. Thomas Mainwaring, "Community Among the Moravian Brethren of Wachovia 1753–1772" (M.A. thesis, University of North Carolina, 1977), 87; Gol-

lin, *Moravians*, 180–83; Spangenberg diary, Fries et al., *Records*, 1: 30–62.

22. Van Laer to Spangenberg, July 2, 1754, LC-MC, R.14.Ba.Nr.2b: 253–54; Kurzen Status der North Carol. Societaet, Dec. 23, 1754, LC-MC, R.14.Ba.Nr.2c: 106; van Laer to Spangenberg, March 15, 1754, LC-MC, R.14.Ba.Nr.2b: 168–70; Spangenberg to Lösch, June 29, 1755, LC-MC, R.14.Ba.Nr.2b: 516–18; [letter from Spangenberg dated May 21, 1754] in Beylage zur XXVIIten Woche des Jünger-Haus Diarii 1754, LC-MC, R.14.Ba.Nr.2b: 218–19; Spangenberg to Weiss, June 27, 1754, LC-MC, R.14.Ba.Nr.2b: 224–26.

23. Spangenberg to Weiss, Nov. 27, 1754, LC-MC, R.14.Ba.Nr.2b: 296–97.

24. Friis to Spangenberg, April 30, 1755, LC-MC, R.14.Ba.Nr.2b: 475–81; Höger to Weiss, Dec. 26, 1754, LC-MC, R.14.Ba.Nr.2b: 375–78; Spangenberg to [the Brr. in Bethabara], June 29, 1755, MA-SP, trans. K. G. Hamilton; Conferenz über den Wachauischen Plan gehalten in Bethl[ehem], Sept. 22, 1755, LC-MC, R.14.Ba.Nr.2b: 596–601 and MA-NP, Wachovia II, folder 2, item 2–5; [announcement of prices and conditions of purchase], Dec. 14, 1756, MA-NP, Wachovia II, folder 4, item 2–8.

25. Friis to Spangenberg, April 30, 1755, LC-MC, R.14.Ba.Nr.2b: 475–81; Extract aus meine Journalen von Frucht [illegible word], [1759–69], March 22, 1759, MA-SP. Profits of wheat and corn based on average yields of 15 and 18 bushels per acre, respectively, (Thorp, "Colonization", 368–9) and prices of 3s. to 3s.6d. and 2s. per bushel ([statements of income and expenses], LC-MC, R.14.Ba.Nr.2c: 40–57, 67–72, 127–32, 177–79). The difference in income per acre was even greater, 57s. versus 36s., if the wheat was sold as flour.

26. [Statement of income and expenses, July–Dec. 1757], LC-MC, R.14.Ba.Nr.2c: 242–44; Spangenberg to [the members in Wachovia], May 25, 1757, MA-SP, trans. K. G. Hamilton

27. Spangenberg to Zinzendorf, Nov. 15, 1757, LC-MC, R.14.Ba.Nr.2c: 202–8; [statement of harvests and mill tolls in 1757], April 23, 1758, LC-MC, R.14.Ba.Nr.2c: 235; annual consumption of approximately 11 bushels per person calculated from Bethabara Accounts, June 1, 1764–May 31, 1765, MA-NP, Wachovia VI, Papiere die Wachau betreffend 1762–64; [statement of income and expenses, Jan.–July 1758], LC-MC, R.14.Ba.Nr.2c: 257–62.

28. [Catalogue of buildings in Bethabara], March 27, [1758], LC-MC, R.14.Ba.Nr.2c: 222–25; [statement of income and expenses, July–Dec.

1757], LC-MC, R.14.Ba.Nr.2c: 242–44; [statement of income and expenses, Jan.–July 1758], LC-MC, R.14.Ba.Nr.2c: 257–62; Bethabara Diary, April 29, Sept. 15, and Oct. 6, 1757, MA-SP; Spangenberg to Lösch, May 3, 1756, LC-MC, R.14.Ba.Nr.2c: 84–87; Mack to Zinzendorf, Feb. 26, 1757, LC-MC, R.14.Ba.Nr.2c: 162–67.

29. [Statement of income and expenses, Oct. 8, 1753–Nov. 10, 1755], LC-MC, R.14.Ba.Nr.2c: 40–57; [statement of income and expenses, Nov. 10, 1755–Feb. 26, 1756], LC-MC, R.14.Ba.Nr.2c: 67–72; [statement of incomes and expenses, Jan.–July 1758], LC-MC, R.14.Ba.Nr.2c: 257–62.

30. Specification derer Sachen, welche von Bethlehem . . . sind geschickt werden, Aug. 10, 1756, LC-MC, R.14.Ba.Nr.2c: 116–18; Bethabara diary extracts, Fries et al., *Records*, 1: 173; Bethabara Diary, Sept. 17, 1757, MA-SP.

31. Ramsey, *Carolina Cradle*, 107, 126, 152–70; Merrens, *Colonial North Carolina*, 162–64; Mitchell, *Commercialism and Frontier*, 189–229; Alexander and John Lowrance Ledger, Manuscript Dept., Perkins Library, Duke Univ.; Lester J. Cappon, ed., *Atlas of Early American History* (Princeton: Princeton Univ. Press, 1976), 28 (this source shows a pottery in Steeds, N.C., but inquires at the Museum of Early Southern Decorative Arts in Winston-Salem, N.C., convince me that no such pottery existed during the colonial period).

32. Monathliche Berechnung . . . in Bethabara, Jan. 1759, LC-MC, R.14.Ba.Nr.2c: 425–30.

33. Spangenberg to die Conferenz in Bethabara, June 13, 1758, LC-MC, R.14.Ba.Nr.2c: 252–53.

34. Spangenberg to van Laer, Jan. 27, 1759, LC-MC, R.14.Ba.Nr.2c: 265–72.

35. Ohnmassgebliches Project zur Besezung des Districts in North Caroline, Sept. 12, 1753, MA-NP, Wachovia II, folder 1, item 2–36; Spangenberg to Hutton, Marschall, and Cossart, Nov. 18, 1754, LC-MC, R.14.Ba.Nr.2b: 290–91; memorabilia and Bethabara diary extracts, Fries et al., *Records*, 1: 157–61, 180; Spangenberg to the Brethren and Sisters [at Bethabara], [Dec. 6, 1756], MA-SP, trans. K. G. Hamilton; vom Weingarten oder Weinbergen, June 9, 1767, MA-SP, Lösch to [?], April 22, 1758, LC-MC, R.14.Ba.Nr.2c: 236; Spangenberg to die Conferenz in Bethabara, June 13, 1758, LC-MC, R.14.Ba.Nr.2c: 252–53.

36. Spangenberg to Lösch, May 3, 1756, LC-MC, R.14.Ba.Nr.2c: 84–87; Cossart to Spangenberg, April 1, 1754, MA-NP, Wachovia V, Correspondence of Spangenberg, item 1; Lösch to Spangenberg, April 22, 1758, LC-MC, R.14.Ba.Nr.2c: 228–34; Extract-Observation von Obst

Baumen, [1758–66], entries for June 6, 1759 and March 18, 1760, MA-SP; Journal Beym Landmessen in Wachau . . . , [1760], entry for March 18, LC-MC, R.14.Ba.Nr.2c: 462–77.

37. Okley to Lösch, April 27, 1756, LC-MC, R.14.Ba.Nr.2c: 65; Bethabara Diary, Jan. 3, 1757, MA-SP; Protocoll der Helfers Conferenz, Feb. 27, 1757, Sept. 30, 1759, and Oct. 31, 1759, MA-SP; Spangenberg to [the Members in Wachovia], May 25, 1757, MA-SP, trans. K. G. Hamilton (in translating this letter, Bishop Hamilton mistranslated "Beutel" as account book rather than bolter); Spangenberg to Johannes [von Watteville], Oct. 21, 1759, LC-MC, R.14.Ba.Nr.2c: 388–91.

38. [Bethabara Accounts, June 1, 1762–May 31, 1763], MA-NP, Wachovia VI, Papiere die Wachau betreffend 1762–64; [account of the *Oeconomy*], MA-SP, Bethabara Diacony Ledger, 1764–72; Carville Earle and Ronald Hoffman, "Staple Crops and Urban Development in the Eighteenth-Century South," *Perspectives in American History* 10 (1976): 7–78; Historischer Bericht, LC-MC, R.14.Ba.Nr.2a: 19–42.

39. Merrens, *Colonial North Carolina*; W. Stitt Robinson, *The Southern Colonial Frontier, 1607–1763* (Albuquerque: Univ. of New Mexico Press, 1979); Peter H. Wood, *Black Majority: Negroes in South Carolina From 1670 through the Stono Rebellion* (New York: Knopf, 1974; New York: Norton, 1975); Converse D. Clowse, *Economic Beginnings in Colonial South Carolina, 1670–1730* (Columbia: Univ. of South Carolina Press, 1971); Lemon, *Best Poor Man's Country*, 161; Eighth and Ninth United States Censuses; Protocoll der Helfers Conferenz, March 9 and June 6, 1759, MA-SP; Christian Fredrich Oerter to Marschall, Sept. 1, 1768, MA-SP, trans. E. Marx; diary/letter of Rev. John Jacob Friis, Fries et al., *Records*, 2: 529–33.

40. Item aus Br. Dixon's Brief, n.d., LC-MC, R.14.Ba.Nr.2c: 605–6; Höger to Weiss, Dec. 26, 1754, LC-MC, R.14.Ba.Nr.2b: 375–78; Conferenz über den Wachauischen Plan gehalten in Bethl[ehem], Sept. 22, 1755, LC-MC, R.14.Ba.Nr.2b: 596–601 and MA-NP, Wachovia II, folder 2, item 2–5; Spangenberg to the Brethren and Sisters [at Bethabara], [Dec. 6, 1756], MA-SP, trans. K. G. Hamilton.

41. Ettwein to Hopson, Nov. 15, 1758, LC-MC, R.14.Ba.Nr.2c: 263–64; Ettwein to Spangenberg, Jan. 6, 1759, LC-MC, R.14.Ba.Nr.2c: 280–81.

42. [Accounts of the store and of the *Oeconomy*], MA-SP, Bethabara Diacony Ledger, 1764–72; Converse D. Clowse, *Measuring Charleston's Overseas Commerce, 1717–1767: Statistics From the Port's Naval Lists* (Washington, D.C.: Univ. Press of America, 1981), 55; Ettwein to die Conferenz in Bethlehem, Jan. 18, 1762, LC-MC, R.14.Ba.Nr.2c: 576–80;

Ettwein to Marschall, May 12, 1765, MA-NP, Wachovia III, folder 3, item 15.

43. Bethabara diary extracts, Fries et al., *Records*, 1: 133, 211; [catalogue of buildings in Bethabara], March 27, [1758], LC-MC, R.14.Ba.Nr.2c: 222–25; Protocoll der Helfers Conferenz, Sept. 26, 1759, MA-SP.

44. Bericht an das Unit. Diener Department, Aug. 3, 1770, MA-SP, Reports to the Unity Elders Conference, translation from extract in Fries et al., *Records*, 2: 614; Bethabara diary extracts, Fries et al., *Records*, 1: 211; for Brother Joh. Schaub at the Opening of the Brethren's Store in Bethabara, July 9, 1759, MA-SP, trans. K. G. Hamilton.

45. Zettel appear throughout the Bethabara Diacony Ledger, 1764–72, MA-SP and in the Aug. 3, 1770 Bericht cited in note 44.

46. Okley to W. Maulsby, [April 27, 1756], LC-MC, R.14.Ba.Nr.2c: 65; Donald R. Lennon and Ida Brooks Kellam, *The Wilmington Town Book, 1743–1778* (Raleigh: Div. of Archives and History, 1973), 3n–4n; Spangenberg to Weiss, Sept. 13, 1755, LC-MC, R.14.Ba.Nr.2b: 594–95; Historischer Bericht, LC-MC, R.14.Ba.Nr.2a: 19–42.

47. Bridenbaugh, *Myths & Realities*, 150; Ettwein to John Hopson, Nov. 15, 1758, LC-MC, R.14.Ba.Nr.2c: 263–64; Protocoll der Engen Conferenz, Jan. 3 and 23, 1759, MA-SP; Ettwein to Spangenberg, Jan. 6, 1759, LC-MC, R.14.Ba.Nr.2c: 280–81; Ettwein to Spangenberg, Jan. 29, 1759, LC-MC, R.14.Ba.Nr.2c: 282–83.

48. Spangenberg to van Laer, Jan. 27, 1759, LC-MC, R.14.Ba.Nr.2c: 265–72; [accounts for John and Richard Lyon], MA-SP, Bethabara Diacony Ledger, 1764–72; Protocoll der Helfers Conferenz, Nov. 4, 1759, MA-SP.

49. Wachovia church book and Bethabara diary extracts, Fries et al., *Records*, 1: 234–35; extract from *South Carolina Gazette*, Feb. 7, 1761, in Hamer et al., *Papers of Henry Laurens*, 3: 59; Lösch to Spangenberg, Feb. 18, 1761, LC-MC, R.14.Ba.Nr.2c: 553–60; Ettwein to die Conferenz in Bethlehem, Feb. 28, 1761, LC-MC, R.14.Ba.Nr.2c: 549–52.

50. Lösch to Spangenberg, Feb. 18, 1761, LC-MC, R.14.Ba.Nr.2c: 553–60; Ettwein to die Conferenz in Bethlehem, Feb. 28, 1761, LC-MC, R.14.Ba.Nr.2c: 549–52; Protocoll der Wöchentlicher Conferenz, Jan. 2, 1762, MA-SP; Ettwein's Visit to Governor William Tryon at Brunshwig in North Carolina, Fries et al., *Records*, 1: 338–41; Extract aus Br. Dixon's Brief, n.d., LC-MC, R.14.Ba.Nr.2c: 605–6; Ettwein to die Conferenz in Bethlehem, Jan. 18, 1762, LC-MC, R.14.Ba.Nr.2c: 576–80; Ettwein to die Conferenz in Bethlehem, Sept. 9, 1762, MA-NP, Wachovia III, folder 1, item 1–9.

51. Gammern to Nathanael [Seidel], Sept. 2, 1764, MA-NP, Wachovia III, folder 2, item 1–46; Graff to Nathanael [Seidel], April 7, 1766, MA-NP, Wachovia III, folder 2, item 1–71; [editors' note], Hamer et al., *Papers of Henry Laurens*, 5: 735–36; Protocoll der Helfers Conferenz, Oct. 10, 1766, MA-SP.

52. An die Unitaets Helfer, Oct. 15, 1770, MA-SP, Reports to the Unity; Ettwein's Visit to Governor William Tryon at Brunshwig in North Carolina, Fries et al., *Records*, 1: 338–41; diary extracts, Fries et al., *Records*, 1: 356. There is no evidence to support Lawrence Lee's claim that the Brethren felt a continuing desire to trade with Wilmington and were frustrated in this because residents of the Cape Fear region heard rumors about them that "turn[ed] suspicion into antagonism and create[d] a reluctance to promote the profits of the Brethren" (Lawrence Lee, *The Lower Cape Fear in Colonial Days* [Chapel Hill: Univ. of North Carolina Press, 1965], 174).

53. [Catalogue of residents], Dec. 31, 1762, Fries et al., *Records*, 1: 253–55; Catalogue of . . . Inhabitants, [April 1766], Fries et al., *Records*, 1: 343–45; [statement of income and expenses, June 1, 1760–May 31, 1761], LC-MC, R.14.Ba.Nr.2c: 567–69; Bethabara Accounts, June 1, 1762–May 31, 1763, MA-NP, Wachovia VI, Papiere die Wachau betreffend 1762–64; [membership list of the Single Brothers Choir, Aug. 30, 1768] filed in MA-SP, Classen und Besuche der Led. Brr. u. Knaben in Salem [1765–1788]; [account of earnings and losses], MA-SP, Bethabara Diacony Ledger, 1764–72.

54. [Accounts of the gunsmith, gunstocker, *Oeconomy*, potter, saddler, and store], MA-SP, Bethabara Diacony Ledger, 1764–72.

55. Extract aus Br. Dixon's Brief, n.d., LC-MC, R.14.Ba.Nr.2c: 605–6; Ettwein to die Conferenz in Bethlehem, Jan. 18, 1762, LC-MC, R.14.Ba.Nr.2c: 576–80; [accounts of the store and the *Oeconomy*], MA-SP, Bethabara Diacony Ledger, 1764–72.

56. Bethabara diary extracts, Fries et al., *Records*, 1: 244; Ettwein to [a conference in Bethlehem], Aug. 19, 1761, LC-MC, R.14.Ba.Nr.2c: 565–66; Ettwein to Spangenberg, Jan. 18, 1762, LC-MC, R14.Ba.Nr.2c: 581–82; 10 Jährige Observation von Säen und Ernden zu Bethabara, [1758–69], MA-SP; Extract aus meine Journalen von Frucht [illegible word], [1759–69], MA-SP; [statement of assets in the *Oeconomy*], May 31, 1761, LC-MC, R.14.Ba.Nr.2c: 567–69; Bethabara Accounts, June 1, 1762–May 31, 1763, MA-NP, Wachovia VI, Papiere die Wachau betreffend 1762–64; Bethabara Accounts, June 1, 1764–May 31, 1765, MA-NP, Wachovia VI, Papiere die Wachau betreffend 1762–64; [inventory of

fruit trees planted], April 22, 1758, LC-MC, R.14.Ba.Nr.2c: 561–62; memorabilia, Fries et al., *Records*, 1: 382–86.

57. Lösch to Spangenberg, Feb. 27, 1761, LC-MC, R.14.Ba.Nr.2c: 561–62; Bethabara Accounts, June 1, 1762–May 31, 1763, MA-NP, Wachovia VI, Papiere die Wachau betreffend 1762–64; Böhler to die Conferenz in der Wachau, Oct. 25, 1762, MA-SP; [catalogue of residents], Dec. 31, 1762, Fries et al., *Records*, : 253–55; memorabilia, Fries et al., *Records*, 1: 279–83; Bethabara Accounts, June 1, 1762–May 31, 1763, MA-NP, Wachovia VI, Papiere die Wachau betreffend 1762–64; Bethabara Accounts, June 1, 1764–May 31, 1765, MA-NP, Wachovia VI, Papiere die Wachau betreffend 1762–64.

58. [Note dated Nov. 3, 1771] on back of An des Department der Helfer in U. Aelt. Collegio, Sept. 2, 1771, MA-SP.

59. This is abundantly clear from Bethabara Accounts, June 1, 1762 - May 31, 1763, MA-NP, Wachovia VI, Papiere die Wachau betreffend 1762–64; Bethabara Accounts, June 1, 1764–May 31, 1765, MA-NP, Wachovia VI, Papiere die Wachau betreffend 1762–64; [various accounts], MA-SP, Bethabara Diacony Ledger, 1764–72.

60. Ettwein to Nathanael [Seidel], Dec. 6, 1762, MA-NP, Wachovia III, folder 1, item 1–15; Protocoll der Helfers Conferenz, May 2, 1760, Jan. 16, 1764, Sept. 19, 1766, and Aug. 14, 1769, MA-SP; Protocoll der Wöchentlicher Conferenz, Feb. 28, July 25, and Dec. 19, 1763, MA-SP; Bethabara diary extracts, Fries et al., *Records*, 1: 250, 391; Pro Memoria Noch wegen Stadt Bau u. Stadt Platz, Jan. 8, 1762, LC-MC, R.14.Ba.Nr.2c: 616–18; Reuter to Spangenberg, March 30, 1764, LC-MC, R.14.Ba.Nr.2c: 190–91; Historischer Bericht, LC-MC, R.14.Ba.Nr.2a: 19–42.

61. Bethabara diary extracts, Fries et al., *Records*, 1: 274; [lease for Cate], Oct. 21, 1767, MA-SP, Bills of Sale; bills of sale dated Aug. 9, 1769, March 28, Aug. 24, and Oct. 12, 1771, MA-SP, Bills of Sale; Henry Laurens' Journal, 1766–73, 46, Robert Scott Small Library–Manuscript Section, College of Charleston; Schropp to Nathanael [Seidel], April 14, 1767, MA-NP, Wachovia III, folder 2, item 1–83; [Salem account], MA-SP, Bethabara Diacony Ledger, 1764–72.

62. Buying and reselling an annual average of 4,964 pounds of deer skin should have generated sales between Moravians and non-Moravians of between £1158 and £1738, North Carolina.

63. Protocoll einer Conferenz in Bethabara, Aug. 7, 1759, LC-MC, R.14.Ba.Nr.2c: 357–61; Extract aus meines Anmerkungen . . . von Aller Land Zahmen Vieh, [1758–66], entry for Aug. 24, 1762, MA-SP; Betha-

bara diary extracts, Fries et al., *Records*, 1: 249, 290; Carolinische Conferenz in Directorial Collegio, July 26, 1763, MA-NP, Wachovia VI, Papiere die Wachau betreffend 1762–64, item 1; F. W. Marshall's Notes Concerning Wachovia, Feb. 1, 1764, Fries et al., *Records*, 1: 293–94; Protocoll der Helfers Conferenz, Dec. 4 and 6, 1764 and Feb. 24, 1766, MA-SP; [out-lots account], MA-SP, Bethabara Diacony Ledger, 1764–72.

64. For Brother Joh. Schaub at the Opening of the Brethren's Store in Bethabara, July 9, 1759, MA-SP, trans. K. G. Hamilton; Bethabara Accounts, June 1, 1762–May 31, 1763, MA-NP, Wachovia VI, Papiere die Wachau betreffend 1762–64; Protocoll der Helfers Conferenz, Aug. 13, 1764 and Aug. 19, 1767, MA-SP; Ettwein to Marschall, [Nov. 1765], MA-SP, trans. K. G. Hamilton; Schropp to Oeconomats Conf. in Bethlehem, Nov. 23, 1766, MA-NP, Wachovia III, folder 2, item 1–79; Schropp to [?], Nov. 20, 1766, MA-SP, trans. E. Marx; [store account], MA-SP, Bethabara Diacony Ledger, 1764–72.

65. Bethabara Accounts, June 1, 1763–May 31, 1764, MA-NP, Wachovia VI, Papiere die Wachau betreffend 1762–64; Spangenberg to Lösch, Feb. 6, 1758, LC-MC, R.14.Ba.Nr.2c: 213–14; Spangenberg to die Conferenz in Bethabara, April 17, 1762, LC-MC, R.14.Ba.Nr.2c: 592–600; Ettwein to die Conferenz in Bethlehem, Jan. 18, 1762, LC-MC, R.14.Ba.Nr.2c: 576–80; Bethabara diary extracts, Fries et al., *Records*, 1: 235.

66. [Salem account], MA-SP, Bethabara Diacony Ledger, 1764–72.

CHAPTER 6
Law and Politics Moravian Style

1. Conf. des Directorii zu Zeyst, Aug. 26, 1767, MA-SP, Conferences-Decisions of U.E.C. concerning Salem 1763, 1765, 1767, translation from extract in Fries et al., *Records*, 2: 599–600.

2. Neither signatures nor handwriting provide a means of identifying English speakers in Wachovia because even men known to have spoken and written English still wrote German in German script and signed their names in German.

3. Laura Becker, "The People and the System: Legal Activities in a Colonial Pennsylvania Town," *Pennsylvania Magazine of History and Biography* 105 (1981): 135–49. The Moravians' experience offers an interesting contrast to Becker's account of assimilation among Reading's Germans. Most of the latter belonged to either the Lutheran or Reformed Church and arrived either in family groups or individually. Becker

maintains that the "essentially disorganized" nature of this migration, compared to that of sectarians like the Moravians, facilitated the newcomers' adjustment to English law by placing them in relative isolation from their fellow Germans and thus reducing their ability to maintain German traditions. In the Moravians' case, though, sectarian clannishness was an important factor in the speed with which an immigrant group mastered the law of their host country. Unity leaders recognized the necessity of learning the law and used the church's almost military chain of command to effect it. For other discussions of German settlers' response to Anglo-American law and politics, see George Fenwick Jones, *The Salzburger Saga: Religious Exiles and Other Germans Along the Savannah* (Athens: Univ. of Georgia Press, 1984) and Elizabeth A. Kessel, "Germans on the Maryland Frontier: A Social History of Fredrick County, Maryland, 1730–1800" (Ph.D. dissertation, Rice Univ., 1981).

4. Spangenberg to [?], Aug. 4, 1753, MA-NP, Wachovia II, folder 1, item 2–32, translation from undated copy in Fries et al., *Records*, 2: 526–27; Spangenberg diary, Fries et al., *Records*, 1: 30–62.

5. Hutton to Spangenberg, n.d., LC-MC, R.14.Ba.Nr.2b: 11–12 (most of this letter appears in Fries et al., *Records*, 2: 515, but the final paragraph does not, for some reason); Bethabara diary, Fries et al., *Records*, 1: 84; [Lösch's receipt for a law book], Sept. 7, 1754, LC-MC, R.14.Ba.Nr.2b: 248; Benzien to Christian Heinrich [Rauch], Feb. 26, 1756, MA-SP, trans. K. G. Hamilton; [inventory of the congregational library], MA-SP, Mobillien Inventaria des Diaconats von der Wachau. . . , 1766.

6. Bethabara diary, Fries et al., *Records*, 1: 84; Levering, *Bethlehem*, 211. For a more complete discussion of Moravian concerns about resentment among the populace in North Carolina, see chapter 7.

7. "An Act for Establishing the Church. . .", 1741, in Walter Clark, *The State Records of North Carolina*, 16 vols. beginning with number 11 (Raleigh: P. M. Hale, 1886–1907) 23: 187–91; Instructions for Jacob Rogers, Minister of Dobbs Parish, June 19, 1758, Fries et al., *Records*, 1: 196–98.

8. Edward M. Holder, "Community Life in Wachovia 1752–1780" (M. A. thesis, Univ. of North Carolina, 1929); "An Act for encouraging the People known by the Name of *Unitas Fratrum*. . . to settle in His Majesty's Colonies in America," Anno 22 George II (1749), chapter 30; Protocoll der Helfers Conferenz, July 30, 1764, MA-SP.

9. Protocoll einer Conferenz in Bethabara, Aug. 7, 1759, LC-MC, R.14.Ba.Nr.2c: 357–61; Journal Beym Landmessen in Wachau. . ., [1760], entry for Feb. 29, LC-MC, R.14.Ba.Nr.2c: 462–77.

10. Protocoll einer Conferenz in Bethabara, Aug. 7, 1759, LC-MC, R.14.Ba.Nr.2c: 357–61; Spangenberg to Ettwein, Jan. 20, 1761, LC-MC, R.14.Ba.Nr.2c: 541–46; Protocoll der Wöchentlicher Conferenz, May 30, 1763, MA-SP.

11. Davis to Antes, Oct. 22, 1754, LC-MC, R.14.Ba.Nr.2b: 529–30; Okley to Davis, June 30, 1755, LC-MC, R.14.Ba.Nr.2b: 532–33. For other examples of this tactic, see Bethabara diary extracts, Fries et al., *Records,* 1: 252, 303.

12. Bethabara diary extracts, Fries et al., *Records,* 1: 330.

13. Spangenberg to van Laer, Jan. 27, 1759, LC-MC, R.14.Ba.Nr.2c: 265–72; Levering, *Bethlehem,* 210–13.

14. Vorschlage wegen einer Corporation in Salem, April 1767, LC-MC, R.14.A.Nr.44: 22–27; Conf. des Directorii zu Zeyst, Aug. 16, 1767, MA-SP, Conferences-Decisions of U.E.C. concerning Salem 1763, 1765, 1767, translated extract in Fries et al., *Records,* 2: 596–99.

15. Paul Conkin, "The Church Establishment in North Carolina, 1765–1776," *North Carolina Historical Review* 32 (1955): 1–30; John M. Garland, "The Non-Ecclesiastical Activities of an English and North Carolina Parish: A Comparative Study," *North Carolina Historical Review* 50 (1973): 32–51; Clark, *State Records,* 23: 187–91; Jack P. Greene, *The Quest for Power: The Lower Houses of the Assembly in the Southern Royal Colonies, 1689–1776* (Chapel Hill: Univ. of North Carolina Press, 1963), 352–53.

16. Benziens Relation seiner Reise nach Wachau, Cape Fear, New Bern, und wieder züruck nach Bethlehem, Nov. 21, 1755, LC-MC, R.14.Ba.Nr.2b: 619–30; Spangenberg to Zinzendorf, Aug. 1–19, 1756, LC-MC, R.14.Ba.Nr.2c: 119–22; Spangenberg to Weiss, Sept. 3, 1754, LC-MC, R.14,Ba.Nr.2b: 240–47.

17. The decision to request a separate parish is mentioned in an untitled and undated document filed amidst the minutes of a Bethlehem conference held in August 1754 and probably originating in that conference, LC-MC, R.14.Ba.Nr.2b: 235; [draft of a petition to the North Carolina assembly], n.d., MA-NP, Wachovia II, folder 4, item 2-2; Extract aus einer Conf. vom 6ten Apr. 1755 zur Instruction vor die Brr. Dav. Nitschman u. Benzien, LC-MC, R.14.Ba.Nr.2b: 407.

18. Benziens Relation seiner Reise nach Wachau, Cape Fear, New Bern, und wieder züruck nach Bethlehem, Nov. 21, 1755, LC-MC, R.14.Ba.Nr.2b: 619–30; Spangenberg to Zinzendorf, Aug. 1–19, 1756, LC-MC, R.14.Ba.Nr.2c: 119–22.

19. "An Act, for erecting that Part of Rowan County called Wachovia into a distinct Parish," Clark, *State Records,* 23: 438–39.

20. Spangenberg to Zinzendorf, Aug. 1–19, 1756, LC-MC, R.14.Ba.Nr.2c: 119–22. It is also clear that at least some of Wachovia's neighbors understood what the Brethren were up to; see, for example, Theodorus Swaine Drage, Rector of St. Luke's Parish to the Secretary [of the Society for the Propagation of the Gospel], Feb. 28, 1771, in William L. Saunders, *The Colonial Records of North Carolina*, 10 vols. (Raleigh: P.M. Hale, 1886–90) 8: 502–7.

21. Names of the vestrymen are on various papers in MA-SP, Rowan County-Dobbs Parish Papers; Benzien to Corbin, Sept. 17, 1756, MA-NP, Wachovia III, folder 3, item 1–19; Benzien to Zinzendorf, Oct. 13, 1756, LC-MC, R.14.Ba.Nr.2c: 141–42; Spangenberg to Your Excel. [Arthur Dobbs], July 28, 1756, MA-NP, Wachovia II, folder 3, item 1–15; Ramsey, *Carolina Cradle*, 205.

22. Extracts from the Minutes of the Aeltesten Conferenz, Aufseher Collegium, and Grosse Helfers Conferenz, Fries et al., *Records*, 2: 773; [Dobbs Parish account], MA-SP, Bethabara Diacony Ledger, 1764–72; Protocoll der Helfers Conferenz, April 25, 1768, April 17 and Dec. 4, 1769, MA-SP; [minutes of a vestry meeting], June 14, 1757, MA-SP, Rowan County-Dobbs Parish Papers, also in Fries et al., *Records*, 1: 427.

23. Spangenberg to die Brüder in Wachau, Feb. 27, 1756, LC-MC, R.14.Ba.Nr.2c: 29; Benzien to Weiss, May 26, 1756, LC-MC, R.14.Ba.Nr.2c: 36–39; Bethabara Diary, Sept. 20, 1756, MA-SP; Rogers to the Dobbs Parish Vestry, March 15, 1762, MA-SP, Rowan County-Dobbs Parish Papers; Spangenberg to die Conf. in Bethabara, April 17, 1762, LC-MC, R.14.Ba.Nr.2c: 592–600; Marschall to the Board of Elders at Bethabara, June 24, 1766, MA-SP, trans. K. G. Hamilton.

24. Rogers to Spangenberg, Feb. 11, 1759, LC-MC, R.14.Ba.Nr.2c: 284–85.

25. Conkin, "Church Establishment." It is impossible to say how many Anglicans there were in the backcountry. In the case of Rowan County, all one can say is that the number probably fell somewhere between the 200 who signed a petition to the governor and assembly of North Carolina in 1769 (Saunders, *Colonial Records*, 8: 154–55) and the 7,000 reported there by T. S. Drage, Rector of St. Luke's Parish, the following year (Drage to the Secretary [of the Society for the Propagation of the Gospel], Feb. 28, 1771, Saunders, *Colonial Records*, 8: 502–7).

26. Patricia U. Bonomi and Peter R. Eisenstadt, "Church Adherence in the Eighteenth-Century British American Colonies," *William and Mary Quarterly*, 3rd ser., 39 (1982): 245–86, especially 266–68; Drage to Tryon, May 29, 1770, Saunders *Colonial Records*, 8: 202–10; [petition from Rowan County], [1770], Saunders, *Colonial Records*, 8: 219.

Notes to Pages 161–166

27. [Dobbs Parish account], MA-SP, Bethabara Diacony Ledger, 1764–1772; Protocoll der Helfers Conferenz, Dec. 4, 1769, MA-SP; Fries et al., *Records:* passim.

28. Spangenberg to Zinzendorf, Nov. 15, 1757, LC-MC, R.14.Ba.Nr.2c: 202–8; Spangenberg to [?], Aug. 4, 1753, MA-NP, Wachovia II, Folder 1, item 2–32, undated translation in Fries et al., *Records*, 2: 526–27; Spangenberg to Johannes [von Watteville], Sept. 15, 1759, LC-MC, R.14.Ba.Nr.2c: 423–24; Historischer Bericht, LC-MC, R.14.Ba.Nr.2a: 19–42.

29. Cossart to Dobbs, Dec. 15, 1754, LC-MC, R.14.Ba.Nr.1: 9–11; Metcalf to Spangenberg, March 5, 1763, LC-MC, R.14.A.Nr.44: 12–19; Carolinische Conferenz in Directorial Collegio, July 26, 1763, MA-NP, Wachovia VI, Papiere die Wachau betreffend 1762–64, item 1; Conditionen, welche man zu einer Charter für Salem proponiren könnte, n.d., LC-MC, R.14,A.Nr.44: 28–29; Paul M. McCain, "Magistrates Courts in Early North Carolina," *North Carolina Historical Review* 48 (1971): 23–30.

30. Carolinische Conferenz in Directorial Collegio, July 26, 1763, MA-NP, Wachovia VI, Papiere die Wachau betreffend 1762–64, item 1; Bericht des Directorii an des U.V. Coll. wegen der Amer. Conferenzen..., [March 30–April 27, 1767], MA-SP, Conferences-Decisions of U.E.C. concerning Salem 1763, 1765, 1767, translated extract in Fries et al., *Records*, 2: 596; Conf. des Directorii zu Zeyst, Aug. 26, 1767, MA-SP, Conferences-Decisions of U.E.C. concerning Salem 1763, 1765, 1767, translated extract in Fries et al., *Records*, 2: 599–600.

31. Corbitt, *North Carolina Counties*, 199–200.

32. Paul M. McCain, *The County Court in North Carolina Before 1750*, Historical Papers of the Trinity College Historical Society, 31 (Durham, N.C.: Duke Univ. Press, 1954); Clark, *State Records*, 23: 252–67, 332–41, 563–75.

33. Ohnmassgebliches Project zur Besezung des Districts in North Caroline, Sept. 12, 1753, MA-NP, Wachovia II, folder 1, item 2–36; Lösch to Benzien, April 19, 1756, LC-MC, R.14.Ba.Nr.2c: 96–97; Spangenberg to [the Members in Wachovia], May 25, 1757, MA-SP, trans. K. G. Hamilton; [North Carolina] Council Journal, May 17, 1757, Saunders, *Colonial Records*, 5: 810; Bethabara diary extracts, Fries et al., *Records*, 1: 192; [minutes of the Rowan County court meeting, October 1758], Archives of the North Carolina State Library, Rowan County-Minutes of Court of Pleas and Quarter Sessions, C. R. 85.301.2: 245–49.

34. Memorabilia, Fries et al., *Records*, 1: 382–86; memorabilia, Fries

et al., *Records*, 1: 430–37; Spangenberg to van Laer, Jan. 27, 1759, LC-MC, R.14.Ba.Nr.2c: 265–72; Ettwein to the Conference in Bethlehem, Jan. 18, 1762, LC-MC, R.14.Ba.Nr.2c: 576–80.

35. Wachovia diary extracts, Fries et al., *Records*, 1: 386–87; McCain, "Magistrates Courts"; Consignation der Schulden, Feb. 1, 1760, LC-MC, R.14.Ba.Nr.2c: 299.

36. Diary extracts, Fries et al., *Records*, 1: 271, 287, 289, 337, 392, 410; Spangenberg to [the Members in Wachovia], May 25, 1757, MA-SP, trans. K. G. Hamilton; Ettwein to die Conferenz in Bethlehem, Jan. 18, 1762, LC-MC, R.14.Ba.Nr.2c: 576–80.

37. The Regulators criticized public officials in general for being corrupt (Ekirch, *"Poor Carolina"*, 164–96) and Jacob Lösch, personally, for alleged involvement in a land fraud (Bethabara diary extracts, Fries et al., *Records*, 1: 451–52), but they do not seem to have criticized the performance or judicial integrity of any Moravian justice.

38. Fries et al., *Records*, passim.

39. Benzien to Dobbs, March 12, 1757, MA-SP, Rowan County-Dobbs Parish Papers; Spangenberg to van Laer, Jan. 27, 1759, LC-MC, R.14.Ba.Nr.2c: 265–72; Spangenberg to [the Members in Wachovia], May 25, 1757, MA-SP, trans. K. G. Hamilton; Marvin L. Michael Kay and William S. Price, Jr., " 'To Ride the Wood Mare': Road Building and Militia Service in Colonial North Carolina, 1740–1775," *North Carolina Historical Review* 57 (1980): 361–409; Bethabara diary extracts, Fries et al., *Records*, 1: 110. For a more complete account of Moravian attitudes toward war at this time, see Glenn Weaver, "Moravians During the French and Indian War," *Church History* 24 (1955): 239–56.

40. Benzien to Dobbs, March 12, 1757, MA-SP, Rowan County-Dobbs Parish Papers; [North Carolina] Council Journal, May 17, 1757, Saunders, *Colonial Records*, 5: 810; Spangenberg to van Laer, Jan. 27, 1759, LC-MC, R.14.Ba.Nr.2c: 265–72.

41. Bethabara diary extracts, Fries et al., *Records*, 1: 98; memorabilia, Fries et al., *Records*, 1: 279–83; memorabilia, Fries et al., *Records*, 1: 382–86; Bethabara Diary, Feb. 16, 1756, MA-SP; Protocoll der Helfers Conferenz, May 6, 1767, MA-SP; Journal Beym Landmessen in Wachau . . ., [1760], LC-MC, R.14.Ba.Nr.2c: 462–77.

42. Bethabara diary extracts, Fries et al., *Records*, 1: 108, 124, 163, 180–81, 249, 251; [statement of income and expenses for 1759], LC-MC, R.14. Ba.Nr.2c: 498; [statement of income and expenses, June 1, 1759 - May 31, 1760], LC-MC, R.14.Ba.Nr.2c: 533; [statement of income and expenditures, June 1, 1760 - May 31, 1761], LC-MC, R.14.Ba.Nr.2c: 567–

69; Bethabara Accounts, June 1, 1762 - May 31, 1763 MA-NP, Wachovia VI, Papiere die Wachau betreffend 1762–64; extracts from Minutes of the Aufseher Collegium, Fries et al., *Records*, 2: 702.

43. Charles S. Sydnor, *Gentlemen Freeholders* (Chapel Hill: Univ. of North Carolina Press, 1952), chaps. 2–4; Clark, *State Records*, 25: 299, 425; Jack P. Greene, *All Men Are Created Equal: Some Reflections on the Character of the American Revolution* (Oxford: Clarendon Press, 1976), especially 12–17.

44. Benzien to Christian Heinrich [Rauch], Feb. 26, 1756, MA-SP, trans. K. G. Hamilton; [deed dated June 21, 1758], LC-MC, R.14.Ba.Nr.2c: 254–55.

45. F. W. Marshall's Notes concerning Wachovia, Fries et al., *Records*, 1: 293–94; Extract der vom Directorio mit Geschw. Marschalls am 30 Mart 1767 zu Zeist gehalten Conf. die Wachau betreffend, MA-SP, Conferences-Decisions of U.E.C. concerning Salem 1763, 1765, 1767, translated extract in Fries et al., *Records*, 2: 596–97.

46. Bethabara Diary, Oct. 19, 1757, MA-SP; Bethabara diary extracts, Fries et al., *Records*, 1: 231, 236, 284, 391, 470.

47. "An Act to Regulate Elections . . . ," Clark, *State Records*, 23: 523–26; Underhill to Venerable gentlemen, Aug. 23, 1757, MA-NP, Wachovia II, folder 3, item 1–36; Bethabara diary extracts, Fries et al., *Records*, 1: 469.

48. Ekirch, *"Poor Carolina"*, 177–78.

49. Merrens, *Colonial North Carolina*, 54–55; memorabilia, Fries et al., *Records*, 1: 206–8; Surry County Tax Roll, 1771, Archives of the North Carolina State Library, Leg. Papers 11.1; Bethabara diary extracts, Fries et al., *Records*, 1: 470.

50. Hamilton and Hamilton, *History*, 34–94; Hamilton, "Recognition," passim.

51. Spangenberg diary, Fries et al., *Records*, 1: 30–62; Br. Böhlers Memoranda betreffend Wachau, [Dec. 1754], LC-MC, R.14.Ba.Nr.2b: 337–46.

52. Conferenz über den Wachauischen Plan gehalten in Bethl[ehem], Sept. 22, 1755, LC-MC, R.14.Ba.Nr.2b: 596–601 and MA-NP, Wachovia II, folder 2, item 2–5; Protocoll der Helfers Conferenz, July 29, 1767, MA-SP; [untitled report], June 16, 1771, MA-SP, Reports to the Unity, 1771; diary extracts, Fries et al., *Records*, 1: 214, 353–55, 462–65.

53. Bethabara diary extracts, Fries et al., *Records*, 1: 214; [Untitled and undated document filed with minutes of a conference held in Beth-

lehem in August 1754], LC-MC, R.14.Ba.Nr.2b: 235; [draft of a petition to the assembly of North Carolina], n.d., MA-NP, Wachovia II, folder 4, item 2–2; Spangenberg to Weiss, Sept. 3, 1754, LC-MC, R.14.Ba.Nr.2b: 240–47; Br. P. Böhlers Reis Diarium von Wachau nach Newbern, Edenton u. so wieder zürück nach Wachau von 30ten Sept. bis 28ten Oct. [17]54, LC-MC, R.14.Ba.Nr.2b: 347–50; Br. Böhlers Memoranda betreffend Wachau in North Carolina, n.d. LC-MC, R.14.Ba.Nr.2b: 337–46; Böhler to Zinzendorf, Dec. 16, 1754, LC-MC, R.14.Ba.Nr.2b: 333–36.

54. Extract aus einer Conf. von 6ten April 1755 zur Instruction vor die Brr. Dav. Nitschman u. Benzien, LC-MC, R.14.Ba.Nr.2b: 407; Bethabara diary extracts, Fries et al., *Records*, 1: 129; Benzien to Spangenberg, May 30, 1755, LC-MC, R.14.Ba.Nr.2b: 502–3; Benzien to Spangenberg, July 8, 1755, LC-MC, R.14.Ba.Nr.2b: 545; Spangenberg to Benzien, June 30, 1755, LC-MC, R.14.Ba.Nr.2b: 519–22; Benziens Relation seiner Reise nach Wachau, Cape Fear, Newbern und wieder züruck nach Bethlehem, Nov. 21, 1755, LC-MC, R.14.Ba.Nr.2b: 619–30.

55. Ekirch, *"Poor Carolina"*, 86–160; Greene, *Quest for Power*, 39–45; Benziens Relation seiner Reise nach Wachau, Cape Fear, Newbern und wieder züruck nach Bethlehem, Nov. 21, 1755, LC-MC, R.14.Ba.Nr.2b: 619–30.

56. Benziens Relation seiner Reise nach Wachau, Cape Fear, Newbern und wieder züruck nach Bethlehem, Nov. 21, 1755, LC-MC, R.14.Ba.Nr.2b: 619–30; [North Carolina] Council Journal, Oct. 9–15, 1755, Saunders *Colonial Records*, 5: 509–19; Journal of the House, Oct. 9–15, 1755, Saunders, *Colonial Records*, 5: 539–58.

CHAPTER 7
Getting on with the Neighbors

1. Bethabara diary extracts, Fries et al., *Records*, 1: 470; Ettwein to die Conferenz in Bethlehem, Jan. 18, 1762, LC-MC, R.14.Ba.Nr.2c: 576–80.

2. Rhys Isaac, *The Transformation of Virginia, 1740–1790* (Chapel Hill: Univ. of North Carolina Press, 1982), especially 143–77.

3. Spangenberg to [?], Jan. 9, 1754, MA-NP, Wachovia V, Correspondence of Spangenberg, item 22.

4. Hamilton and Hamilton, *History*, 84–85, 143; Lovejoy, *Religious Enthusiasm*, 209–13; Weaver, "Moravians During the French and Indian War"; *The North Carolina Gazette*, Nov. 28, 1755, endorsed copy in LC-MC, R.14.Ba. Nr.2c: 93–94.

5. Regulator Advertisement Number 4, in William S. Powell, James K. Huhta, and Thomas J. Farnham, eds., *The Regulators in North Carolina: A Documentary History, 1759–1776* (Raleigh: State Dept. of Archives and History, 1971), 76; Among the numerous discussions of the Regulators, the one I find most convincing is that contained in Ekirch's *"Poor Carolina"*.

6. Interim Instrument in My Ld. Granville's Hand, n.d., MA-NP, Wachovia II, folder 1, item 4–8; [endorsement on copy of] *The North Carolina Gazette*, Nov. 28, 1755, LC-MC, R.14.Ba.Nr.2c: 93–94; Bethabara diary extracts, Fries et al., *Records*, 1: 150, 417.

7. Bethabara diary extracts, Fries et al., *Records*, 1: 245.

8. Ettwein to Laurens, [June 24, 1762], Hamer et al., *Papers of Henry Laurens*, 3: 101–5; Ettwein's Visit to Governor William Tryon at Brunshwig in North Carolina, Fries et al., *Records*, 1: 338–41.

9. Bethabara diary, Fries et al., *Records*, 1: 84.

10. Ettwein to Marschall, [Nov. 1765], MA-SP, trans. K. G. Hamilton; Marschall to Ettwein, Sept. 22, 1765, MA-SP, trans. K. G. Hamilton.

11. [Instructions for Jacob Rogers], June 19, 1758, LC-MC, R.14.Ba.Nr.2c: 248–51, translation from copy in Fries et al., *Records*, 1: 196–98.

12. Schropp to Oeconomats Conferenz in Bethlehem, Nov. 23, 1766, MA-NP, Wachovia III, folder 2, item 1–79; Schroppe, etc. to [?], Nov. 20, 1766, MA-SP, trans. E. Marx.

13. Bethabara diary extracts, Fries et al., *Records*, 1: 245.

14. Bethabara diary extracts, Fries et al., *Records*, 1: 391.

15. Conf. des Directorii zu Zeyst, Aug. 26, 1767, MA-SP, Conferences-Decisions of U.E.C. concerning Salem 1763, 1765, 1767, translation from extract in Fries et al., *Records*, 2: 599–600; Bethabara diary extracts, Fries et al., *Records*, 1: 355.

16. Bethabara diary extracts, Fries et al., *Records*, 1: 469–70; An des Department der Helfer im U. Aelt. Collegio, Sept. 2, 1771, MA-SP, Reports to the Unity, 1771.

17. Conferenz über den Wachauischen Plan gehalten in Bethl[ehem], Sept. 22, 1755, LC-MC, R.14.Ba.Nr.2b: 596–601 and MA-NP, Wachovia II, folder 2, item 2–5; Bethabara diary extracts, Fries et al., *Records*, 1: 113, 164; diary/letter of Rev. John Jacob Friis, Fries et al., *Records*, 2: 529–33.

18. Spangenberg to van Laer, Jan. 27, 1759, LC-MC, R.14.Ba.Nr.2c: 265–72; memorabilia, Fries et al., *Records*, 1: 430–37 and 2: 658–66.

19. Spangenberg to White, The intended State of the Brethrens

Settlement in Wachovia in North Carolina, Jan. 17, 1754, LC-MC, R.14.Ba.Nr.2b: 117; Spangenberg to [the Members in Wachovia], May 25, 1757, MA-SP, trans. K. G. Hamilton.

20. Bischoff, Hofman, and Ettwein to die Conferenz in Bethlehem, [April 26, 1760], LC-MC, R.14.Ba.Nr.2c: 488–89.

21. Memorabilia, Fries et al., *Records*, 1: 382–86; for Brother Joh. Schaub at the Opening of the Brethren's Store in Bethabara, July 9, 1759, MA-SP, trans. K. G. Hamilton; Historischer Bericht, LC-MC, R.14.Ba.Nr.2a: 19–42.

22. For Brother Joh. Schaub at the Opening of the Brethren's Store in Bethabara, July 9, 1759, MA-SP, trans. K. G. Hamilton; Spangenberg to the Brethren and Sisters [at Bethabara], [Dec. 6, 1756], MA-SP, trans. K. G. Hamilton.

23. For Brother Joh. Schaub at the Opening of the Brethren's Store in Bethabara, July 9, 1759, MA-SP, trans. K. G. Hamilton; Protocoll der Helfers Conferenz, April 17, 1759, MA-SP.

24. Spangenberg to Lösch, May 3, 1756, LC-MC, R.14.Ba.Nr.2c: 84–87.

25. Bethabara diary extracts, Fries et al., *Records*, 1: 278.

26. Bethabara diary extracts, Fries et al., *Records*, 1: 246; Laurens to Ettwein, April 7, 1762, Hamer et al., *Papers of Henry Laurens*, 3: 92–95; Hooker, *Carolina Backcountry*, 77–78, 241; Smyth, *Tour*, 1: 216; Drage to the Secretary [of the Society for the Propagation of the Gospel], Feb. 28, 1771, Saunders, *Colonial Records*, 8: 502–7.

27. Bethabara diary extracts, Fries et al., *Records*, 1: 245, 469.

28. Salem diary extracts, Fries et al., *Records*, 2: 816.

29. Protocol der Helfers Conferenz, April 17, 1757, and Aug. 19, 1766, MA-SP; Bethabara diary extracts, Fries et al., *Records*, 1: 303, 330, 451, 452, 455; Besondere Observations und einige Bedeutung, May 19, 1767, MA-SP; depositions filed in *Marshall v. Lovelace* (1801), Archives of the North Carolina State Library, Supreme Court Records, Case #298.

30. Bethabara diary extracts, Fries et al., *Records*, 1: 417, 451–52, 454.

31. Frohock to Fanning, April 27, 1765 in Powell, Huhta, and Farnham, *The Regulators*, 17–19.

32. Corbitt, *North Carolina Counties*, 199–200; Bethabara diary extracts, Fries et al., *Records*, 1: 469 and 2: 732; [extracts from] Marshall's Reports to U.E.C., Fries et al., *Records*, 2: 621; The Bagge Manuscript, Fries et al., *Records*, 2: 650–54; [extracts] From the Bagge MS, Fries et al., *Records*, 2: 753–55; [petition] Concerning the Division of Rowan County, Fries et al., *Records*, 1: 425–26.

33. Pauline Maier, "Popular Uprisings and Civil Authority in Eighteenth-Century America," *William and Mary Quarterly*, 3rd ser., 27 (1970): 3–35; Richard Maxwell Brown, "Violence and the American Revolution," in Stephen G. Kurtz and James H. Hutson, eds., *Essays on the American Revolution* (Chapel Hill: Univ. of North Carolina Press, 1973; New York: Norton, 1973), 81–120; Gary B. Nash, "Social Change and the Growth of Prerevolutionary Urban Radicalism," in Young, ed., *The American Revolution*, 3–36; Edward Countryman, "'Out of the Bounds of the Law': Northern Land Rioters in the Eighteenth Century," in Young, ed., *American Revolution*, 37–69; Whittenburg, "Planters, Merchants, and Lawyers."

Conclusion

1. Roche quoted in Patricia U. Bonomi, *A Factious People: Politics and Society in Colonial New York* (New York: Columbia Univ. Press, 1971), 27.

2. Barth, *Ethnic Groups and Boundaries*; Curtin, *Cross-Cultural Trade*; Frederick B. Tolles, *Quakers and the Atlantic Culture* (New York: Macmillan, 1960); William H. TeBrake, *Medieval Frontier: Culture and Ecology in Rijnland* (College Station: Texas A & M Univ. Press, 1985); Gerald D. Suttles, *The Social Order of the Slum: Ethnicity and Territory in the Inner City* (Chicago: Univ. of Chicago Press, 1968); Gordon W. Allport, "Formation of In Groups," in Arnold Dashefsky, ed., *Ethnic Identity in Society* (Chicago: Rand McNally College Pub., 1976), 73–89.

3. I have discussed the link between land and relations between different ethnic groups in Daniel B. Thorp, "Land and Pluralism in Early America," in *Les Etats-Unis: Conformismes et Dissidences. Actes du Groupe de Recherche et Etudes Nord Américaines* (Aix-en-Provence: Univ. de Provence, 1987, 91–102. See also, Alan B. Anderson and James S. Frideres, *Ethnicity in Canada: Theoretical Perspectives* (Toronto: Butterworths, 1981), 134; D. Aidan McQuillan, "Territory and Ethnic Identity," in James R. Gibson, ed., *European Settlement and Development in North America* (Toronto: Univ. of Toronto Press, 1978), 136–69.

4. TeBrake, *Medieval Frontier*, 48.

5. Stephenie G. Wolf, *Urban Village: Population, Community, and Family Structure in Germantown, Pennsylvania, 1683–1800* (Princeton: Princeton Univ. Press, 1976) (Franklin quote on 138); Lemon, *Best Poor Man's Country*; Laura L. Becker, "Diversity and Its Significance in an Eighteenth-Century Pennsylvania Town," in Zuckerman, *Friends and Neighbors*, 196–221.

6. Benzien to Dobbs, March 12, 1757, MA-SP, Rowan County-Dobbs

Parish Papers; Michael Zuckerman, "The Fabrication of Identity in Early America," *William and Mary Quarterly*, 3rd ser., 34 (1977): 183–214; Richard S. Dunn, *Sugar and Slaves: The Rise of the Planter Class in the English West Indies, 1624–1713* (Chapel Hill: Univ. of North Carolina Press, 1972; New York: Norton, 1973), 18.

7. Zuckerman, "Fabrication of Identity"; Roderick Nash, *Wilderness and the American Mind* (New Haven: Yale Univ. Press, 1967) (Bradford quote on 22–3); Entwurf zu dem Settlement die Brüder in North-Carolina, [Oct. 1753], LC-MC, R.14.Ba.Nr.2a: 7–14; John Mack Faragher, *Sugar Creek: Life on the Illinois Prairie* (New Haven: Yale Univ. Press, 1986) (Latrobe quote on 134); Bethabara diary, Fries et al., *Records*, 1: 96.

8. Jerry L. Surratt, "The Moravian as Businessman: Gottlieb Schober of Salem," *North Carolina Historical Review* 60 (1983): 1–23; Fries, Wright, and Hendricks, *Forsyth*, 83–112.

9. Larry E. Tise, *Government*, vol. 6 in *Winston-Salem in History*, 13 vols. (Winston-Salem: Historic Winston, Inc., 1966–77), 15–23.

10. Surratt, "Dissent"; Extracts from Results of the Synod, 1818, Fries et al., *Records*, 7: 3558–68.

Selected Bibliography

Published Sources

Allport, Gordon W. "Formation of In Groups." In *Ethnic Identity in Society*, edited by Arnold Dashefsky, 73–89. Chicago: Rand McNally College Pub., 1976

Anderson, Alan B., and James S. Frideres, *Ethnicity in Canada: Theoretical Perspectives*. Toronto: Butterworths, 1981.

Bailyn, Bernard. *Voyagers to the West: A Passage in the Peopling of America on the Eve of the Revolution*. New York: Knopf, 1986.

Barth, Fredrik. *Ethnic Groups and Boundaries*. Boston: Little, Brown, 1969.

Becker Laura L. "Diversity and Its Significance in an Eighteenth-Century Pennsylvania Town." In *Friends and Neighbors: Group Life in America's First Plural Society*, edited by Michael Zuckerman, 196–221. Philadelphia: Temple Univ. Press, 1982.

———. "The People and the System: Legal Activities in a Colonial Pennsylvania Town." *Pennsylvania Magazine of History and Biography* 105 (1981): 135–49.

Beeman, Richard. *The Evolution of the Southern Backcountry: A Case Study of Lunenburg County, Virginia, 1746–1832*. Philadelphia: Univ. of Pennsylvania Press, 1984.

Blankenburg, Walter. "Die Musik der Brüdergemeine in Europa." In *Unitas Fratrum*, edited by Mari P. van Buijtenen, Cornelis Dekker, and Huib Leeuwenberg, 351–86. Utrecht: Rijksarchief in Utrecht, 1975.

Bonomi, Patricia U. *A Factious People: Politics and Society in Colonial New York*. New York: Columbia Univ. Press, 1971.

Bonomi, Patricia U., and Peter R. Eisenstadt. "Church Adherence in the Eighteenth-Century British American Colonies." *William and Mary Quarterly,* 3rd ser., 39 (1982): 245–86.

Boyd, William K., ed. *Some Eighteenth Century Tracts Concerning North Carolina.* Raleigh: North Carolina Historical Commission, 1927; Spartanburg, S.C.: The Reprint Co., 1973.

Brawley, James S. *Rowan County: A Brief History.* Raleigh: North Carolina Dept. of Cultural Resources, 1974.

Bridenbaugh, Carl. *Myths & Realities: Societies in the Colonial South.* Baton Rouge: Louisiana State Univ. Press, 1952; New York: Atheneum, 1963.

Brigham, Clarence S. *History and Bibliography of American Newspapers, 1690–1820,* 2 vols. Worcester, Mass.: American Antiquarian Society, 1947.

Brown, Dale. *Understanding Pietism.* Grand Rapids, Mich.: William B. Eerdmans, 1978.

Brown, Richard Maxwell. "Violence and the American Revolution." In *Essays on the American Revolution,* edited by Stephen G. Kurtz and James H. Hutson, 81–120. Chapel Hill: Univ. of North Carolina Press, 1973; New York: Norton, 1973.

Butner, Jo Conrad. "A New Town in Wachovia." In *The Three Forks of Muddy Creek,* edited by Frances Griffin. Vol. 5 of an ongoing series under the same title and editor. Winston-Salem, N.C.: Old Salem, Inc., 1978.

Cappon, Lester J., ed. *Atlas of Early American History.* Princeton: Princeton Univ. Press, 1976.

Clark, Walter. *The State Records of North Carolina,* 16 vols. Raleigh: P.M. Hale, 1886–1907.

Clowse, Converse D. *Economic Beginnings in Colonial South Carolina, 1670–1730.* Columbia: Univ. of South Carolina Press, 1971.

———. *Measuring Charleston's Overseas Commerce, 1717–1767: Statistics From the Port's Naval Lists.* Washington, D.C.: Univ. Press of America, 1981.

Conkin, Paul. "The Church Establishment in North Carolina, 1765–1776." *North Carolina Historical Review* 32 (1955): 1–30.

Corbitt, David L. *The Formation of North Carolina Counties, 1663–1943.* Raleigh: State Dept. of Archives and History, 1950.

Coulter, E. Merton. "The Granville District." *James Sprunt Historical Publications* 13 (1913), no. 1: 33–56.

Countryman, Edward. "'Out of the Bounds of the Law': Northern Land Rioters in the Eighteenth Century." In *The American Revolution:*

Explorations in the History of American Radicalism, edited by Alfred F. Young, 37–69. Dekalb: Northern Illinois Univ. Press, 1976.

Curtin, Philip D. *Cross-Cultural Trade in World History*. Cambridge: Cambridge Univ. Press, 1984.

Davis, David Brion. *The Problem of Slavery in Western Culture*. Ithaca, N.Y.: Cornell Univ. Press, 1966.

Degn, Christian. *Die Schimmelmanns im Atlantischen Dreieckshandel: Gewinn und Gewissen*. Neumünster: D. Wachholz, 1974.

Doggett, Coleman A. "The Moravian Foresters." *Journal of Forest History* 31 (1987): 19–24.

Dunn, Richard S. *Sugar and Slaves: The Rise of the Planter Class in the English West Indies, 1624–1713*. Chapel Hill: Univ. of North Carolina Press, 1972; New York: Norton, 1973.

Earle, Carville, and Ronald Hoffman. "Staple Crops and Urban Development in the Eighteenth-Century South." *Perspectives in American History* 10 (1976): 7–78.

Eisenstadt, S.N. "The Place of Elites and Primary Groups in the Absorption of New Immigrants in Israel." *American Journal of Sociology* 57 (1951): 222–31.

Ekirch, A. Roger. *"Poor Carolina": Politics and Society in Colonial North Carolina, 1729–1776*. Chapel Hill: Univ. of North Carolina Press, 1981.

Erb, Peter C., ed. *Pietists: Selected Writings*. Classics of Western Spirituality. New York: Paulist Press, 1983.

Les Etats-Unis: Conformismes et Dissidences. Actes du Groupe de Recherche et Etudes Nord Américaines. Aix-en-Provence: Univ. de Provence, 1987.

Faragher, John Mack. *Sugar Creek: Life on the Illinois Prairie*. New Haven: Yale Univ. Press, 1986.

Fries, Adelaide. *Customs and Practices of the Moravian Church*. 3rd ed. Winston-Salem, N.C.: Board of Christian Education and Evangelism, 1973.

Fries, Adelaide, Stuart Thurman Wright, and J. Edwin Hendricks. *Forsyth: The History of a County on the March*. Revised edition. Chapel Hill: Univ. of North Carolina Press, 1976.

Fries, Adelaide, Kenneth G. Hamilton, Douglas L. Rights, and Minnie J. Smith, eds. *Records of the Moravians in North Carolina, 11 vols. Raleigh: North Carolina Historical Commission, 1922–69*.

Fulbrook, Mary. *Piety and Politics: Religion and the Rise of Absolutism in England, Württemberg and Prussia*. Cambridge: Cambridge Univ. Press, 1983.

Garland, John M. "The Non-Ecclesiastical Activities of an English and North Carolina Parish: A Comparative Study." *North Carolina Historical Review* 50 (1973): 32–51.

Gollin, Gillian L. *Moravians in Two Worlds.* New York: Columbia Univ. Press, 1967.

Greene, Jack P. *All Men Are Created Equal: Some Reflections on the Character of the American Revolution.* Oxford: Clarendon Press, 1976.

————. *The Quest for Power: The Lower Houses of Assembly in the Southern Royal Colonies, 1689–1776.* Chapel Hill: Univ. of North Carolina Press, 1963.

Haller, Mabel. *Early Moravian Education in Pennsylvania.* Nazareth, Pa.: Moravian Historical Society, 1953.

Hamer, Phillip, M., George C. Rogers, Jr., David R. Chestnutt, C. James Taylor, and Peggy J. Clark, eds. *The Papers of Henry Laurens,* 11 vols. to date. Columbia: Univ. of South Carolina Press, 1968– .

Hamilton, J. T. "The Recognition of the Unitas Fratrum as an Old Episcopal Church by the Parliament of Great Britain in 1749." *Transactions of the Moravian Historical Society,* Special Series, 2 (1925): part 2.

Hamilton, J. T., and Kenneth G. Hamilton. *History of the Moravian Church.* Winston-Salem, N.C.: Interprovincial Board of Christian Education, Moravian Church in America, 1967.

Handbook of North Carolina. Raleigh: State Board of Agriculture, 1893.

Hecht, Irene W.D. "The Virginia Muster of 1624/25 as a Source for Demographic History." *William and Mary Quarterly,* 3rd ser., 30 (1973): 65–92.

Heimert, Alan, and Perry Miller, eds. *The Great Awakening.* Indianapolis: Bobbs-Merrill, 1967.

Hinshaw, Seth B. *The North Carolina Quaker Experience.* Davidson, N.C.: Briar Patch Press, 1984.

Hoffman, Ronald, Thad W. Tate, and Peter J. Albert, eds. *An Uncivil War: The Southern Backcountry during the American Revolution.* Charlottesville: Univ. Press of Virginia, 1985.

Hooker, Richard J., ed. *The Carolina Backcountry on the Eve of the Revolution: The Journal and Other Writings of Charles Woodmason, Anglican Itinerant.* Chapel Hill: Univ. of North Carolina Press, 1953.

Isaac, Rhys. "Evangelical Revolt: The Nature of the Baptists' Challenge to the Traditional Order in Virginia, 1765 to 1775." *William and Mary Quarterly,* 3rd ser., 31 (1974): 345–68.

————. *The Transformation of Virginia, 1740–1790.* Chapel Hill: Univ. of North Carolina Press, 1982.

James, Hunter. *Old Salem: Official Guidebook.* Winston-Salem, N.C.: Old Salem, Inc., 1971.

Jones, George Fenwick. *The Salzburger Saga: Religious Exiles and Other Germans Along the Savannah.* Athens: Univ. of Georgia Press, 1984.

Jordan, Winthrop D. *White Over Black: American Attitudes Toward the Negro, 1550–1812.* Chapel Hill: Univ. of North Carolina Press, 1968.

Kanter, Rosabeth Moss. *Commitment and Community.* Cambridge: Harvard Univ. Press, 1972.

Kay, Marvin L. Michael. "The North Carolina Regulation, 1766–1776." In *The American Revolution: Explorations in the History of American Radicalism,* edited by Alfred F. Young, 71–123. Dekalb: Northern Illinois University Press, 1976.

Kay, Marvin L. Michael, and William S. Price, Jr. "'To Ride the Wood Mare': Road Building and Militia Service in Colonial North Carolina, 1740–1775." *North Carolina Historical Review* 57 (1980): 361–409.

Kessler, Werner. "Die Evangelische Brüdergemeine im Deutschen Raum von der Entstehung Herrnhuts an bis heute." In *Unitas Fratrum,* edited by Mari P. van Buijtenen, Cornelis Dekker, and Huib Leeuwenberg, 55–92. Utrecht: Rijksarchief in Utrecht, 1975.

Klein, Rachel N. "Ordering the Backcountry: The South Carolina Regulation." *William and Mary Quarterly,* 3rd ser., 38 (1981): 661–80.

Kulikoff, Alan. *Tobacco and Slaves: The Development of Southern Cultures in the Chesapeake, 1680–1800.* Chapel Hill: Univ. of North Carolina Press, 1986.

Kurtz, Stephen G., and James H. Hutson. *Essays on The American Revolution.* Chapel Hill: Univ. of North Carolina Press, 1973; New York: Norton, 1973.

Lee, Lawrence. *The Lower Cape Fear in Colonial Days.* Chapel Hill: Univ. of North Carolina Press, 1965.

Lemon, James T. *The Best Poor Man's Country: A Geographical Study of Early Southeastern Pennsylvania.* Baltimore: Johns Hopkins Univ. Press, 1972; New York: Norton, 1976.

Lennon, Donald R., and Ida Brooks Kellam. *The Wilmington Town Book, 1743–1778.* Raleigh: Div. of Archives and History, 1973.

Levering, Joseph M. *A History of Bethlehem, Pennsylvania, 1742–1892.* Bethlehem: Times Pub. Co., 1903.

Lovejoy, David S. *Religious Enthusiasm in the New World.* Cambridge: Harvard Univ. Press, 1985.

Maier, Pauline. "Popular Uprisings and Civil Authority in Eighteenth-Century America." *William and Mary Quarterly,* 3rd ser., 27 (1970): 3–35.

McCain, Paul M. "Magistrates Courts in Early North Carolina." *North Carolina Historical Review* 48 (1971): 23–30.

———. *The County Court in North Carolina Before 1750.* Historical Papers of the Trinity College Historical Society, 31. Durham, N.C.: Duke Univ. Press, 1954.

McQuillan, D. Aidan. "Territory and Ethnic Identity." In *European Settlement and Development in North America*, edited by James R. Gibson, 136–69. Toronto: Univ. of Toronto Press, 1978.

Merrens, H. Roy. *Colonial North Carolina in the Eighteenth Century.* Chapel Hill: Univ. of North Carolina Press, 1964.

Meyer, Henry H. *Child Nature and Nurture According to Nicholaus Ludwig von Zinzendorf.* New York: Abingdon Press, 1928.

Mitchell, Robert D. *Commercialism and Frontier: Perspectives on the Early Shenandoah Valley.* Charlottesville: Univ. Press of Virginia, 1977.

Molnar, Amedeo. "Die Böhmische Brüderunität. Abriss Ihrer Geschichte." In *Unitas Fratrum*, edited by Mari P. van Buijtenen, Cornelis Dekker, and Huib Leeuwenberg, 15–34. Utrecht: Rijksarchief in Utrecht, 1975.

Nash, Gary B. "Social Change and the Growth of Prerevolutionary Urban Radicalism." In *The American Revolution: Explorations in the History of American Radicalism*, edited by Alfred F. Young, 3–36. Dekalb: Northern Illinois Univ. Press, 1976.

Nash, Roderick. *Wilderness and the American Mind.* New Haven: Yale Univ. Press, 1967.

Neisser, Georg. *A History of the Beginnings of Moravian Work in America.* Translated by William N. Schwarze and Samuel H. Gapp. Bethlehem, Pa.: Moravian Archives, 1955.

Oldendorp, C.G.A. *History of the Mission of the Evangelical Brethren on the Caribbean Islands of St. Thomas, St. Croix, and St. John.* Translated and edited by Arnold R. Highfield and Vladimir Barac. Ann Arbor, Mich.: Karoma Pub., 1987.

Phillips, Catherine. *Memoirs of the Life of Catherine Phillips.* Philadelphia: Budd & Bartram, 1798.

Powell, William S. *The Carolina Charter of 1663.* Raleigh: State Dept. of Archives and History, 1954.

Powell, William S., James K. Huhta, and Thomas J. Farnham, eds. *The Regulators in North Carolina: A Documentary History, 1759–1776.* Raleigh: State Dept. of Archives and History, 1971.

Ramsey, Robert W. *Carolina Cradle: Settlement of the Northwest Carolina Frontier, 1747–1762.* Chapel Hill: Univ. of North Carolina Press, 1964.

Reichel, Levin T. *The Moravians in North Carolina*. Philadelphia: Lippincott, 1857.

Rights, Douglas L. "The Trading Path to the Indians." *North Carolina Historical Review* 8 (1931): 403–26.

Robinson, W. Stitt. *The Southern Colonial Frontier, 1607–1763*. Albuquerque: Univ. of New Mexico Press, 1979.

Rumple, Jethro. *A History of Rowan County, North Carolina*. Salisbury, N.C.: J.J. Bruner, 1881; Baltimore: Baltimore Regional Pub. Co., 1974.

Rutman, Darrett B., and Anita H. Rutman. "'More True and Perfect Lists': The Reconstruction of Censuses for Middlesex County, Virginia, 1668–1704." *Virginia Magazine of History and Biography* 88 (1980): 37–74.

———. *A Place in Time: Middlesex County, Virginia, 1650–1750*. New York: Norton, 1984.

Saunders, William L. *The Colonial Records of North Carolina*, 10 vols. Raleigh: P.M. Hale, 1886–90.

Schattschneider, David A. "The Missionary Theologies of Zinzendorf and Spangenberg." *Transactions of the Moravian Historical Society* 22 (1975): 213–33.

Sessler, Jacob John. *Communal Pietism Among Early American Moravians*. New York: Henry Holt, 1933; New York: AMS Press, 1971.

Smyth, J.F.D. *A Tour in the United States of America*, 2 vols. London: G. Robinson, J. Robson, and J. Stewell, 1784.

Stinchcombe, Arthur L. "Social Structures and Organizations." In *Handbook of Organizations*, edited by James G. March, 142–91. Chicago: Rand McNally, 1965.

Stoeffler, F. Ernest. *German Pietism During the Eighteenth Century*. Leiden: E.J. Brill, 1973.

Surratt, Jerry L. *Gottlieb Schober of Salem: Discipleship and Ecumenical Vision in an Early Moravian Town*. Macon, Ga.: Mercer Univ. Press, 1983.

———. "The Moravian as Businessman: Gottlieb Schober of Salem." *North Carolina Historical Review* 60 (1983): 1–23.

———. "The Role of Dissent in Community Evolution among Moravians in Salem, 1772–1860." *North Carolina Historical Review* 52 (1975): 235–55.

Suttles, Gerald D. *The Social Order of the Slum: Ethnicity and Territory in the Inner City*. Chicago: Univ. of Chicago Press, 1968.

Sydnor, Charles S. *Gentlemen Freeholders*. Chapel Hill: Univ. of North Carolina Press, 1952.

TeBrake, William H. *Medieval Frontier: Culture and Ecology in Rijnland.* College Station: Texas A & M Univ. Press, 1985.

Tillson, Albert H., Jr. "The Localist Roots of Backcountry Loyalism: An Examination of Popular Political Culture in Virginia's New River Valley." *Journal of Southern History* 54 (1988): 387–404.

Thorp, Daniel B. "Assimilation in North Carolina's Moravian Community." *Journal of Southern History* 52 (1986): 20–42.

———. "Chattel With a Soul: The Autobiography of a Moravian Slave." *Pennsylvania Magazine of History and Biography* 112 (1988): 433–51.

———. "The City That Never Was: Count von Zinzendorf's Original Plan for Salem." *North Carolina Historical Review* 61 (1984): 36–58.

———. "Land and Pluralism in Early America." In *Les Etats-Unis: Conformismes et Dissidences. Actes du Groupe de Recherche et Etudes Nord Américaines,* 91–102. Aix-en-Provence: Univ. de Provence, 1987.

Tise, Larry E. *Government.* Vol. 6 in *Winston-Salem in History,* 13 vols. Winston-Salem: Historic Winston, Inc., 1966–77.

Tolles, Frederick B. *Quakers and the American Culture.* New York: Macmillan, 1960.

Towlson, Clifford W. *Moravian and Methodist.* London: Epworth Press, 1957.

Vacovsky, Adolf. "History of the 'hidden seed' (1620–1722)." In *Unitas Fratrum,* edited by Mari P. van Buijtenen, Cornelis Dekker, and Huib Leeuwenberg, 35–54. Utrecht: Rijksarchief in Utrecht, 1975.

van Buijtenen, Mari P., Cornelis Dekker, and Huib Leeuwenberg, eds. *Unitas Fratrum.* Utrecht: Rijksarchief in Utrecht, 1975.

van der Linde, Jan Marinus. "Herrnhuter im Karibischen Raum." In *Unitas Fratrum,* edited by Mari P. van Buijtenen, Cornelis Dekker, and Huib Leeuwenberg, 241–60. Utrecht: Rijksarchief in Utrecht, 1975.

Wattenberg, Ben J., ed., *The Statistical History of the United States from Colonial Times to the Present.* New York: Basic Books, 1976.

Weaver, Glenn. "Moravians During the French and Indian War." *Church History* 24 (1955): 239–56.

Weinlick, John R. "Colonial Moravians, Their Status Among the Churches." *Pennsylvania History* 26 (1959): 213–25.

———. *Count Zinzendorf.* Nashville, Tenn.: Abingdon Press, 1956.

Wesley, John. *The Works of the Rev. John Wesley,* 10 vols. New York: J. and J. Harper, 1826–27.

Whittenburg, James P. "Planters, Merchants, and Lawyers: Social Change and the Origins of the North Carolina Regulation." *William and Mary Quarterly,* 3rd ser., 34 (1977): 215–38.

Wolf, Stephanie G. *Urban Village: Population, Community, and Family Structure in Germantown, Pennsylvania, 1683–1800.* Princeton: Princeton Univ. Press, 1976.

Wood, Peter H. *Black Majority: Negroes in Colonial South Carolina From 1670 through the Stono Rebellion.* New York: Knopf, 1974; New York: Norton, 1975.

Wrigley, E.A., and R.S. Schofield. *The Population History of England, 1541–1871.* Cambridge: Harvard Univ. Press, 1981.

Young, Alfred F., ed. *The American Revolution: Explorations in the History of American Radicalism.* Dekalb: Northern Illinois Univ. Press, 1976.

Zinzendorf, Nicholaus Ludwig, Count von. *Nine Public Lectures on Important Subjects in Religion Preached in Fetter Lane Chapel in London in the Year 1746.* Translated and edited by George W. Forell. Iowa City: Univ. of Iowa Press, 1973.

———. *Sixteen Discourses on the Redemption of Man by the Death of Christ Preached at Berlin.* London: 1740.

Zuckerman, Michael. "The Fabrication of Identity in Early America." *William and Mary Quarterly,* 3rd ser., 34 (1977): 183–214.

———, ed. *Friends and Neighbors: Group Life in America's First Plural Society.* Philadelphia: Temple Univ. Press, 1982.

Theses and Dissertations

Hendricks, Christopher Edwin. "The Planning and Development of Two Moravian Congregation Towns: Salem, North Carolina and Gracehill, Northern Ireland." M.A. thesis, the College of William and Mary in Virginia, 1987.

Hinman, William. "Philip Gottlieb Reuter, First Surveyor of Wachovia." M.A. thesis, Wake Forest Univ., 1985.

Holder, Edward M. "Community Life in Wachovia 1752–1780." M.A. thesis, Univ. of North Carolina, 1929.

Hughes, Kaylene. "Populating the Back Country: The Demographic and Social Characteristics of the South Carolina Frontier, 1730–1760." Ph.D. diss., Florida State Univ., 1985.

Kessel, Elizabeth A. "Germans on the Maryland Frontier: A Social History of Fredrick County, Maryland, 1730–1800." Ph.D. diss., Rice Univ., 1981.

Lenius, Susan. "Slavery and the Moravian Church in North Carolina." Honors thesis in history, Moravian College, Bethlehem, Pa., 1974.

Mainwaring, W. Thomas. "Community Among the Moravian Brethren of Wachovia, 1753–1772." M.A. thesis, Univ. of North Carolina, 1977.

Merrell, James H. "Natives in a New World: The Catawba Indians of Carolina, 1650–1800." Ph.D. diss., The Johns Hopkins Univ., 1982.

Thorp, Daniel B. "Moravian Colonization of Wachovia, 1753–1772: The Maintenance of Community in Late Colonial North Carolina." Ph. D. diss., The Johns Hopkins Univ., 1982.

Woosley, Robert W., Jr. "The Ethics of the Moravians in Wachovia." M.A. thesis, Southeastern Baptist Theological Seminary, 1956.

Index

Rogers, Jacob, 76, 159–61, 185–86
Rogers, Johanna, 76
Rogers, Polly, 76
Rowan, Matthew, 176
Rowan County, 30, 194, 196–97; economy of, 33–34, 112, 118, 125, 127, 173; government of, 32, 165–68, 173; population of, 30–32, 34, 173; religion in, 32–33, 161, 165, 238; society in, 32, 34
Rutman, Anita, 49
Rutman, Darrett, 49

Sabbath, 18, 150, 166
St. Christopher, 202
St. Luke's Parish, 33, 161, 165
St. Thomas, 52, 53
Salem, 6, 46, 49–52, 66, 70–71, 108–10, 143–44, 146–47, 155, 164, 169, 172, 187, 205
Salisbury, 125, 141, 167, 169, 175, 186
Sauter, Michael, 103
Schaff, Jeremias, 65
Schaub, Johannes, 65, 134
Schmid, George, 190
Schnepf, Daniel, 36
Schober, Andreas, 74
Schober, Gottlieb, 74
schools, 71, 72, 75
Schropp, Mattheus, 186
Schubert, August, 100–4, 184, 223
Seidel, Christian, 86, 188
Select Conference, 85, 87
servants, 144
Seven Years War. *See* French and Indian War
sex: ratios, 42, 44, 47–49, 51–52; roles, 44–45, 73, 82–83, 144; segregation, 60, 64
Shallow Ford, 170
Shenandoah Valley, Va., 49
Shepard, Mr., 192, 195
silk, 129–30
slaves: in Bethlehem, 54; in Wacho-

via, 54–56, 144; Moravian view of, 52–55
Smyth, J. F. D., 110, 193
socialization
—of children, 49, 59, 62, 68–75
—of individuals, 59–63, 77–80
societies, 17, 20–21, 46–47, 141, 158, 189, 194–96
Spangenberg, August Gottlieb: explores Wachovia, 29, 119, 149, 153, 179; life of, 28–29; role of in Wachovia, 41, 44, 46, 63, 69–70, 84, 92, 99, 109, 112–13, 120–21, 133–34, 145, 149, 151, 154, 159, 165, 171, 174, 189, 190–92
Spener, Philipp Jakob, 13, 15, 17, 61
Spönhauer, Margaret Elizabeth, 219, 221
Springhill, 135–36
Starkey, John, 176
Steiner, Jacob, 137
Stoeffler, Ernest, 16
Stotz, Peter, 36
Surry County, 34, 165, 173–74, 194, 197
Swann, Samuel, 175–76
Sydnor, Charles, 171

TeBrake, William, 201
Tomes, Nancy, 3
Town Fork, 31, 113, 117, 169, 195
trade
—between Moravians and non-Moravians, 35–36, 56, 107, 114–18, 122–23, 125, 127–28, 130–38, 141–47, 189–92, 200, 233
—international, 128–30, 132–38, 141
—regional, 114–18, 122–23, 125, 127–28, 130–31, 133–38, 140–44, 233
—regulation of, 83, 96, 108–11, 128, 130–34, 145–46, 186, 189–92, 203–4
—*See also* specific commodities, e.g. deerskin

The Moravian Community in Colonial North Carolina
was designed by Dariel Mayer, composed by Graphic
Composition, Inc., printed by Cushing-Malloy, Inc., and
bound by John H. Dekker & Sons, Inc. The book is set in
Palatino. Text stock is 60-lb. Glatfelter Natural Antique.